W9-CFG-093

EXAM CRAM™

PSAT/NMSQT®

Steven W. Dulan

Advantage Education

CERTIFICATION

PSAT/NMSQT® Exam Cram

International Standard Book Number: 0-7897-3444-3

Library of Congress Catalog Card Number: 2005929964

Printed in the United States of America

First Printing: September 2005

08   07   06   4   3   2

Trademarks

Warning and Disclaimer

Bulk Sales

Que Publishing offers excellent discounts on this book when ordered in quantity for bulk purchases or special sales. For more information, please contact

U.S. Corporate and Government Sales
1-800-382-3419
corpsales@pearsontechgroup.com

For sales outside the U.S., please contact

International Sales
international@pearsoned.com

Publisher
Paul Boger

Executive Editor
Jeff Riley

Acquisitions Editor
Carol Ackerman

Development Editor
Songlin Qiu

Managing Editor
Charlotte Clapp

Project Editor
Mandie Frank

Indexer
Aaron Black

Proofreader
Carla Lewis

Technical Editor
Jim Persell

Publishing Coordinator
Sharry Lee Gregory

Designer
Gary Adair

About the Author

Steve Dulan has been involved with PSAT preparation since 1989, when, as a former U.S. Army Infantry Sergeant, and undergraduate student at Michigan State University, Steve became a PSAT instructor. He has been helping students to prepare for success on the PSAT and other standardized exams ever since. Steve scored in the 99th percentile on every standardized test he has ever taken. After graduating from Michigan State, Steve attended The Thomas M. Cooley Law School on a full Honors Scholarship based on his 99th percentile score on the Law School Admission Test (LSAT). While attending law school, Steve continued to teach standardized test prep classes (including ACT, SAT, PSAT, GRE, GMAT, and LSAT) an average of 30 hours each week, and tutored some of his fellow law students in a variety of subjects and in essay exam writing techniques. Professor Dulan has also served as an instructor at Baker University, Cleary University, Lansing Community College, The Ohio State University-Real Estate Institute, and The Thomas M. Cooley Law School. Guest lecturer credits include: Michigan State University, University of Michigan, Detroit College of Law, Marquette University, Texas Technical University, University of Miami, and Wright State University.

Thousands of students have benefited from Steve's instruction, coaching, and admissions consulting, and have gone on to their colleges of choice. Steve's students have gained admission to some of the most prestigious institutions of higher learning in the world, and have received numerous scholarships of their own. Since 1997, Steve has served as the president of Advantage Education (www.study-smart.com), a company dedicated to providing effective and affordable test prep education in a variety of settings including classes and seminars at high schools and colleges around the country, summer College Prep Camps at the University of Michigan, and one-on-one via the Internet worldwide. The information and techniques included in this book are the result of Steve's experiences with test preparation students at all levels over many years.

Acknowledgements

I would like to acknowledge the contribution of the faculty and staff of Advantage Education. You are not only the smartest, but also the best. Special thanks to: Jennifer Kostamo, a quiet genius who almost always keeps her composure no matter how often she is rudely interrupted by me; Josh Singer, our math whiz; and, Pamela Chamberlain, our brilliant, versatile, and hard-working contributor/editor. All of you put in extra effort to make this book a success.

Thanks to Carol Ackerman of Que Certification for her help throughout this project. Her good nature and positive attitude were greatly appreciated.

Most importantly, I would like to acknowledge the single biggest contributor to this work: my wife, colleague, co-author, editor, typist, employee, boss, and friend: Amy Dulan. None of this would have been possible without your hard work and dedication.

About the Technical Editor

Jim Persell has a B.S. in psychology and sociology from Northwest Missouri State University, a B.A. in education from Upper Iowa University, and a Masters in technology and curriculum from the University of Phoenix. He's been an educator for the past 10 years and has played a major role in writing his school district's curriculum and helping to implement technology into the classroom.

We Want to Hear from You!

As the reader of this book, *you* are our most important critic and commentator. We value your opinion and want to know what we're doing right, what we could do better, what areas you'd like to see us publish in, and any other words of wisdom you're willing to pass our way.

As an executive editor for Que Certification, I welcome your comments. You can email or write me directly to let me know what you did or didn't like about this book—as well as what we can do to make our books better.

Please note that I cannot help you with technical problems related to the topic of this book. We do have a User Services group, however, where I will forward specific technical questions related to the book.

When you write, please be sure to include this book's title and author as well as your name, email address, and phone number. I will carefully review your comments and share them with the author and editors who worked on the book.

Email: feedback@quepublishing.com

Mail: Jeff Riley
Executive Editor
Que Certification
800 East 96th Street
Indianapolis, IN 46240 USA

For more information about this book or another Que Certification title, visit our website at www.examcram.com. Type the ISBN (excluding hyphens) or the title of a book in the Search field to find the page you're looking for.

Contents at a Glance

Table of Contents

Introduction: Getting Started

This book includes general information about the PSAT and chapters with specific information on each of the test sections, as well as two simulated tests.

In an ideal situation, you will be reading this at least three to four weeks before you take your actual PSAT exam. If that is not the case, even just a few hours of study and practice can have a positive impact on your PSAT score.

If you have enough time between now and your actual PSAT exam, (at least three weeks) you should work through this entire book. Some of the material is meant to be used as realistic practice material to get you ready for the whole experience of taking a PSAT exam.

As you work through the simulated tests, you should be aware that they are not actual exams. They are reasonably accurate simulations written by experienced experts. They contain basically the same mix of question types as a real PSAT. If you work through all the material provided, you can rest assured that there won't be any surprises on test day. Generally, students tend to score a little better on each successive practice test. But, PSAT exams are sensitive to individual conditions such as fatigue and stress. Therefore, the time of day that you take your practice exams, your environment, and other things that might be going on in your life can have an impact on your scores. Don't get worried if you see some score fluctuation because of a bad day or because the practice test revealed weaknesses in your knowledge or skills. Simply use the information that you gather to help you improve.

In our experience, the students who see the largest increases in their scores are the ones who put in consistent effort over several weeks. Try to keep your frustration to a minimum if you are struggling. And, try to keep from becoming overconfident when everything is going your way.

What This Book Will Not Do

This book is not a substitute for regular textbooks or course work. It will not teach you everything you need to know about the subject matter tested on the PSAT. Although the PSAT is primarily considered a skills-based test, you will be required to have a basic understanding of certain mathematical concepts and standard written English. This book will introduce you to some of those concepts, but it will not provide an in-depth review.

The focus of this book is on helping you to maximize your PSAT score. Each chapter includes specific test-taking strategies, some content area review, and practice questions.

About the PSAT

The PSAT is a standardized test that provides firsthand practice for the SAT. It is also used to qualify you for the National Merit Scholarship Corporation (NMSC) scholarship programs. In fact, the full name of the test is PSAT/NMSQT (Preliminary SAT/National Merit Scholarship Qualifying Test.) The PSAT is not a direct measure of a student's abilities. It is not an IQ test. The PSAT is certainly not a measure of your value as a person. It is not even a perfect predictor of how well you will do on the SAT. The PSAT doesn't measure your natural, inborn ability. If it did, we wouldn't have had the successes that we have had in raising past students' scores on PSAT exams.

The PSAT actually measures a predictable set of skills and some specific knowledge. It is "trainable," meaning that you can do better on your PSAT if you put time in learning the knowledge and perfecting the skills that are tested.

More information on the structure of the PSAT is shown in Table IN.1.

Table IN.1 PSAT Structure	
Critical Reading	
48 questions	Two 25-minute sections
Content	*Number of Questions*
Sentence Completions	13
Passage Based Reading	35

(continued)

Table IN.1 PSAT Structure (continued)	
Mathematics	
38 questions	Two 25-minute sections
Content	*Number of Questions*
Multiple Choice	28
Student-produced Response	10
Writing Skills	
39 questions	One 30-minute section
Content	*Number of Questions*
Identifying Sentence Errors	14
Improving Sentences	20
Improving Paragraphs	5

A company called The College Board decides exactly what is going to be on your PSAT exam. These experts consult with classroom teachers at the high school and college level. They look at high school and college courses, and they consult with educators and specialized psychologists called "*psychometricians*" (measurers of the mind), who know a lot about the human brain and how it behaves under a variety of conditions.

Registering for the PSAT

You have to register for the PSAT in advance. You can't just show up on test day with a #2 pencil and expect to start right in. The best source of information for everything regarding PSAT is, not surprisingly, the PSAT website: www.PSAT.org. There is also a strong chance that a pre-college counselor at your school has a PSAT Registration Book, which includes all the information that you will need for your registration.

National Merit Scholarships

Other than practicing for the SAT, the next most common reason for students to take the PSAT is to try to qualify for a National Merit Scholarship.

The National Merit Scholarship is administered by the National Merit Scholarship Corporation and recognizes the top 50,000 scorers out of more than a million students who take the test each year. In order to qualify, you must take the test during your third year of high school (usually called your junior year). Approximately 16,000 of the top 50,000 are named as semi-finalists. The remaining students are sent Letters of Commendation. About 15,000 out of the 16,000 become finalists by qualifying based on academic standards. Approximately 8,200 of the finalists actually receive Merit Scholarship awards, which are valued at a minimum of $2,500. In some cases, these scholarships amount to full scholarships, which can be renewed for up to four years of college. Each year, about 1,600 of the top 50,000, who are not finalists, are awarded special scholarships of varying amounts. Detailed information about these scholarships can be found online at www.nationalmerit.org.

A Note on Scoring the Practice Tests

The practice tests in this book are created by experts to simulate the question types, difficulty level, and content areas that you will find on your real PSAT. Scoring worksheets as well as scoring tables are included in Appendix D at the end of the book. The worksheets should only be used as a guide to computing approximate test scores. Actual PSAT exams are scored with scales that are unique to each test form. Do not get overly worried about your test scores; your goal should be to learn something from every practice experience and to get used to the format and types of questions on the PSAT.

Preparing for the PSAT

The Self Assessment should be your first step. It will help you to focus on areas of strength and weakness in your knowledge base and skill set.

There is a detailed explanation for each of the practice questions in this book. You will probably not need to read each and every one of them. Sometimes, when you look back over a practice test that you took, you can tell right away why you got a particular question wrong. We have heard many students call these errors "stupid mistakes." We suggest that you refer to these errors as "concentration errors." Everyone makes them from time to time, and you should not get overly upset or concerned when they occur. There is a good chance that your focus will be much better on the real test as long as you train yourself properly using this book. You should note the difference between those concentration errors and any questions that you get wrong because of a lack of understanding or holes in your knowledge base. If you have the time, it is probably worth reading the explanations for any of the questions that were at all difficult for you. Sometimes, students get questions correct but for the wrong reasons, or because they simply guessed in correctly. While you are practicing, you should mark any questions that you want to recheck and be sure to read the explanations for those questions.

PSAT Versus SAT

The PSAT, or Preliminary SAT, is almost identical to the SAT. However, the PSAT does not include an essay-writing section. Both tests have a "guessing penalty," which means that test takers lose an extra fraction of a point when they mark a question incorrectly. If you leave a question blank on either the PSAT or the SAT, you basically lose one raw point.

If you mark a question incorrectly, you lose an extra $\frac{1}{4}$ point. So, you have to think carefully about whether to guess. Additional stress can make the PSAT and SAT seem harder than they actually are.

Key Test-taking Strategies

Following is a general discussion of important information that should help you to approach the PSAT with confidence. Additional chapters in the book include strategies and techniques specific to each of the PSAT sections.

KSA

Cognitive psychologists, the ones who study learning and thinking, use the letters *K*, *S*, and *A* to refer to the basic parts of human performance in all activities, ranging from academics to athletics, playing music to playing games. The letters stand for **K**nowledge, **S**kills, and **A**bilities. As mentioned previously, the PSAT measures certain predictable areas of knowledge, and it measures a specific set of skills. You probably already understand this since you are reading this book. In fact, thousands and thousands of students have successfully raised their PSAT scores through study and practice.

The human brain stores and retrieves factual knowledge a little bit differently from the way it acquires and executes skills. Knowledge can generally be learned fairly quickly and is fairly durable, even when you are under stress.

Skills, on the other hand, require repetition to be even near perfect. Psychologists use the term, "perfectly internalized skills," which means that the skills are executed automatically, without any conscious thought.

Take, for example, shoe-tying. It is highly unlikely that you can remember the exact moment you tied your shoes this morning. The reason that you probably cannot remember actually tying your shoes is because, as an adult shoe tier, you have perfectly internalized the skill of shoe-tying over many repetitions.

We want you to internalize the skills that you will need on the PSAT so that you don't have to spend time and energy figuring out what to do during the exam. We are hoping that you will be well into each section while some of your less-prepared classmates are still reading the directions and trying to figure out exactly what they are supposed to be doing.

We suggest that you do sufficient practice so that you will develop your test-taking skills, and, specifically, good PSAT-taking skills. While you practice, you should distinguish between practice that is meant to serve as a learning experience and practice that is meant to be a realistic simulation of your actual PSAT.

During practice that is meant for learning, it is okay to "cheat." What we mean is that you should feel free to disregard the time and just think about how the questions are put together and even stop to look up information in textbooks, or on the Internet, or look at the explanations in the back of the book. It is even okay to talk to others about what you are learning during your "learning practice." But, you also need to do some simulated testing practice, where you time yourself carefully and try to control as many variables in your environment as you can. Some research shows that you will have an easier time executing your skills and remembering information when the environment that you are testing in is similar to the environment where you studied and practiced. It is important to note that you should not attempt any timed practice tests when you are mentally or physically exhausted. This will only add more unwanted stress to an already stressful situation.

You learn factual information by studying, and you acquire skills through practice. There is some overlap between these actions and, hopefully, you will do some learning while you practice, and vice versa. In fact, research shows that repetition is important for both information storage and skills acquisition.

But, there is a large difference between knowledge and skills: Knowing about a skill, or understanding how the skill should be executed, is not the same as actually *having* that skill. For instance, you might be told all about a skill such as driving a car with a standard (stick shift) transmission, or playing the piano, or typing on a computer keyboard. You could have a great teacher, have wonderful learning tools, and pay attention very carefully. You might *understand* everything perfectly. But, the first few times that you actually attempt the skill, you will probably make some mistakes. In fact, you will probably experience some frustration because of the gap between your *understanding* of the skill and your actual ability to *perform* the skill.

Perfecting skills takes practice. You need repetition to create the pathways in your brain that control your skills. Therefore, you shouldn't be satisfied with simply reading this book and then saying to yourself, "I get it." You will not reach your full PSAT scoring potential unless you put in sufficient time practicing as well as understanding and learning.

Later in this book, we'll go into detail about the facts that make up the "knowledge base" that is essential for PSAT success. First, we need to tell you about the skills and strategies.

Strategic Thinking

In college, there will be stress that arises from sources such as family expectations, fear of failure, heavy workload, competition, and difficult subjects. The PSAT, like the SAT, tries to create similar stresses. The *psychometricians* (specialized psychologists who study the measurement of the mind), who contribute to the design of standardized tests, use *artificial stressors* to test how you will respond to the stress of college.

The main *stressor* is the time limit. The time limits are set on the PSAT so that most students cannot finish all the questions in the time allowed. So, you will have to get used to the idea that you will probably leave some questions blank on each section. You should try to answer as many questions as you can, and then go back to the questions you skipped if you have time remaining in each section.

Another stressor is the element of surprise that is present for most students. If you practice enough, there should be no surprises on test day. The PSAT is very predictable.

Relax to Succeed

Probably the worst thing that can happen to a test taker is to panic. Research shows that there are very predictable results when a person panics. To panic is to have a specific set of easily recognizable symptoms: sweating, shortness of breath, muscle tension, increased pulse rate, tunnel vision, nausea, light-headedness and, in rare cases, even loss of consciousness.

These symptoms are the results of chemical changes in the brain brought on by some stimulus. The stimulus does not even have to be external. Therefore, we can panic ourselves just by thinking about certain things.

The stress chemical in your body called *epinephrine*, more commonly known as *adrenalin*, brings on these symptoms. Adrenalin changes the priorities in your brain activity. It moves blood and electrical energy to some parts of the brain and away from others. Specifically, it increases brain activity in the areas that control your body and reduces activity in the parts of your brain that are involved in complex thinking.

Therefore, panic makes a person stronger and faster, and also less able to perform the type of thinking that is important on a PSAT exam.

It is not a bad thing to have a small amount of adrenalin in your bloodstream because of a healthy amount of excitement about your exam. But, you should be careful not to panic before or during an exam.

You can control your adrenalin levels by minimizing the unknown factors in the PSAT testing process. The biggest stress-inducing questions are: "What do the PSAT writers expect?" "Am I ready?" "How will I do on test day?" If you spend time and energy studying and practicing under realistic conditions before your test day, you'll have a much better chance of controlling your adrenalin levels and handling the exam with no panic.

The goals of your preparation should be to learn about the test, acquire the knowledge and skills that are being measured by the test, and learn about yourself and how you respond to the different parts of the exam.

The *psychometricians*, and other experts who work on the design of PSAT exams, refer to certain parts of the PSAT as "artificial stressors." In other words, they are actually trying to create a certain level of stress in you. They are doing this because the PSAT is a practice SAT and the SAT is supposed to tell college admissions officials something about how you will respond to the stress of college exams.

You should also consider which question types you will try on test day and which ones you will just make an educated guess on. You need to be familiar with the material that is tested on each section of your PSAT. As you work through this book, make an assessment of the best use of your time and energy. Concentrate on the areas that will give you the highest score in the amount of time that you have until the exam. This will result in a feeling of confidence on test day even when you are facing very challenging questions.

Specific Relaxation Techniques

Following is some useful information on how to be as relaxed and confident as possible on test day.

Be Prepared

The more prepared you feel, the less likely it is that you'll be stressed on test day. Study and practice consistently during the time between now and your test day. Be organized. Have your supplies and lucky testing clothes ready in advance. Make a practice trip to the test center before your test day.

Know Yourself

Get to know your strengths and weaknesses on the PSAT and the things that help you to relax. Some test takers like to have a slightly anxious feeling to help them focus. Others folks do best when they are so relaxed that they are almost asleep. You will learn about yourself through practice.

Rest

The better rested you are, the better things seem. As you get fatigued, you are more likely to look on the dark side of things and worry more, which hurts your test scores.

Nutrition

Sugar is bad for stress and brain function in general. Consuming refined sugar creates biological stress that has an impact on your brain chemistry. Keep sugar consumption to a minimum for several days before your test. If you are actually addicted to caffeine, (you can tell that you are if you get headaches when you skip a day) get your normal amount. Don't forget to eat regularly while you're preparing for the PSAT. It's not a good idea to skip meals simply because you are experiencing some additional stress. It is also important to eat something before you take the PSAT. An empty stomach might be distracting and uncomfortable on test day.

Do the Easy Stuff First

Get familiar with the format of each section of the PSAT so that you can recognize portions that are likely to give you trouble. Mark as many correct answers as you can early on, and then go back and work on the harder questions. You don't have to get all the questions right in order to get a great score on the PSAT.

Each of the questions on a PSAT test is worth the same number of points as every other question. Some questions are harder than others. So, you are foolish if you waste time and energy on a hard question while other less difficult questions are still waiting. If time permits, you can always come back and work on the challenging problems in the final minutes. You cannot skip from one section to another but you can skip around within a section as much as necessary.

This strategy helps with both time management and stress reduction.

Breathe

If you feel yourself tensing up, slow down and take deeper breaths. This will relax you and get more oxygen to your brain so that you can think more clearly.

Take Breaks

You cannot stay sharply focused on your PSAT for the whole time in the testing center. You are certainly going to have distracting thoughts, or times when you just can't process all the information. When this happens, you should close your eyes, clear your mind, and then start back on your test. This process should take only a minute or so. You could pray, meditate, or just picture a place or person that helps you to relax. Try thinking of something fun that you have planned for right after your PSAT. Remember that you cannot skip from one section to another on the PSAT. However, you can skip any troublesome questions within a section and come back to them later if you have time.

Have a Plan of Attack

Know how you are going to work through each part of the exam. There is no time to make up a plan of attack on test day. Hopefully you will do enough practice that you internalize the skills you need to do your best on each section, and you won't have to stop to think about what to do next.

Manage the Grid

Avoid the common mistake of marking the answer to each question on your answer grid right after you finish the question. Do *not* go directly to your "bubble sheet" after each question. This is dangerous and a waste of time. It's dangerous because you might mark the wrong space on your answer grid. It wastes time since you have to find your place on the answer sheet and then find your place back in the test booklet. You don't waste a lot of time with each question, but, it can add up over the course of an entire test section and could cost you enough time to get a few more questions done.

Answer a series of questions, circling your choice in the test booklet. Then, transfer that set of answers to the answer sheet. Filling in circles can be a good activity to keep you busy when you simply need a break.

You Own Your Test Booklet

A PSAT test booklet is meant to be used by one test taker only. You will not have any scratch paper on test day. You are expected to do any note taking or figuring on the booklet itself. Your score comes only from the answers that you mark on the answer sheet.

Be Aware of Time

You should time yourself on test day. You should time yourself on some of your practice exams. We suggest that you use an analog (dial face) watch. You can turn the hands on your watch back from noon to allow enough time for the section that you are working on. For instance, if you are working on a PSAT Writing Skills section, which is 30 minutes long, you can turn your watch back to 11:30 and set it on the desk in front of you. You will be finished when the hands on your watch point to 12:00. Similarly, if you are working on any other section, set your watch to 11:35 and, again, you will be done at noon. This method has the added benefit of helping you to forget about the outside world while you are testing. All that matters during the test is your test. All of life's other issues will have to be dealt with after your test is finished. You might find this attitude easier to attain if you lose track of what time it is in the "outside world."

Guessing

Never guess at random! For every incorrect answer that you mark, you lose an extra $\frac{1}{4}$ point. If you leave a question blank, you only lose one point. Because there are five possible answer choices for each question, you only have a $\frac{1}{5}$ chance of guessing correctly. The odds reach the break-even point when you can eliminate one answer choice that you are certain is incorrect. If you can eliminate at least one choice, go ahead and guess. Obviously, the more choices you can eliminate before you guess, the better off you'll be.

Changing Answers

Most testers should not change an answer once they make a decision. But, some testers tend to be much more accurate when they do make a change— meaning, if they change an answer, they are more likely to change it *to* the correct answer, rather than *from* the correct answer. You can only learn this about yourself by doing practice exams and paying attention to any changes that you made.

What to Expect on Test Day

Do a Dry Run

Make sure that you know how long it will take to get to the testing center and where you will park, alternative routes, and so on. If you are testing in a place that is new to you, try to get into the building between now and test day so that you can absorb the sounds and smells, find out where the bathrooms and snack machines are, and so on.

Wake Up Early

You generally have to be at the testing center by 8:00 a.m. Set two alarms if you have to. Leave yourself plenty of time to get fully awake before you have to run out the door.

Dress for Success

Wear loose, comfortable, clothes in layers so that you can adjust to the temperature. Remember your watch. There might not be a clock in your testing room.

Fuel Up

Eat something without too much sugar in it on the morning of your test. Get your normal dose of caffeine, if any. (Test day is not the time to "try coffee" for the first time!)

Bring Supplies

Bring your driver's license (or passport), your admission ticket, several #2 pencils, a good eraser or two, and your calculator. You can check the PSAT website for up-to-date information about which calculators are acceptable. If you need them, bring your glasses or contact lenses. You won't be able to eat or drink while the PSAT is in progress, but you can bring a snack for the break time if you wish.

Warm Up Your Brain

Read a newspaper or something similar so that the PSAT isn't the first thing you read on test day.

Plan a Mini-vacation

Most students find it easier to concentrate on their exam preparation and on their PSAT if they have a plan for some fun right after the test. Plan something that you can look forward to as a reward for all the hard work and energy that you're putting in. Then, when it gets hard to concentrate, you can say, "If I do my work now, I'll have tons of fun right after the exam!"

The chapters in this book cover the specific sections on the PSAT. There are additional strategies and practice questions in each chapter. The full-length Practice Tests can be found directly following these content-area chapters. Plan to take one full-length test about one week prior to the actual PSAT. Read the explanations for the questions that you missed, and review the content-area chapters as necessary. Remember, practice as much as you can under realistic testing conditions to maximize your PSAT score.

Self-Assessment

This section will assist you in evaluating your current readiness for the PSAT. Sample questions representing each section of the PSAT are included to help you to pinpoint areas of strength and weakness in your knowledge base and your skill set. Make an honest effort to answer each question, and then review the explanation that follows. Don't worry if you are unable to answer many or most of the questions at this point. The rest of the book contains information and resources to help you to maximize your PSAT score.

 Even if you already know that your strength is either verbal or math, attempt all the questions in this section. The PSAT is probably unlike any test you've ever taken, and now is a good time to familiarize yourself with the types of questions that will appear on the PSAT.

Verbal Assessment

This portion of the PSAT tests your ability to effectively understand and use standard written English. It also assesses your critical thinking skills as well as your vocabulary. Following are sample questions, similar to those that might appear on the PSAT:

Critical Reading—Sentence Completion

Select the best word or words to complete the following sentences.

1. The film had a divergent effect on viewers: it was _____ by critics as the most influential of the decade and, at the same time, _____ to the public, who found the focus of the film to be offensive.

   (A) applauded .. agreeable

   (B) shunned .. despicable

   (C) rejected .. pleasing

   (D) donned .. enticing

   (E) hailed .. loathsome

2. The cast members nervously watched Jeff on the stage opening night, worried that his performance would echo the terrible _____ he had experienced earlier in the week.

   (A) introduction

   (B) scenery

   (C) rehearsal

   (D) atmosphere

   (E) plot

3. Unlike the daily satisfaction most Americans experience from an over-abundance of food, thousands of _____ villagers in Moldavia have barely enough food to survive.

   (A) impoverished

   (B) prosperous

   (C) affluent

   (D) insolvent

   (E) flourishing

4. The researchers unveiled _____ new equipment that detected _____ illnesses sooner than any other equipment on the market.

   (A) traditional .. discernible

   (B) conventional .. vicious

   (C) pioneering .. infirm

   (D) revolutionary .. emerging

   (E) controversial .. morose

5. The actress was well known for her _____ behavior; her reactions in the face of even the slightest disruption were highly unpredictable.

   (A) vigilant

   (B) impetuous

   (C) assiduous

   (D) anticipated

   (E) foreseeable

Critical Reading—Sentence Completions— Answer Key and Explanations

1. The best answer is **E**. Because the sentence indicates that the film had a divergent effect, you should be looking for answer choices that contradict one another; the critics felt one way, whereas the general public felt another way. *Hailed* means enthusiastically praised, and *loathsome* means highly offensive, which are contradictory terms that correctly describe the feelings of the critics and the public, respectively. The word pairs *applauded* and *agreeable* and *shunned* and *despicable* do not contradict each other; the word pairs *rejected* and *pleasing* and *donned* and *enticing* do not fit the context of the sentence; therefore, answer choices A, B, C, and D are incorrect.

2. The best answer is **C**. To answer this question, you must know the meaning of the word *rehearsal*, which means a practice or run-through. The members were nervous because of Jeff's "terrible rehearsal," which is the only choice that logically fits into the context of the sentence. The other words could relate to a play, but do not effectively complete the sentence; therefore, answer choices A, B, D, and E are incorrect.

3. The best answer is **A**. The sentence begins with "unlike," which indicates that the information before the comma is contradictory to the information after the comma; Americans are described as being satisfied, whereas the Moldavian villagers are described as being something other than satisfied. *Impoverished* means poor, and thus could be used to describe someone with barely enough food to survive; *prosperous* and *affluent* mean to be rich and successful; therefore, eliminate answer choices B and C. *Insolvent* means unable to meet debts, which doesn't fit with the context, so eliminate answer choice D. *Flourishing* means thriving or prospering, so eliminate answer choice E.

4. The best answer is **D**. In the sentence, the first blank is an adjective that describes the equipment, and the second blank is an adjective that describes illnesses. Because the equipment is described as *new*, it doesn't make sense that it would also be *traditional* or *conventional*; eliminate answer choices A and B. The remaining answer choices contain words that could fit into the first blank, so now look at the second blank. Based on the context of the sentence, it makes sense that *revolutionary*, new equipment would be able to detect *emerging* illnesses. *Infirm* and *morose* are not words that would be used to describe an illness, so eliminate answer choices C and E.

5. The best answer is **B**. In this sentence, the information following the semicolon gives a definition for the word that fits into the blank. Because the definition indicates that her behavior would be *unpredictable*, eliminate answer choices D and E, which have opposite meanings to *unpredictable*. *Vigilant* means *watchful*, and *assiduous* means *persistent* or *diligent*—neither of which fit the context of the sentence. Therefore, eliminate answer choices A and C.

Critical Reading—Passage-Based Reading

Select the best answers to the questions following the passage.

This is a recently written passage focusing on the physical attributes and inspirational design of the Lincoln Memorial.

The Lincoln Memorial, located on the National Mall in Washington, D.C., is one of the most profound symbols of American Democracy in the world. Dedicated in 1922, it won the prestigious Gold Medal of the American Institute of Architects for its architect, Henry Bacon. The
5 physical presence of the memorial is exceptionally impressive. There are a total of 36 Doric columns around the building, each representing one of the 36 states of the union at the time of Lincoln's death in 1865. Stones from various states were used in the construction of the memorial. The names of the 48 states in the Union at the time of the memo-
10 rial's completion are carved on the outside walls. The North wall of the Lincoln Memorial boasts the 16th president's second inaugural address, while on the South wall, the Gettysburg Address is proudly carved. Above the statue of Abraham Lincoln are the words: "In this Temple, as in the hearts of the people, for whom he saved the Union, the memory
15 of Abraham Lincoln is enshrined forever."

Designed by famed American sculptor Daniel Chester French and carved by the Piccirilli Brothers, the statue is three times the size of an average adult. There are also two paintings by artist Jules Guerin depicting important events of Lincoln's tenure as president, including
20 a painting titled "Emancipation." In front of the building is a set of long steps, which lead directly into the open entranceway. The rectangular reflecting pool in front of the structure provides a calm and serene atmosphere where visitors can ponder the ideals in which Abraham Lincoln so strongly believed.

25 In addition to its structural magnificence, the Lincoln Memorial is known as a place where citizens can assemble to draw attention to those causes and issues that continue to divide the country. From all walks of

life, people come to be awed by the spirit of President Lincoln's fierce determination to save the Union and his extraordinary compassion
30 towards those who had been denied their freedom. Perhaps the reason the Lincoln Memorial holds such a special place in the hearts of all Americans is because it serves as a place to celebrate things that unite us as a nation, as well as a place to focus on the things that still divide us. It is also possible that people come by the millions to be inspired by
35 the strength and compassion of President Lincoln's great vision. As a potent symbol of American democracy, the Lincoln Memorial continues to inspire the world with its simple and dignified message of freedom.

1. As used in line 11, the word "boasts" most nearly means

   (A) engraves

   (B) downplays

   (C) exhibits

   (D) is proud of

   (E) is well-liked

2. The primary purpose of the passage is to

   (A) account for the popularity of President Lincoln

   (B) highlight the significance of the Lincoln Memorial

   (C) explain how the Lincoln Memorial was constructed

   (D) introduce the concept of presidential memorials

   (E) describe the history of the Civil War

3. The phrase "…including a painting titled 'Emancipation'" is used by the author to illustrate

   (A) how much Abraham Lincoln contributed to the construction of the Lincoln Memorial

   (B) how important the physical appearance of the Lincoln Memorial is to visitors

   (C) the manner in which Lincoln convinced visitors to adopt his ideals

   (D) the significance of Lincoln's work toward ensuring freedom for all American citizens

   (E) how strongly American citizens supported Lincoln's message of peace and serenity

4. In line 23, "ideals" refers to

(A) Daniel Chester French's plans to carve the statue of Lincoln

(B) the calming effect of the reflecting pool

(C) Lincoln's honorable and noble principles

(D) the important events depicted in Guerin's paintings

(E) Lincoln's desire to construct the memorial

5. The opening sentence of the passage (lines 1–3) introduces a sense of

(A) patriotism

(B) wonder

(C) mystery

(D) fanaticism

(E) treachery

Critical Reading—Passage-Based Reading—Answer Key and Explanations

1. The best answer is **C**. The passage states that "The North wall of the Lincoln Memorial boasts the 16th president's second inaugural address…" Based on the context of the passage, the word "boasts" is intended to indicate that President Lincoln's second inaugural address is exhibited on the North Wall. The word "boasts" can be used to suggest pride, but not in this context, so eliminate answer choice D. Answer choices A, B, and E are not supported by the context of the passage.

2. The best answer is **B**. The passage describes the physical attributes and inspirational design of the Lincoln Memorial. Details in the passage highlight the significance of the structure. The passage mentions that Lincoln had "great vision," but the focus of the passage is not Lincoln's popularity; eliminate answer choice A. The passage includes information on the materials used to construct the Memorial, but does not explain how the Memorial was constructed; eliminate answer choice C. The passage provides information on the Lincoln Memorial specifically, but does not introduce the concept of presidential memorials in general; eliminate answer choice D. There is no discussion of the history of the Civil War in the passage, so eliminate answer choice E.

3. The best answer is **D**. The phrase "...including a painting titled 'Emancipation'" immediately follows a discussion of Jules Guerin's paintings that depict important events of Lincoln's tenure as president. The passage goes on to say that Lincoln had extraordinary compassion toward those who had been denied their freedom. It is most likely that the author introduced the concept of "emancipation," which relates to freedom, to emphasize the significance of Lincoln's work toward ensuring freedom for all American citizens. Answer choices A, B, C, and E are not supported by information in the passage.

4. The best answer is **C**. An "ideal" is an honorable or worthy principle. The context of the passage supports this definition and use of the word "ideals." Answer choices A, B, D, and E are not supported by information in the passage.

5. The best answer is **A**. The opening sentence of the passage states that "The Lincoln Memorial, located on the National Mall in Washington, D.C., is one of the most profound symbols of American Democracy in the world." The passage goes on to emphasize President Lincoln's "fierce determination to save the Union," as well as his "great vision." These details best support a sense of "patriotism." "Treachery" has a negative connotation, which is not supported by the passage, so eliminate answer choice E. Answer choices B, C, and D do not accurately convey the sense introduced by the first sentence.

Writing Skills—Identifying Sentence Errors

For each sentence, select the underlined portion that includes an error. Select answer choice E if there is no error.

1. The negative <u>effects</u> of nitrogen-based fertilizers <u>have been</u> widely

              A   B

publicized, yet scientists <u>has</u> not managed to find <u>an acceptable</u>

                         C   D

replacement. <u>No error</u>

        E

2. The Broadway musical *The Mambo Kings*, <u>based</u> on the novel by Oscar

A

Hijuelos, a Pulitzer Prize–winning author, <u>depicting</u> the journey of the

B

Castillo <u>brothers</u> <u>from Havana</u> to New York City in the 1950s. <u>No error</u>

              C   D   E

3. The new <u>oven</u> at the restaurant, which <u>uses</u> circulating fans <u>for to cook</u>

          A   B   C

food, may decrease preparation time <u>by</u> half. <u>No error</u>

                                 D   E

4. The <u>author, whose</u> upbringing in a rural community <u>has</u>

          A   B

<u>influenced her writing</u>, <u>attempts to</u> overcome the misconceptions about

           C   D

rural life in her novels and literary articles. <u>No error</u>

                                   E

5. <u>In contrast to</u> most other professors, Dr. James <u>chose to</u> lecture on new

      A   B

material before the midterm exam, not realizing that the students <u>were</u>

                                                C

<u>preoccupied to</u> reviewing their notes for the test. <u>No error</u>

   D   E

Writing Skills—Identifying Sentence Errors—Answer Key and Explanations

1. The best answer is **C**. The verb "has" is a singular verb, and must be used with a singular noun. The noun "scientists" is plural, and must be followed by the plural verb "have." Therefore, the underlined word "has" is incorrect.

2. The best answer is **B**. This sentence as it is written is an incomplete sentence, because of the use of the verb form "depicting." To correct the sentence, you could use either the present tense verb "depicts," or the past tense verb "depicted."

3. The best answer is **C**. To make this sentence correct in standard written English, you should remove the word "for" in the underlined portion "for to cook." Therefore, answer choice C is correct because it contains an error.

4. The best answer is **E**. This sentence is correct as it is written. Don't be afraid to select answer choice E; the test requires you to first decide whether or not there are any errors, and then identify those errors. It is possible that the sentence might not contain any errors.

5. The best answer is **D**. To make this sentence correct in standard written English, you should replace the word "to" in the underlined portion "preoccupied to" with the word "with." The phrase "preoccupied with" is idiomatic, which means that it reflects common usage in standard written English. Therefore, answer choice D is correct because it contains an error.

Writing Skills—Improving Sentences

Select the answer choice that creates the most effective sentence. Answer choice A repeats the underlined portion.

1. Distracted by noisy teenagers at the library, <u>a quiet area to study was what Mandy desperately needed to find</u> if she planned on finishing her homework.

   (A) a quiet area to study was what Mandy desperately needed to find

   (B) Mandy desperately needed to find a quiet area to study

   (C) Mandy's need to find a quiet area to study was desperate

   (D) a quiet area to study for which Mandy desperately needed to find

   (E) Mandy's desperate need to find an area to study that was quiet

2. The rest of his family was already at the hospital <u>when Jack had been told that</u> his son had been in an accident.

   (A) when Jack had been told that

   (B) when it was learned by Jack that

   (C) when Jack learned that

   (D) then Jack was told that

   (E) and then Jack learned

3. <u>Standing</u> on the bank of the river, the tugboat appeared to be barely moving.

(A) Standing

(B) Standing as I was

(C) By standing

(D) Positioned

(E) From my position

4. <u>Having first-rate computer skills, a pleasant and professional demeanor, and his filing experience,</u> Michael is considered the top contender for the position at my firm.

(A) Having first-rate computer skills, a pleasant and professional demeanor, and his filing experience,

(B) Having first-rate computer skills, a pleasant and professional demeanor, and also his filing experience,

(C) With his first-rate computer skills, pleasant and professional demeanor, and having filing experience,

(D) Because of his first-rate computer skills, pleasant and professional demeanor, and filing experience,

(E) By having first-rate computer skills, a pleasant and professional demeanor, and having filing experience,

5. Most adults should <u>know that regular exercise helps to maintain</u> a healthy weight and reduces the risk of cardiovascular disease.

(A) know that regular exercise helps to maintain

(B) know that exercise regularly maintains

(C) know that regular exercise may, by helping to maintain

(D) have known that regular exercise not only maintains

(E) have the knowledge that regular exercise maintains

Writing Skills—Improving Sentences— Answer Key and Explanations

1. The best answer is **B**. The replacement for the underlined portion that most clearly indicates that Mandy was distracted by the noise and

needed to find a quiet place to study is "Mandy desperately needed to find a quiet area to study." Eliminate answer choices A and D, which suggest that the quiet study area was distracted by the noisy teenagers. Answer choices C and E are awkward and should be eliminated as well.

2. The best answer is **C**. The replacement for the underlined portion that most clearly indicates the sequence of events is "when Jack learned that." This section is also in the active voice, which is preferred on the PSAT. Answer choices A, B, D, and E are awkward and do not effectively convey the idea that Jack's family was already at the hospital.

3. The best answer is **E**. The sentence as it is written contains a misplaced modifier. The action of "standing" appears to be contributed to the tugboat, which does not make sense; eliminate answer choice A. Eliminate answer choices C and D for the same reason. Only the phrase "from my position" clearly indicates that "I" was on the bank of the river observing the tugboat. Eliminate answer choice B because it is awkward.

4. The best answer is **D**. It is important to use parallel expressions within a sentence. As it is written, the sentence is clumsy. The replacement for the underlined portion that most clearly states Michael's qualifications is "Because of his first-rate computer skills, pleasant and professional demeanor, and filing experience." Eliminate answer choices A, B, C, and E because they are awkward and do not include parallel expressions.

5. The best answer is **A**. The sentence as it is written is clear and concise, and maintains parallel construction between the verb forms. Eliminate answer choice B because the word "regularly" should not be used to describe the verb "maintains." Eliminate answer choices C, D, and E because they are wordy and awkward.

Writing Skills—Improving Paragraphs

This passage is an early draft of an essay. Select the best answers to the questions following the passage.

(1) Many people believe that the best thing about having money is using it to help others. (2) Actor/director/producer Paul Newman is no exception. (3) For years, Newman concocted his own recipe of an oil and vinegar based salad dressing and distributed it around to friends and family. (4) Every year he would receive enthusiastic praise and requests for more until he finally decided that he had a marketable product on his hands. (5) With that thought in mind, in 1982 Newman began his company, *Newman's Own*.

(6) The product line, found in grocery stores and markets across the country, features salsas, popcorn, lemonade, pasta sauces, and more.

(7) From the beginning, Newman had at least two important driving forces behind his company's establishment. **(8)** First, all of *Newman's Own* products were derived from natural ingredients and included no preservatives. **(9)** The ingredients must have been fresh and of high quality. **(10)** Second, it was decided that all profits from the products' sales would be given to charitable or educational organizations. **(11)** To date, over $150 million has been donated to a variety of charities, projects, and education groups.

(12) Ten years after *Newman's Own* was established, Paul Newman's daughter Nell decided to jump on the bandwagon. **(13)** She suggested to her father that a new line of food products be added to the company's offerings. **(14)** Beginning with organic pretzels, *Newman's Own Organics: The Second Generation* is now well-established, with items ranging from organic cookies to pet food. **(15)** Nell Newman added a twist to her branch of the company by suggesting that company employees decide which charities to support. **(16)** Over $2 million has been given to such causes as wildlife preservation, medical research, and senior citizen groups.

1. In context, what is the best way to deal with sentence 5?

    (A) Leave it as it is.

    (B) Move it to the beginning of the second paragraph.

    (C) Connect it to sentence 6 with a comma.

    (D) Move it to the end of the first paragraph.

    (E) Start a new sentence after "mind" and delete "in 1982."

2. Of the following, which is the best version of the underlined portion of sentence 9 (reproduced below)?

    The ingredients <u>must have been</u> fresh and of high quality.

    (A) (As it is now)

    (B) had to be

    (C) will have been

    (D) must of been

    (E) has to have been

3. Which of the following sentences is best to insert between sentences 10 and 11?

   (A) Many charities were selected to receive money.

   (B) Sales of the products were insignificant.

   (C) This decision proved to be extremely important for the charities.

   (D) Some charities also received money from government sources.

   (E) Many grocery store managers generally contribute to charities.

4. Which phrase, if inserted at the beginning of sentence 13 (reproduced below), best fits the context?

   She suggested to her father that a new line of food products be added to the company's offerings.

   (A) Certain that the company was not going to be successful,

   (B) Despite the increasing cost of all-natural ingredients,

   (C) Building on the large amounts of money already donated to the company,

   (D) Instead of focusing on fresh, natural ingredients,

   (E) Convinced that the company should focus on organic ingredients,

5. The primary effect of the final paragraph (sentences 12–16) is to

   (A) contrast the ideas presented in the first and second paragraphs

   (B) describe a continuation of the ideas discussed in the essay

   (C) explain the contradictions within the essay

   (D) use persuasion to change the reader's opinion

   (E) summarize the ideas introduced in the preceding paragraph

Writing Skills—Improving Paragraphs— Answer Key and Explanations

1. The best answer is **A**. The sentence is best as it is written and where it is placed within the paragraph. Moving it to the beginning of the second paragraph or to the end of the first paragraph would disrupt the flow of ideas within the essay. Eliminate answer choices B and D. Connecting sentence 5 to sentence 6 with a comma would create a comma splice,

which is grammatically incorrect. Eliminate answer choice B. Starting a new sentence after "mind" would create an incomplete sentence; eliminate answer choice E.

2. The best answer is **B**. It is important to maintain parallel construction within a paragraph. The sentences preceding sentence 9 are in the past tense, so sentence 9 should also be in the past tense. Eliminate answer choices A, C, and E because they are not in the past tense. It is never correct to say "must of," so eliminate answer choice D.

3. The best answer is **C**. The best sentence to insert between sentences 10 and 11 will logically lead the reader from one sentence to the next. Sentence 10 states that all profits would be given to charitable organizations, and sentence 11 states that over $150 million has been donated so far. The sentence "This decision proved to be extremely important for the charities" effectively ties those two ideas together. Eliminate answer choices A, B, D, and E because they contain irrelevant information.

4. The best answer is **E**. The sentence that most effectively explains why Nell suggested adding new products is "Convinced that the company should focus on organic ingredients," answer choice E. Eliminate answer choice A because the essay indicates that the company was already successful. Eliminate answer choice C because the money was donated to charities, not to the company. Eliminate answer choices B and D because they are not supported by the context of the essay.

5. The best answer is **B**. The final paragraph serves to continue the ideas presented earlier in the essay. It describes the continued success of the company and indicates that even more money was donated to worthy causes. Answer choices A, C, D, and E are not supported by the essay.

 You should now have a good idea of the types of questions found on the different Verbal sections of the PSAT. If this is your weak area, refer specifically to the chapters in the book that focus on strengthening your verbal skills.

Math Assessment

This portion of the PSAT tests your ability to effectively apply mathematical concepts, including arithmetic, algebra, geometry, and data analysis. It also assesses your critical thinking skills. Following are sample questions, similar to those that might appear on the PSAT:

Multiple Choice

Solve the problems and select the best answer.

1. If $z = m(m - 4)$, then $z - 4 = ?$

  (A) $m^2 - 4m - 4$

  (B) $m^2 - m$

  (C) $m^2 + 4m - 4$

  (D) $m^2 - 4m + 4$

  (E) $m^2 - 8$

2. All numbers divisible by both 3 and 8 are also divisible by which of the following numbers?

  (A) 5

  (B) 6

  (C) 9

  (D) 21

  (E) 38

3. What is the area of the triangle in the figure below?

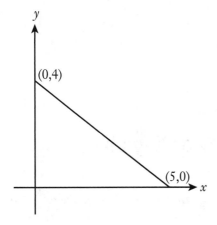

  (A) 4.5

  (B) 9.0

  (C) 10.0

  (D) 12.5

  (E) 20.0

4. If each of the longhaired dogs staying at the kennel weighs less than twenty pounds, which of the following must be true?

(A) There is one longhaired dog staying at the kennel that weighs more than twenty pounds.

(B) No longhaired dog weighing less than twenty pounds is staying at the kennel.

(C) All longhaired dogs not staying at the kennel weigh more than twenty pounds.

(D) No longhaired dog that weighs twenty pounds or more is staying at the kennel.

(E) All dogs that weigh less than twenty pounds are staying at the kennel.

5. If $x/5 = x^2$, the value of x can be which of the following?

I. $-\dfrac{1}{5}$

II. $\dfrac{1}{5}$

III. 1

(A) I only

(B) II only

(C) III only

(D) I and III only

(E) I, II, and III

Multiple Choice—Answer Key and Explanations

1. The correct answer is **A**. You are given that $z = m(m-4)$. Therefore, the best way to solve this problem is to substitute the quantity $m(m - 4)$ for z in the second equation given in the question, as follows:

➤ $z - 4$ is equivalent to $m(m - 4) - 4$

➤ Apply the distributive property to get $m^2 - 4m - 4$, answer choice A.

If you incorrectly divided the second two elements of the equation by 4, you would get answer choice B. You would get either answer choice C or D if you did not effectively keep track of the negative signs in the equation. If you did not correctly apply the distributive property, you would get answer choice E.

2. The correct answer is **B**. The best approach to solving this problem is to find one number that is divisible by both 3 and 8, and then determine which of the answer choices also goes into that number. When you multiply 3 times 8, you get 24, which means that 24 is one number that is divisible by both 3 and 8. Of the answer choices, only 6 also goes into 24, so answer choice B must be correct. None of the other answer choices is a divisor of 24.

3. The correct answer is **C**. To correctly answer this question, you must remember that the area of a triangle is calculated using the formula $A = \frac{1}{2}(bh)$, where b is the base of the triangle and h is the height of the triangle. The base of the triangle extends from the origin in the (x,y) coordinate plane, $(0,0)$ to the point $(5,0)$. This means that the base is 5. The height of the triangle extends from the origin in the (x,y) coordinate plane, $(0,0)$ to $(0,4)$. The height of the triangle is 4. Plug these values into the formula:

➤ $A = \frac{1}{2}(bh)$

➤ $A = \frac{1}{2}(5 \times 4)$

➤ $A = \frac{1}{2}(20)$

➤ $A = 10$, answer choice C.

4. The correct answer is **D**. The best way to answer this question is to look at the answer choices given and decide whether each choice is true, based on the information given in the question, or false because it contradicts information given in the question.

➤ Answer choice A states that one longhaired dog staying at the kennel weighs more than twenty pounds; this contradicts information in the question, which states that all the longhaired dogs staying at the kennel weigh less than twenty pounds. Eliminate answer choice A.

➤ Answer choice B states that no longhaired dog weighing less than twenty pounds is staying at the kennel, which is also contradictory to the statement in the question regarding the weight of the longhaired dogs. Eliminate answer choice B.

➤ Answer choice C states that all longhaired dogs not staying at the kennel weigh more than twenty pounds. This is not a logical inference based on the information given in the question, so eliminate answer choice C. The question tells you that all the longhaired dogs that are staying at the kennel are under 20 pounds but doesn't really tell you anything about any dogs that are not staying at the kennel.

➤ Answer choice D states that no longhaired dog that weighs twenty pounds or more is staying at the kennel. This must be true because the question tells you that any longhaired dog that is staying at the kennel weighs less than 20 pounds. Answer choice D is true, and therefore, correct.

➤ Answer choice E states that all dogs that weigh less than twenty pounds are staying at the kennel. This is also an illogical statement, not supported by information given in the question because you only know about the weight of the longhaired dogs staying at the kennel, not anything about any other type of dog. Eliminate answer choice E.

5. The correct answer is **B**. The best way to approach this question is to apply reason, and eliminate the Roman numerals that cannot be true. For example, x^2 must be a positive number because any nonzero number squared is positive. Therefore, Roman Numeral I cannot be true. At this point, you can eliminate answer choices A, D, and E, which all contain Roman Numeral I. Now look at Roman Numeral III because it is an easier number to work with. Substitute 1 for x in the given equation:

➤ $x/5 = x^2$

➤ $\frac{1}{5}$ does not equal 1^2

Now you can eliminate answer choice C, which leaves answer choice B as the only possible correct answer. To check the math, substitute $\frac{1}{5}$ for x in the given equation:

➤ $\dfrac{\frac{1}{5}}{5} = 5^2$

➤ $\frac{1}{5}$ divided by 5 is the same as 5 times 5, which equals 25. 5^2 also equals 25. Because the equation is satisfied, one possible value of x is $\frac{1}{5}$.

Student-Produced Response

Solve the following problems.

1. If $a(b + c) = 127$ and $ac = 82$, what is the value of ab?

2. The perimeter of a rectangular playground is 350 yards. If the length of one side of the playground is 75 yards, what is the area of the playground, in square yards?

3. For what value of c would the following system of equations have an infinite number of solutions?

$24a - 15b = 108$

$72a - 45b = 9c$

4. If line l, which is not shown on the following graph, intersects line MO between M and O and passes through point P (0,1), what is one possible slope of line l?

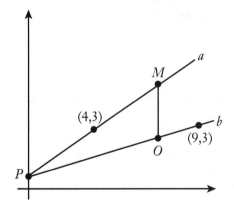

5. The following table shows the results of a survey conducted on a group of 32 students in a class that would soon be graduating from college. The students were asked to indicate whether they had 0, 1, 2, 3, or 4 different part-time jobs while in college. After the survey was completed, a new student joined the class, and the mean number of part-time jobs held became equivalent to the original mode number of part-time jobs per student. What number of part-time jobs did the new student hold during college?

Part-time Jobs Held in College Per Graduating Student	
Number of Part-time Jobs Held	Number of Graduating Students
0	2
1	1
2	2
3	14
4	13

Student-Produced Response—Answer Key and Explanations

1. **The answer is 45.** The first step in solving this problem is to apply the distributive property in the first equation, as follows:

   ➤ $a(b + c) = 127$

   ➤ $ab + ac = 127$

   You are given that $ac = 82$, so substitute 82 for ac in the first equation, and solve for ab:

   ➤ $ab + 82 = 127$

   ➤ $ab = 127 - 82$

   ➤ $ab = 45$

2. **The answer is 7,500.** To solve this problem, you must remember that the perimeter of a rectangle is calculated by using the formula $P = 2l + 2w$, where l is the length and w is the width. You are given that the perimeter is 350 and the length of one side is 75. Substitute these values into the formula, as follows:

   ➤ $350 = 2l + 2(75)$—Note that you can make either the length or the width equal to 75 at this point. We chose to make the width equal to 75, and will now solve for the length.

   ➤ $350 = 2l + 150$

   ➤ $350 = 2l + 150$

   ➤ $200 = 2l$

   ➤ $100 = l$

You now have both the length (100) and the width (75) of the rectangular playground. To calculate the area, multiply the length by the width: $100 \times 75 = 7,500$.

3. **The answer is 36.** Systems of equations will have an infinite number of solutions when the equations are equal to each other. The first step in solving this problem is to recognize that the second equation is exactly three times the value of the first equation:

➤ $72a = 3(24a)$, $45b = 3(15b)$, so $9c$ must equal $3(108)$. Solve for c:

➤ $9c = 3(108)$

➤ $9c = 324$

➤ $c = 36$

4. **The answer is** $\dfrac{2}{9} < x < \dfrac{1}{2}$ **or .222 < x < .5.** To answer this question, first draw line l on the diagram shown:

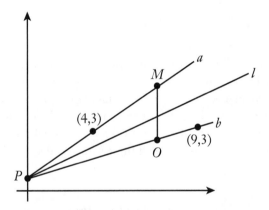

Line l lies somewhere between lines a and b. You are given that point P is at $(0,1)$. Because you have two points on line a and two points on line b, you can find the slope of each of those lines. Calculate the slope of a line using the formula $\dfrac{y_1 - y_2}{x_1 - x_2}$:

➤ Slope of line $a = \dfrac{(1-3)}{(0-4)} = \dfrac{-2}{-4} = \dfrac{1}{2}$

➤ Slope of line $b = \dfrac{(1-3)}{(0-9)} = \dfrac{-2}{-9} = \dfrac{2}{9}$

Therefore, the slope of line l must be somewhere between $\frac{1}{2}$ and $\frac{2}{9}$. If you grid in any value that falls between $\frac{1}{2}$ and $\frac{2}{9}$, you will be correct.

5. **The answer is 0.** The first step in solving this problem is to recognize that the original mode number of part-time jobs per student is 3. Mode is the number or range of numbers in a set that occurs the most frequently. A total of 14 students held 3 part-time jobs, so 3 is the mode. To calculate the mean number (average) of part-time jobs, you must first determine the total number of part-time jobs, as follows:

➤ 2 students held 0 jobs; $2 \times 0 = 0$

➤ 1 student held 1 job; $1 \times 1 = 1$

➤ 2 students held 2 jobs; $2 \times 2 = 4$

➤ 14 students held 3 jobs; $14 \times 3 = 42$

➤ 13 students held 4 jobs; $13 \times 4 = 52$

➤ $0 + 1 + 4 + 42 + 52 = 99$

You are given that, after the 33rd student joins the survey, the mean is equivalent to the original mode number of jobs (3). Because 99 (the total number of part-time jobs) divided by 33 (the total number of students in the survey) equals 3 (the mean), the new student must have held zero jobs during college. If the student held 1, 2, 3, or 4 jobs, the total number of jobs would be 99 + 1, 2, 3, or 4. None of these sums divided by 33 equals 3.

You should now have a good idea of the types of questions found on the different Math sections of the PSAT. If this is your weak area, refer specifically to the chapters in the book that focus on strengthening your math skills.

Now that you've assessed your readiness for the PSAT, you can begin to work on the remaining sections of the book. Focus first on the areas in which you need the most improvement, and apply the strategies and techniques provided. The old adage "practice makes perfect" really holds true here, so be sure to try all the practice questions included in the chapters, as well as the two full-length practice tests at the end of the book.

Critical Reading Section

Terms You'll Need to Understand

✓ Vocabulary in context
✓ Cognates
✓ Antonym
✓ Synonym
✓ Prefix
✓ Suffix
✓ Introductory phrase
✓ Transitional phrase
✓ Inference
✓ Imply
✓ Assumption

Concepts You'll Need to Master

✓ Determining the meaning of words using context
✓ Using introductory and transitional phrases to select appropriate word or words
✓ Drawing conclusions based on information presented in the reading passage
✓ Locating important details within a reading passage
✓ Comparing and contrasting information presented in one or more reading passages

The PSAT Critical Reading Section is designed to measure the skills required to carefully read and understand sentences and passages written in standard written English. The section includes Sentence Completion questions and Passage Based Reading questions. A total of 48 multiple-choice questions will test your critical reading skills. In this chapter, we'll give you useful strategies and techniques, an overview of the question types, and a breakdown of the critical reading skills that will be tested. At the end of the chapter, you will find some sample practice questions and explanations.

You will probably not recognize every word that appears in the PSAT Sentence Completion section. If you don't know the meaning of a particular word, don't panic. You can use context clues to eliminate answer choices that clearly do not fit the meaning of the sentence. You should also consider related words, prefixes, and suffixes during the process of elimination. If you can narrow the answer choices down to three or four possible candidates (in other words, eliminate at least one answer choice), it is in your best interest to make an educated guess.

Sentence Completion

A strong vocabulary is the cornerstone of critical reading. The best way to develop a large and varied vocabulary is by reading. In addition to reading more, you might want to review the vocabulary list included as Appendix A at the end of this book.

The PSAT includes both vocabulary in context and logic-based Sentence Completion questions that are designed to test your grasp of the English language. There will be a total of 13 Sentence Completion questions on the PSAT, each consisting of a sentence with either one or two blanks, and five answer choices from which to select the appropriate word or words to put into those blanks. You should select the best possible answer.

General Strategies

PSAT Sentence Completion questions usually test the standard meaning of a word. Pay attention to the logic of the sentence. Try to predict a word to insert in the blank or blanks as you read the sentence, and then look for your word or a *synonym* of your word among the answer choices. A *synonym* is a word that has the same meaning as another word. You should also look for *antonyms*, which are words that have the opposite meaning of your predicted word. If you locate any words among the answer choices that have a meaning opposite to the word that you would like to insert in the blank, eliminate those answer choices.

It often helps to use Latin roots, prefixes, and suffixes to figure out what hard words mean. Look for *cognates* from French, Spanish, or Italian (the modern version of Latin) if you recognize them. A *cognate* is a word that means the same or nearly the same thing in more than one language. For example, the word *amigo*, which means friend in Spanish, the word *ami*, which means friend in French, and the word *amicable*, which means friendly in English, all come from the Latin root word for friend, *amicus*. These words are considered *cognates*.

Let the context of the sentences guide you. Make sure that you understand what's going on in the sentence, and pay attention to introductory and transitional words and phrases in each sentence that might suggest a continuation, contrast, or comparison. Figure 1.1 shows a table of commonly used introductory and transitional words and phrases.

WORDS OR PHRASES THAT SUGGEST CONTINUATION	WORDS OR PHRASES THAT SUGGEST CONCLUSION
Furthermore Moreover In addition	Therefore Thus In other words

WORDS OR PHRASES THAT SUGGEST COMPARISON	WORDS OR PHRASES THAT SUGGEST CONTRAST	WORDS OR PHRASES THAT SUGGEST EVIDENCE
Likewise Similarly Just as Like	But Whereas Although Despite However	Because Since As a result of Due to

Figure 1.1 Introductory and transitional words and phrases.

If the question requires you to fill in two blanks, focus on one blank at a time. You can start with either the first or the second blank. Remember that if one word in the answer choice doesn't fit within the context of the sentence, you can eliminate the entire answer choice. Work on both blanks together only if you have not been able to eliminate all of the incorrect answers.

When you think that you have the correct answer, read the entire sentence silently to yourself, using your choice(s) in the blank(s). If the sentence makes sense, mark your answer.

Remember that the difficulty level increases as you move through the Sentence Completion questions. Move quickly through the less difficult questions and skip those that give you trouble the first time through. Mark them on your test booklet and come back to them later if you have time.

Passage Based Reading

There are a total of 35 Passage Based Reading questions designed to test how well you understand information presented in the passages. Each passage ranges from about 100 words up to about 800 words in length, and discusses subjects in the areas of humanities, social studies, natural sciences, and literary fiction. You might be tested on one longer passage, or be asked to consider two shorter, related passages. In either case, the passage or passages will be followed by a series of questions, each with five answer choices. You should select the best possible answer for each question.

The Passage Based Reading sections are not meant to test your knowledge about a particular subject. You should answer all the questions based only on the information presented in the passage or passages, not on any prior knowledge that you might have of the subject. You might be asked to draw a conclusion (inference), but you should only do so based on what the writer's words actually say or imply.

General Strategies

Probably the biggest mistake that you could make is to read these passages as though you are studying for a high school exam. The open-book aspect of the Passage Based Reading sections means that you should read in a way that helps your brain to work through the information efficiently. You should not read slowly and carefully as though you will have to remember the information for a long period of time. You should read loosely and only dwell on information that you are sure is important because you need it to answer a question. This type of reading should be very goal oriented. If the information you are looking at does not help to answer a question that the test writers find important, you should not linger over it. The best scores on this section are usually earned by students who have two key skills: paraphrasing and skimming. These skills are discussed in more detail later.

Following are some specific strategies to apply to the Passage Based Reading sections of the PSAT:

Read the Question Stems First

The single most powerful strategy for reading is to read the question stems first. The question stems are the prompts, or *stimuli* that appear before the five answer choices. Don't read the answer choices before you read the passage. Most of the answer choices are wrong and, in fact, are referred to by testing professionals as "distractors." If you read them before you read the passage, you will be much more likely to get confused. The questions themselves, though, might contain useful information. You might find that the questions refer to specific names or terms repeatedly. You will find other questions that contain references to the line numbers that are printed down the left side of the passage. These can be very useful in focusing your attention and energy on the parts of the passage that are likely to lead to correct answers to questions.

Each of the passages has numbered lines. Some of the questions will refer to a particular line or lines. When you read a question that contains a line reference, locate those lines in the passage and make a note in the margin so that you know where to begin to find the answer to the question.

Read for Main Idea First

The main idea has three components: **topic** ("What"), **scope**, ("What about it") and **purpose** ("Why did the author write this"). If you can answer these three questions, you understand the main idea.

Too often, students confuse the topic with the main idea. The topic of a passage only answers the question "What." If that is all you notice, you are missing some very important information.

So, read a little more slowly at the beginning until you get a grip on the three components of the main idea and then you can shift to the next higher gear and skim the rest of the passage.

Skim

Don't use context clues the first time that you skim through a passage. When you come to a word or phrase that is unfamiliar, just read past it. There is always time to come back if you need to. But, there is strong chance that you won't need to bother figuring out exactly what that one word or phrase means in order to answer the bulk of the questions that follow the passage. If you waste some of your precious time, you'll never get it back. With perseverance and practice, you will start to get comfortable with a less than perfect understanding of the passage.

The goal at this stage is to get a general understanding of the structure of the passage so that you can find what you are looking for when you refer to the passage. You should pay attention to paragraph breaks and try to quickly determine the subtopic for each paragraph. The first sentence is not always the topic sentence. So, don't believe those who say that you can read the first and last sentence of each paragraph and skip the rest of the sentences completely. You are better off skimming over all the words even if you end up forgetting most of what you read almost immediately.

Remember that you can write in your test booklet. So, when you see a topic word, circle it. If you can sum up a paragraph in a word or two, jot it down in the margin. Remember that the idea at this stage is not to waste time. Keep moving through the material.

Read actively throughout this section of the PSAT. That is, think about things such as the tone and the purpose of the passage. This technique will help you to stay focused on the material, and, ultimately, will allow you to select the best answer to the questions.

Read and Answer the Questions

Start at the beginning of each group of questions. Read the question and make sure that you understand it. Paraphrase it if you need to. This means to put the question into your own words. If you paraphrase, keep your language simple, as though explaining the passage to a sixth grader.

Go back to the part of the passage that will probably contain the answer to your question. Some of the questions on the PSAT ask you draw conclusions based on the information that you read. However, even these questions should be answered based on the information in the passage. There will always be some strong hints, or evidence, that will lead you to an answer.

Some of the questions contain references to specific lines of the passage. The trick in those cases is to read a little before and a little after the specific line that is mentioned. At least read the entire sentence that contains the line that is referenced.

Some of the questions don't really tell you where to look for the answer, or, they are about the passage as a whole. In those cases, think about what you learned about the passage while you were skimming it. Note the subtopics for the paragraphs, and let them guide you to the part of the passage that contains the information for which you are looking.

One of the important skills rewarded by the PSAT is the ability to sift through text and find the word or concept for which you are looking. This skill improves with practice.

It is possible for an answer choice to be both true *and* wrong. The answer that you choose must respond correctly to the question being asked. Simply being true is not enough to make an answer correct. The best answer will always supported by details, inference, or tone.

Predict an Answer

Once you have found the information in the passage that will provide the answer you are looking for, try to answer the question in your mind. Do this before you look at the answer choices. Remember that four out of every five answer choices are incorrect. Not only are they incorrect, but also they were written by experts to confuse you. They are less likely to confuse you if you have a clear idea of an answer before you read the answer choices. Try to predict an answer for the question, and then skim the choices presented and look for your answer. You might have to be a little flexible to recognize it. Your answer might be there dressed up in different words. If you can recognize a paraphrase of your predicted answer, choose it. Mark the question in your test booklet if you are unsure. Use a mark that will be easy to spot when you are looking back through the test. For example, circle or put a star next to the question number. Whatever symbol you decide to use, be consistent so that the mark always means the same thing every time you use it. Remember that you can always come back to the question later if there is time.

Process of Elimination

Elimination is the process that most test takers use for all the questions that they answer. It is reliable, but slow. It is useful to you as a backup strategy for the questions for which either you cannot predict an answer, or your prediction is not listed as a choice.

The process of elimination is a good tool. It just shouldn't be the only tool in your box. It can be hard to break the habit of always applying the process of elimination. You have developed this habit because you have been given too much time on most exams that you have taken.

There are a couple of different reasons that teachers tend to allow long periods of time for exams. The first is that teachers have to allow enough time for even the slower students to have a fair chance to answer questions. The second is that testing time for students is often break time for the instructor. He or she might be able to catch up on paper work or read a newspaper during the time that students are testing. These factors tend to lead to students who get used to a leisurely pace on exams.

Don't be afraid to refer back to the passage repeatedly, and don't be reluctant to skip around within the question group that accompanies each of the passages. In fact, many students report success with a strategy of actually skipping back and forth between passages. This plan won't work for everyone. It probably would just create confusion for most test takers. But, if you feel comfortable with it after trying it on practice tests, we can't think of any reason not to do it on test day.

It is important that you know the difference between information that is stated directly in the passage, assumptions, and inferences. The reading passages will contain factual information about which you may be asked. They will also include information about which you will be asked to make an assumption or an inference. To answer inference questions, you should look for evidence that supports the correct answer. You won't find the answer on the page in black and white. Instead, you'll find clues that are meant to lead you to the correct answer.

An *assumption* is unstated evidence. It is the missing link in an author's argument. Following is a classic example of a conclusion based on stated evidence and unstated evidence (assumption):

Socrates is a man.

Therefore, Socrates is mortal.

Because you are given that Socrates is a man, the conclusion that Socrates is mortal *must* be based on the assumption that men are mortal.

Socrates is a man. (Stated Evidence)

Men are mortal. (Unstated Evidence)

Therefore, Socrates is mortal. (Conclusion)

Some of the evidence is not stated, but the final conclusion leads you to the existence of that missing evidence, or assumption.

An *inference* is a conclusion based on what is stated in the passage. You can infer something about a person, place, or thing by reasoning through the descriptive language contained in the reading passage. In other words, the author's language *implies* that something is probably true.

Passage Based Reading Question Types

Following is a list of the types of questions you are likely to encounter on the PSAT Passage Based Reading sections. We have also included specific approaches to each question type. You will begin to recognize the different question types as you work through the sample questions and practice exams.

1. **Main Idea/Point of View.** These questions might ask about the main idea of the passage as a whole, or about a specific paragraph. They also ask about the author's point of view or perspective, and the intended audience.

Answer these questions according to your understanding of the three components of the main idea mentioned previously (**topic**, **scope**, and **purpose**). It is also worth noting that the incorrect choices are usually either too broad or too narrow. You should eliminate the answer choices that focus on a specific part of the passage and also eliminate the answer choices that are too general and could describe other passages besides the one on which you are working.

2. **Specific Detail.** These questions can be as basic as asking you about some fact that is easily found by referring to a part of the passage. Often, they are a bit more difficult because they ask you to interpret the information that is referred to.

   Refer to the passage to find the answer to these questions. Use line or paragraph references in the questions if they are given. Sometimes the answer choices are paraphrased, so don't just choose the answers that contain words that appeared in the passage. Make sure that the choice you select is responsive to the question being asked.

3. **Conclusion/Inference.** These questions require the test taker to put together information in the passage and use it as evidence for a conclusion. You will have to find language in the passage that will cause you to arrive at the inference that the question demands. (To "*infer*" is to draw a conclusion based on information in the passage.)

   Although you have to do a bit of thinking for these questions, you should be able to find very strong evidence for your answers. If you find yourself creating a long chain of reasoning and including information from outside the passage when "selling" the answer to yourself, stop and reconsider. The PSAT rewards short, strong connections between the evidence in the passage and the answer that is credited.

4. **Extrapolation.** These questions ask you to go beyond the passage itself and find answers that are probably true based on what you know from the passage. They can be based on the author's tone or on detailed information in the passage.

   You need to be sensitive to any clues about the author's tone or attitude and any clues about how the characters in the passage feel. Eliminate any choices that are outside the scope of the passage. As with the inference questions above, the PSAT rewards short, strong connections between the passage and the correct answers.

5. **Vocabulary In Context.** These questions will ask what a specific word means from the passage. The context of the passage should lead you to an educated guess even if you don't know the specific word being asked about.

The best way to answer these questions is the simplest way; just read the answer choices back into the sentence mentioned in the question stem and choose the one that changes the meaning of the sentence the least.

This is a simulated PSAT Critical Reading Section in format. Time yourself strictly on these practice questions so that you can begin to learn how to pace yourself. Read the directions carefully, and tear out the accompanying answer sheet found on page 27 before you begin answering the questions. Mark the answer sheet with your choices. Make educated guesses as necessary, only after you have eliminated at least one answer choice. Remember, the PSAT has a "guessing penalty," so you should never make random guesses. If you don't know the answer or cannot eliminate at least one answer choice, it's better to leave the question blank on your answer sheet.

Now that you've got a good feel for how to approach the questions found in the PSAT Critical Reading section, try these sample questions. Be sure to read the explanations to help you gain a better understanding of why the correct answer is correct.

Practice Questions

Time—25 Minutes
25 Questions

> **Directions:** For each question, select the best answer from among the choices listed. Fill in the corresponding circle on your answer sheet.

> Each sentence below has either one or two blanks. Each blank indicates that a word has been omitted from the sentence. Beneath each sentence are five words or sets of words. Select the word or set of words that, when inserted into the sentence in place of the blank(s), best fits the context of the sentence as a whole.

1. Despite Jordan's _____ efforts, the team still suffered a _____ loss.
   - (A) complicated . . modest
   - (B) daring . . beneficial
   - (C) generous . . constructive
   - (D) heroic . . devastating
   - (E) selfish . . desperate

2. While some swimmers moved confidently through the water, others were clearly still _____, splashing awkwardly in the pool.
   - (A) agile
   - (B) insistent
   - (C) uncertain
   - (D) relevant
   - (E) arbitrary

3. In addition to advising the school newspaper staff, Mr. Smith also regularly _____ the senior class regarding community service opportunities.
   - (A) rallied against
   - (B) counseled
   - (C) argued with
   - (D) suppressed
   - (E) emulated

4. Eager to become a member of the workforce, Mandy accepted the job offer with _____.
   - (A) reluctance
   - (B) humility
   - (C) aversion
   - (D) reservation
   - (E) alacrity

5. Muscle aches often yield to a _____ treatment, whereas nerve pain can be quite _____.

    (A) simple . . intractable

    (B) complicated . . troublesome

    (C) mundane . . trite

    (D) preventive . . calibrated

    (E) cursory . . superficial

6. Instead of relying entirely upon circumstantial evidence, the prosecutor sought to gather more _____ proof prior to the trial.

    (A) abstract

    (B) contiguous

    (C) tangible

    (D) benign

    (E) peripheral

Each passage below is followed by several questions based on the content of the passage. Answer the questions based on what is either stated or implied in each passage. Be sure to read any introductory material that is provided.

Questions 7–13 are based on the following passages.

The following passages discuss two different perspectives regarding human dependence on computer technology.

Passage 1

Human reliance on information technology today is quickly progressing all over the world. The technological developments in the areas of computing, networking, and software engineering have aided the transitions from paper to paperless transactions, and text and data
5 media to multimedia. Today, speed, efficiency, and accuracy in the exchange of information have become primary tools for increasing productivity and innovation. Activities as diverse as healthcare, education, and manufacturing have come to depend on the generation, storage, and transmission of electronic information. Computers are
10 not only used extensively to perform the industrial and economic functions of society, but are also used to provide many services upon which human life depends. Medical treatment, air traffic control, and national security are a few examples. Even a small glitch in the operation of these systems can put human lives in danger. Computers are
15 also used to store confidential data of a political, social, economic, or personal nature. This fairly recent and progressive dependence on computer technology signals a real danger for the human race.

Current computer systems offer new opportunities for law breaking and the potential to commit traditional types of crimes in nontra-
20 ditional ways. For example, the threat of identity theft is magnified by our reliance on computers to assist us in everyday activities such as shopping and paying bills. Identity theft refers to all types of crime in which someone wrongfully obtains and uses another person's personal data by way of fraud or deception, typically for economic gain. By
25 making personal and credit information available on the Internet, people open themselves up to the possibility of a criminal obtaining this information and using it for nefarious purposes. This is but one instance of the negative impact that overreliance on computer technology can have on society.

30 As humans continue to make technological advances, so too do they rely more heavily upon those innovations. This is a dangerous progression that must be tempered with common sense and self-restraint. We cannot allow computer technology to control so many aspects of our lives, lest we become victims of our own ingenuity.

Passage 2

On the eve of December 31, 1999, millions of people around the world prepared for the worst—major power outages, the loss of communication networks, airplanes falling from the sky, the end of life as we knew it—all because of the uncertainty surrounding computer sys-
40 tems switching from the year 1999 to the year 2000. However, the end did not come, and today it seems that humans are more dependent upon computer technology than ever before. The so-called "Y2K" phenomenon came and went without so much as a lightbulb flicker. This means, of course, that any threat of future disasters
45 resulting from human dependence on technology is unfounded, and we, as a global society, should continue to rely upon computers to enhance our everyday lives.

It is difficult for most of us to imagine a life without computers. The speed with which we can communicate and the ease with which
50 we can accomplish complicated tasks are but two of the many advantages computer technology offers us. For example, the Federal Drug Administration has recently approved a surgical robot for use in certain surgeries. The robot has three arms that can be moved with pinpoint accuracy. This technology magnifies the skills of an experienced
55 surgeon, who can manipulate the robot's arms while sitting in a chair across the room. In addition, the use of computers in the classroom is now being hailed as an educational revolution. Computer technology is currently integrated into the curriculum of thousands of classrooms, transforming the learning environment of students worldwide.
60 Whereas in the past students were forced to rely on printed materials such as encyclopedias, journals, and newspapers to access information, today this data is available on the Internet with the click of a mouse.

Human dependence on technology is a natural progression in the advancement of our species. Computer technology, specifically, will
65 continue to allow people in all nations on earth to learn, grow, heal, and move forward in their efforts to maximize the human potential. It is imperative that we not only maintain our current relationship with computer technology, but that we also develop and nurture this relationship to the fullest extent possible.

7. In Passage 2, the author's attitude toward computer technology is best described as

   (A) fearful
   (B) apathetic
   (C) critical
   (D) favorable
   (E) sympathetic

8. In line 27, "nefarious" most nearly means

(A) unlawful
(B) admirable
(C) economic
(D) prosperous
(E) sensible

9. The author most likely uses the phrase "a small glitch" (line 13) in order to

(A) acknowledge the fact that human reliance on computer technology is completely safe
(B) emphasize the idea that it is dangerous for humans to rely so heavily on computer technology
(C) cast doubt on the accuracy of any personal data collected on the Internet by criminals
(D) criticize human technological advances in the areas of education, medicine, and national security
(E) disprove the theory that computer technology is unnecessary for human advancement

10. The author in Passage 1 argues that

(A) human dependence on computer technology is a positive indicator of the advancement of the species
(B) human dependence on computer technology should never be allowed under any circumstances
(C) human dependence on computer technology is a key component to the advancement of the species
(D) human dependence on computer technology cannot be accurately measured
(E) human dependence on computer technology can sometimes have a negative impact on society

11. What would be the likely response of the author of Passage 2 to the discussion of identity theft in lines 20–29 of Passage 1?

(A) Identity theft does not pose a serious problem to society.
(B) Identity theft presents a technological challenge that can be solved.
(C) Identity theft is an indication that computer technology has progressed too far.
(D) Identity theft emphasizes the more positive advances of technology.
(E) Identity theft provides evidence of the "Y2K" phenomenon.

12. In line 31, "innovations" most nearly means

(A) future disasters
(B) dangerous activities
(C) complicated tasks
(D) raw data
(E) new concepts

13. The author of Passage 1 and the author of Passage 2 disagree most strongly about

(A) the national security applications of computer technology
(B) the role of robotics in advancing medical treatment
(C) the dangers of increasing technological dependence
(D) the definition of computer technology
(E) the implications of including personal information on the Internet

Questions 14–25 are based on the following passage.

Scientists know very little about the eating habits of our ancestors who lived more than two and a half million years ago. To solve this problem, scientists have started examining chimpanzees' hunting behavior and diet to find clues about our own prehistoric past.

5   It is not difficult to determine why studying chimpanzees might be beneficial. Modern humans and chimpanzees are actually very closely related. Experts believe that chimpanzees share about 98.5% of our DNA sequence. If this is true, humans are more closely related to chimpanzees than to any other animal species.

10   In the early 1960s, Dr. Jane Goodall began studying chimpanzees in Tanzania. Before the 1960s, scientists believed that chimpanzees were strict vegetarians. It was Goodall who first reported that meat was a natural part of the chimpanzee diet. In fact, Goodall discovered that chimpanzees are actually very proficient hunters. Individual

15   chimpanzees have been known to hunt and eat more than 150 small animals each year. Some of the chimpanzees' favorite prey is the colobus monkey, feral pig, and various small antelope species. The red colobus monkey is one of the most important animals in the chimpanzees' diet. In one notable study, the red colobus monkey

20   accounted for more than 80% of the animals eaten by one group of chimpanzees.

Despite these findings, scientists still maintain that chimpanzees are mostly fruit-eating creatures. In fact, meat composes only about 3% of the chimpanzee diet. This is substantially less than the quantity

25   of meat consumed by the average human. Studies show that chimpanzees do most of their hunting in the dry season. August and September appear to be the most popular months for hunting. During the dry season, food shortages in the forest cause the chimpanzees' body weight to drop. Consequently, chimpanzees supple-

30   ment their diets with meat. During the height of the dry season, the estimated meat intake is about 65 grams of meat per day for adult chimpanzees. This is comparable to the quantity of meat eaten by human societies that forage when other food sources are scarce. The chimpanzees' eating habits also closely resemble those of the early

35   human hunter-gatherers.

Humans and chimpanzees are the only members of the Great Ape family that hunt and eat meat on a regular basis. However, like chimpanzees, humans are not truly carnivorous creatures. In fact, most ancient humans ate a diet composed mostly of plants, and even mod-
40 ern humans are considered omnivores because they eat fruits, vegetables, and meat.

Most people assume that food choices are based solely on nutritional costs and benefits. Although it is clear that the hunting habits of chimpanzees are guided mostly by nutritional needs, some aspects
45 of the chimpanzees' behavior are not well explained by nutrition alone. Researchers suggest that chimpanzees might hunt for social gain. For instance, a male chimpanzee might try to demonstrate his competence to other male chimpanzees by killing prey. Chimpanzees might also use meat as a political tool to punish rivals and reward
50 friends. However, a study also shows that female chimpanzees that receive large portions of meat after a hunt have healthier and stronger offspring. This indicates that there might be reproductive benefits to eating meat as well.

The information that scientists have been able to gather regarding
55 chimpanzee hunting behavior is shedding some light on the eating habits of our ancestors. Further investigation is needed, however, to provide stronger evidence regarding this aspect of man's prehistoric past.

14. The main purpose of the passage is to
   (A) explore biological and physiological similarities between humans and chimpanzees
   (B) examine the hunting behavior and diet of chimpanzees and compare them to human activity
   (C) discuss the health benefits of eating and hunting meat while simultaneously predicting the effect of this behavior on chimpanzee offspring
   (D) bring attention to the pioneering research of Dr. Jane Goodall in Tanzania
   (E) educate the public on the impact that tool use had on early human societies

15. It can be inferred from the passage that chimpanzees
   (A) prefer the red colobus monkey to any other prey
   (B) find that the red colobus monkey is the easiest prey to hunt
   (C) only hunt when no other plant food is available
   (D) hunt only during the dry season when other food sources are scarce
   (E) vary their diet depending on environmental factors

16. In line 14, "proficient" most nearly means
   (A) skilled
   (B) individual
   (C) natural
   (D) incompetent
   (E) important

17. The passage supports which of the following statements about the eating habits of chimpanzees?
   (A) Chimpanzee eating habits cannot be studied in the wild.
   (B) The exploration of chimpanzee eating habits is in its infancy.
   (C) Chimpanzee eating habits are directly influenced by social factors.
   (D) It is not possible to determine the exact diet of chimpanzees.
   (E) Chimpanzee eating habits are not related to those of humans.

18. The author most likely makes the comparison between chimpanzees and humans (lines 5–9) in order to suggest that
   (A) chimpanzees are more similar to early humans than to modern humans
   (B) studies of chimpanzees will contribute to an understanding of early humans
   (C) early hunter-gatherers typically ate more meat than did chimpanzees
   (D) data collected on chimpanzees cannot be applied to the study of humans
   (E) it is not possible to compare the eating habits of early humans to modern humans

19. In line 33, "forage" most nearly means
   (A) cultivate crops
   (B) consume meat
   (C) alter their diets
   (D) search for food
   (E) lose weight

20. According to the passage, Dr. Jane Goodall's research was important because
   (A) Dr. Goodall was the first scientist to study chimpanzees in their natural habitat
   (B) Dr. Goodall introduced hunting to the Tanzanian chimpanzees
   (C) Dr. Goodall discovered previously undocumented chimpanzee behavior
   (D) Dr. Goodall had always argued that chimpanzees were actually carnivorous creatures
   (E) Dr. Goodall discovered that red colobus monkeys make up 80% of chimpanzees' diet

21. It can be inferred from the passage that humans and chimpanzees

  (A) share a DNA structure that is more similar than that of any two other animals

  (B) share a history of primitive stone tool use to hunt and scavenge

  (C) both hunt when other food sources are scarce

  (D) differ from other related species

  (E) hunt for social gain and prestige in their communities

22. According to the passage, chimpanzees hunt primarily because of

  (A) increased numbers of colobus monkeys

  (B) their preference for meat over plants

  (C) training provided by Dr. Jane Goodall

  (D) their DNA sequence

  (E) food shortages during the dry season

23. In line 38, "carnivorous" most nearly means

  (A) ancient

  (B) meat eating

  (C) vegetarian

  (D) nutritious

  (E) regulated

24. The description in lines 35–41 emphasizes the

  (A) contrast between the diets of chimpanzees and modern humans

  (B) relationship between chimpanzees and all other Great Apes

  (C) similarity between the diets of ancient and modern humans

  (D) importance of meat in the diets of early and modern humans

  (E) difference between carnivores and omnivores

25. In lines 36–41, the tone can best be described as

  (A) affectionate

  (B) humorous

  (C) somber

  (D) informational

  (E) hostile

Answers and Explanations

Sentence Completion (Questions 1–6)

1. **The best answer is D.** The word "despite" suggests a contrast between the information in the first part of the sentence and the information in the second part of the sentence. The context implies that even though Jordan's "efforts" were one way, the results of the game turned out another way. Jordan's "efforts" were not enough to win; therefore, you can assume that the "loss" was "devastating." For answer choice D to be correct, however, "heroic" must fit in the first blank: The adjective "heroic" appropriately describes Jordan's efforts and correctly contrasts the information in the second portion of the sentence. Answer choices A, B, C, and E do not fit the context of the sentence.

2. **The best answer is C.** The word "while" suggests a contrast between the description of the swimmers in the first portion of the sentence and the description of the other swimmers in the second portion of the sentence. The swimmers in the first portion of the sentence moved "confidently," so the word that describes the other swimmers will have a meaning opposite to "confidently." The only answer choice that is an antonym of "confidently" is "uncertain," so answer choice C is correct. The remaining answer choices do not have meanings opposite to "confidently."

3. **The best answer is B.** To answer this question, you must understand the context of the sentence. The introductory phrase "in addition" indicates that the sentence will provide you with more than one example of what Mr. Smith does to help students. The sentence implies that Mr. Smith "advised" or "informed" the students about community service opportunities. Eliminate answer choices A, C, and D because these suggest that Mr. Smith was against students being involved in community service, which does not make sense. Using the verb "emulated" would mean that Mr. Smith tried to be like the students, which also does not make sense, so eliminate answer choice E. "Counseled" is similar to "advised" or "informed," so answer choice B is the best choice.

4. **The best answer is E.** In the sentence, the situation before the comma helps to describe the event after the comma, thus helping to define the word that best fits in the blank. Because Mandy was "eager" to join the workforce, she would most likely display "eagerness" or "enthusiasm" when accepting a job offer. To determine the correct answer, look for a synonym of "enthusiasm" or "eagerness." "Alacrity" is a synonym of "eagerness," so answer choice E is correct. Even if you do not know the definition of "alacrity," you can still find the correct answer by eliminating choices that are antonyms of "eager" or simply do not make sense in the context. "Reluctance" and "reservation" suggest a lack of enthusiasm, so eliminate answer choices A and D. "Humility" is related to "modesty," and "aversion" suggests staying away from something that you don't like. Neither of these words fit the context of the sentence, so eliminate answer choices B and C.

5. **The best answer is A.** The word "whereas" indicates that there is a contrast between the ease of treating "muscle aches" and the ease of treating "nerve pain." The first portion of the sentence implies that muscle aches are easy to treat; therefore, the word that best completes the second portion of the sentence will suggest that nerve pain is not easy to treat. "Simple" is an appropriate synonym for "easy," and "intractable" describes something that is "difficult to deal with or fix," so answer choice A is correct. Even if you do not know the definition of "intractable," you can still find the answer by eliminating choices that have meanings opposite to "easy" for the first blank, have meanings opposite to "not easy to treat" for the second blank, or simply do not fit the context of the sentence. Answer choice B can be eliminated because "complicated" is the opposite of "easy." Answer choice C can be eliminated because "trite" means "ordinary" or "overused." "Calibrated" does not fit the context of the sentence, so answer choice D can be eliminated. The adjective "superficial" would suggest that nerve pain treatment was "easy," so eliminate answer choice E.

6. **The best answer is C.** To answer this question, you do not need to know the exact definition of "circumstantial evidence." You should, however, understand that "circumstantial" describes something that is both "dependent on other events and conditions," and is "indirect." Hence, the prosecutor is probably looking for "real" or "physical" evidence because "circumstantial evidence" might not be very convincing.

"Tangible" is a synonym of "real" and "physical," so answer choice C is correct. Answer choices A, B, D, and E can be eliminated because they are not synonyms of "real" or "physical."

Passage Based Reading (Questions 7–25)

7. **The best answer is D.** Statements such as "… we, as a global society, should continue to rely upon computers to enhance our everyday lives," and "Computer technology…will continue to allow people in all nations on earth to learn, grow, heal,…" indicate that the author of Passage 2 has a very favorable attitude toward computer technology. Answer choices A and C could apply to the attitude of the author of Passage 1. Answer choices B and E are not supported by Passage 2.

8. **The best answer is A.** The term "nefarious" refers to "wickedness" and comes from the Latin word *nefis*, which means "crime." The context of the passage indicates that "nefarious" most nearly means "unlawful." While the passage states that most identity theft is committed for economic gain, "nefarious" does not mean "economic," so eliminate answer choice C. Answer choices B, D, and E are not supported by the context of the passage.

9. **The best answer is B.** The author of Passage 1 states that "even a small glitch in the operation of these systems can put human lives in danger." This statement indicates the potential danger of overreliance on computer technology, especially regarding services that are essential to survival. Answer choices A, C, D, and E are not supported by the passage.

10. **The best answer is E.** The main idea of Passage 1 is that, although computer technology has contributed to the advancement of the human race, our dependence on this technology can be dangerous. Statements such as "…dependence on computer technology signals a real danger for the human race," and "…dangerous progression…" best support answer choice E.

11. **The best answer is B.** The author of Passage 2 believes that humans should continue to depend on computer technology to make their lives easier, despite any potential problems that might arise from such dependence. It is likely, therefore, that this author would agree that

identity theft is a problem, but that the problem can be solved. Answer choices A, C, D, and E are not supported by the passage.

12. **The best answer is E.** An "innovation" is a "new device or process." The word comes from the Latin root *novare*, which means "to make new." The context of the passage indicates a relationship between "technological advances," which are new developments in technology, and "innovations." Answer choices A, B, C, and D are not supported by the context of the passage.

13. **The best answer is C.** The author of Passage 1 believes that human dependence on computer technology can be dangerous, whereas the author of Passage 2 believes that humans should continue to depend on computer technology to make their lives easier, and that "…any threat of future disasters resulting from human dependence on technology is unfounded…" Therefore, it is most likely that the two authors would disagree most strongly about the dangers of increasing technological dependence. Answer choices A, B, D, and E are either too broad or are not supported by information in the passages.

14. **The best answer is B.** Most of the passage discusses the hunting and eating habits of chimpanzees. However, the passage also compares these behaviors with the hunting and eating habits of both early and modern humans. Answer choice C might have appeared to be correct because the passage does state, "However, a study also shows that female chimpanzees that receive large portions of meat after a hunt have healthier and stronger offspring. This indicates that there might be reproductive benefits to eating meat as well." However, discussing this study is not the main purpose or topic of this passage. Likewise, answer choices A, D, and E are not supported by the passage.

15. **The best answer is E.** The passage states that "… chimpanzees do most of their hunting in the dry season. August and September appear to be the most popular months for hunting. During the dry season, food shortages in the forest cause the chimpanzees' body weight to drop. Consequently, chimpanzees supplement their diets with meat." This indicates that environmental factors influence the diet of chimpanzees. Answer choice A might have appeared to be correct because the passage does say, "The red colobus monkey is one of the most important animals in the chimpanzees' diet. In one notable study, red colobus accounted for more than 80% of the animals eaten by a group

of chimpanzees." However, there is nothing in the passage to indicate that chimpanzees actually prefer the red colobus monkey. There could be other reasons why this particular animal is the source of most of the meat in the chimpanzee diet. Likewise, answer choices B, C, and D are not supported by the passage.

16. **The best answer is A.** The word "proficient" means "having an advanced degree of competency." The context of the passage suggests that chimpanzees are "skilled" hunters and are able to supplement their diets with meat when necessary. Answer choices B, C, and E are words from the passage, but none of them have the same meaning as "proficient." Eliminate answer choice D because it is the opposite of "proficient."

17. **The best answer is C.** According to the passage, "...chimpanzees might hunt for social gain. For instance, a male chimpanzee might try to demonstrate his competence to other male chimpanzees by killing prey. Chimpanzees might also use meat as a political tool to punish rivals and reward friends." These statements clearly indicate that chimpanzee eating habits are directly influenced by social factors. Answer choices A, B, D, and E are not supported by the passage.

18. **The best answer is B.** The passage states that "modern humans and chimpanzees are actually very closely related. Experts believe that chimpanzees share about 98.5% of our DNA sequence." This information suggests that studies of chimpanzees will contribute to an understanding of early humans, which is the theory presented in the first paragraph. Answer choices A, C, D, and E are not supported by information in the passage.

19. **The best answer is D.** The word "forage" refers to the "act of looking or searching for food." The passage indicates that some "...human societies...forage when other food sources are scarce." Answer choices A, B, C, and E are related to eating habits, but do not accurately define "forage."

20. **The best answer is C.** According to the passage, Dr. Goodall discovered that chimpanzees are not strictly vegetarians and that they are actually proficient hunters. This information was not previously known. Answer choices A, B, and D are not supported by the passage. Furthermore, answer choice E is incorrect because red colobus

monkeys did not make up 80% of chimpanzees' diets. Rather, red colobus monkeys made up 80% of the *animals* eaten by the group of chimpanzees studied.

21. **The best answer is C.** The passage states that "humans and chimpanzees are the only members of the Great Ape family that hunt and eat meat on a regular basis." This statement best supports answer choice C. Answer choice A might have appeared to be correct. However, the passage states only that the chimpanzee is more closely related to humans than to any other species. The passage does not state that no two other animals are more closely related. Likewise, answer choices B, D, and E are not supported by the passage.

22. **The best answer is E.** The passage states that "... chimpanzees do most of their hunting in the dry season" when "...food shortages in the forest cause the chimpanzees' body weight to drop. Consequently, chimpanzees supplement their diets with meat." Answer choices A, B, C, and D are not supported by details in the passage.

23. **The best answer is B.** The word "carnivorous" means "meat eating." In the lines preceding the word "carnivorous" the passage states that humans and chimpanzees "...hunt and eat meat on a regular basis." Answer choice C is incorrect because "vegetarian" refers to eating plants. Answer choices A, D, and E are mentioned in the passage, but they do not mean the same thing as "carnivorous."

24. **The best answer is C.** The passage states that "... most ancient humans ate a diet composed mostly of plants, and even modern humans are considered omnivores because they eat fruits and vegetables in addition to meat." This statement supports the concept that the diets of ancient and modern humans are similar. Answer choice A is incorrect because the passage also indicates that humans and chimpanzees have a similar diet. The passage mentions other Great Apes, but it does not discuss the relationship between chimpanzees and other Great Apes, so eliminate answer choice B. Although the description indicates that humans eat meat, it does not emphasize the importance of meat in the diets of early and modern humans, so eliminate answer choice D. Although the passage indicates that there is a difference between carnivores and omnivores, the description does not emphasize this difference, so eliminate answer choice E.

25. **The best answer is D.** The lines indicated in the question are delivered in a purely informational tone. Information is being presented regarding food choices and hunting habits of chimpanzees. Answer choices A, B, C, and E suggest emotions that are not reflected in the passage.

CHAPTER 1
PRACTICE QUESTIONS
ANSWER SHEET

Begin with number 1. There may be fewer than 40 questions-
leave the rest of the answer spaces blank.
Completely erase any unnecessary marks.

SECTION 1			
1 Ⓐ Ⓑ Ⓒ Ⓓ Ⓔ	11 Ⓐ Ⓑ Ⓒ Ⓓ Ⓔ	21 Ⓐ Ⓑ Ⓒ Ⓓ Ⓔ	31 Ⓐ Ⓑ Ⓒ Ⓓ Ⓔ
2 Ⓐ Ⓑ Ⓒ Ⓓ Ⓔ	12 Ⓐ Ⓑ Ⓒ Ⓓ Ⓔ	22 Ⓐ Ⓑ Ⓒ Ⓓ Ⓔ	32 Ⓐ Ⓑ Ⓒ Ⓓ Ⓔ
3 Ⓐ Ⓑ Ⓒ Ⓓ Ⓔ	13 Ⓐ Ⓑ Ⓒ Ⓓ Ⓔ	23 Ⓐ Ⓑ Ⓒ Ⓓ Ⓔ	33 Ⓐ Ⓑ Ⓒ Ⓓ Ⓔ
4 Ⓐ Ⓑ Ⓒ Ⓓ Ⓔ	14 Ⓐ Ⓑ Ⓒ Ⓓ Ⓔ	24 Ⓐ Ⓑ Ⓒ Ⓓ Ⓔ	34 Ⓐ Ⓑ Ⓒ Ⓓ Ⓔ
5 Ⓐ Ⓑ Ⓒ Ⓓ Ⓔ	15 Ⓐ Ⓑ Ⓒ Ⓓ Ⓔ	25 Ⓐ Ⓑ Ⓒ Ⓓ Ⓔ	35 Ⓐ Ⓑ Ⓒ Ⓓ Ⓔ
6 Ⓐ Ⓑ Ⓒ Ⓓ Ⓔ	16 Ⓐ Ⓑ Ⓒ Ⓓ Ⓔ	26 Ⓐ Ⓑ Ⓒ Ⓓ Ⓔ	36 Ⓐ Ⓑ Ⓒ Ⓓ Ⓔ
7 Ⓐ Ⓑ Ⓒ Ⓓ Ⓔ	17 Ⓐ Ⓑ Ⓒ Ⓓ Ⓔ	27 Ⓐ Ⓑ Ⓒ Ⓓ Ⓔ	37 Ⓐ Ⓑ Ⓒ Ⓓ Ⓔ
8 Ⓐ Ⓑ Ⓒ Ⓓ Ⓔ	18 Ⓐ Ⓑ Ⓒ Ⓓ Ⓔ	28 Ⓐ Ⓑ Ⓒ Ⓓ Ⓔ	38 Ⓐ Ⓑ Ⓒ Ⓓ Ⓔ
9 Ⓐ Ⓑ Ⓒ Ⓓ Ⓔ	19 Ⓐ Ⓑ Ⓒ Ⓓ Ⓔ	29 Ⓐ Ⓑ Ⓒ Ⓓ Ⓔ	39 Ⓐ Ⓑ Ⓒ Ⓓ Ⓔ
10 Ⓐ Ⓑ Ⓒ Ⓓ Ⓔ	20 Ⓐ Ⓑ Ⓒ Ⓓ Ⓔ	30 Ⓐ Ⓑ Ⓒ Ⓓ Ⓔ	40 Ⓐ Ⓑ Ⓒ Ⓓ Ⓔ

Writing Skills Section

Terms you'll need to understand

✓ Main clause
✓ Relative clause
✓ Misplaced modifier
✓ Ambiguous pronoun
✓ Participle
✓ Gerund
✓ Parallel construction
✓ Idiom
✓ Rhetorical skill
✓ Redundancy
✓ Relevance
✓ Awkward construction
✓ Context

Concepts you'll need to master

✓ Identifying grammatical errors in sentences
✓ Eliminating awkward or incorrect sentence construction
✓ Eliminating unnecessary words from sentences
✓ Altering sentence structure to make the meaning more clear
✓ Using words and phrases in context
✓ Understanding relationships between sentences and paragraphs

The PSAT Writing Skills Section is designed to measure your ability to understand and interpret standard written English. The section will require you to identify sentence errors, improve sentences, and improve paragraphs. A total of 39 multiple-choice questions will test your basic English and grammar skills. These questions will also assess your ability to make choices about the effectiveness and clarity of a word, phrase, sentence, or paragraph. In this chapter, we'll give you useful strategies and techniques, an overview of some rules of grammar, and a breakdown of the writing skills that will be tested. At the end of the chapter, you will find some sample practice questions and explanations.

General Strategies

You can usually trust your impulses when answering many of the questions on the PSAT Writing Skills Section. In other words, if a sentence sounds right to you, it probably is. You should recognize when and how to apply basic rules of grammar, even if you don't recall what the specific rule is. You can tap into the part of your brain that controls speech and hearing as you read the sentences to yourself, "silently/aloud." This technique is called "sub vocalization," and it triggers the part of your brain that "knows" how English is supposed to sound. Remember, the PSAT Writing Skills Section does *not* require you to state a specific rule, only to apply it correctly.

On the PSAT Writing Skills Section, wordiness and redundancy are never rewarded. Throughout the test, you will be asked to make choices that best express ideas. Usually, the fewer words that you use, the better.

This is not a spelling or capitalization test. Also, although punctuation marks might be helpful in choosing the correct answer in some questions, punctuation is not tested directly on the PSAT.

Remember that this is a timed test. One of your jobs is to get through the material as quickly as you can and correctly answer as many questions as you can. You do not have to do the questions in order in each section. Skip the hard ones, mark them in your test, and come back to them later. This technique will keep you moving through the test, which will give you the best possible chance to maximize your score.

Although "skipping around" is a very useful strategy, it is important that you practice enough to fully develop this skill. Be consistent and manage the answer grid so that you fill in the appropriate bubbles. Also, remember that you cannot skip from one section to another on the PSAT.

Basic Grammar Review

This section is intended to provide an overview of some basic rules of grammar, as well as provide examples of common grammatical mistakes. The PSAT requires you to identify errors in a sentence and to improve the way sentences and paragraphs are written. It will be difficult for you to manage these tasks if you don't understand how to apply the underlying rules of grammar.

Subject-Verb Agreement

A well-constructed sentence will contain a subject and a verb and will express a complete thought. The subject is who or what the sentence is about. The verb tells you either what the subject is doing, or what is being done to the subject. The subject and verb must agree; that is, they must share the same person, number, voice, and tense. Voice defines whether the subject performs the action of the verb or receives the action of the verb. The active voice is usually the preferred mode of writing. The following are examples of sentences in which the subject and verb do not agree, followed by corrected versions of each sentence:

> **Incorrect**: Jill, along with her sisters, *have* graduated from college.
>
> The singular subject *Jill* requires the singular verb *has*. The noun contained within the prepositional phrase (sisters) is not part of the subject.
>
> **Correct**: *Jill*, along with her sisters, *has* graduated from college.
>
> **Incorrect**: Either the students or the teacher *are* at fault.
>
> If subjects are joined by *or* or *nor*, the verb should agree with the closer subject, which, in this case, is the singular subject *teacher*.
>
> **Correct:** *Either* the students *or* the teacher is at fault.

Misplaced Modifiers

A sentence should contain at least one main clause. A complex sentence can contain more than one main clause, as well as one or more relative clauses. Relative clauses follow the nouns that they modify. In order to maintain clarity within a sentence, it is important to place a relative clause near the object that it modifies. The following sentence examples contain misplaced modifiers, followed by revised versions of each sentence:

Misplaced Modifier: Running blindly through the woods, the flashlight was of no use to me.

As it is written, the sentence implies that the flashlight was running blindly through the woods, which does not make sense.

Revised Sentence: The flashlight was of no use to me as I ran blindly through the woods.

Misplaced Modifier: As a child, Jordan's mother often helped him with his homework.

This sentence suggests that Jordan's mother was a child when she helped him with his homework, which does not make sense.

Revised Sentence: When Jordan was a child, his mother often helped him with his homework.

Parallel Construction

Parallel construction, or parallelism, allows a writer to show order and clarity in a sentence or a paragraph, by putting grammatical elements that have the same function in the same form. Parallelism creates a recognizable pattern within a sentence and adds unity, force, clarity, and balance to writing. All words, phrases, and clauses used in parallel construction must share the same grammatical form. The following sentence examples include faulty parallelism, followed by revised versions of each sentence:

Faulty Parallelism: Ava wanted three things out of college: *to get* a good education, *to make* good friends, and *experiencing* life.

In this sentence, the verb forms do not match. The verb phrases "to get" and "to make" include an infinitive (to) and a verb. The word "experiencing" is a participle.

Revised Sentence: Ava wanted three things out of college: *to get* a good education, *to make* good friends, and *to experience* life.

Faulty Parallelism: In my haste to *complete* the project, I was *forgetting* an important element.

In this sentence, the verb forms do not match. The verb phrase "to complete" includes an infinitive (to) and a verb. The word "forgetting" is a participle.

Revised Sentence: In my haste to *complete* the project, I *forgot* an important element.

Nouns and Pronouns

The English language contains two forms of nouns: proper nouns, which name a specific person, place, or object, and common nouns, which name a nonspecific person, place, or object. Proper nouns begin with an uppercase letter, and common nouns do not. Pronouns take the place of either a proper or a common noun. Be sure to maintain consistency in pronoun person and number. It is not grammatically correct to use the plural pronoun "their" to represent neutral gender. Instead, use he/she. This is an example of a major difference between standard written English and the English that we ordinarily use when speaking. A pronoun should be placed so that it clearly refers to a specific noun. If it does not, it is known as an ambiguous pronoun. The following sentence examples contain ambiguous pronouns, followed by revised versions of each sentence:

Ambiguous Pronoun: Jeff and Chadwick left rehearsal early to get *his* guitar repaired.

In this sentence, it is unclear whose guitar is getting repaired.

Revised Sentence: Jeff and Chadwick left rehearsal early to get *Chadwick's* guitar repaired.

Ambiguous Pronoun: Some foods are dangerous for your pets, so *they* should be placed out of reach.

In this sentence, it is unclear what should be placed out of reach: the potentially dangerous foods or your pets.

Revised Sentence: Some foods are dangerous for your pets; *these foods* should be placed out of reach.

Incomplete Sentences

A participle is a verb form that can function as an adjective or an adverb. Present tense participles end in "-ing." When you see a word that ends in "-ing," decide whether it is being used as a verb, an adjective, or an adverb. Other words ending in "-ing" could be verbs acting as nouns. These are called gerunds. Some sentences might contain a participle or a gerund without a verb; these are incomplete sentences (also called fragments), and should be corrected.

Incomplete Sentence: Yesterday, the *winning* float in the parade.

The sentence, as it is written, is incomplete; the word *winning* is being used as an adjective to describe the float. The sentence should be revised so that the *winning float* either performs an action, or has an action performed upon it.

Revised Sentence: Yesterday, the *winning float* in the parade *was displayed* on campus.

Incomplete Sentence: Many school districts *releasing* personal information to third parties.

The sentence, as it is written, is incomplete; it should be revised so that the subject, *many school districts*, is actually performing an action.

Revised Sentence: Many school districts *prohibit releasing* personal information to third parties.

Idiom

Idiom refers to the common or everyday usage of a word or phrase. Idiom is part of standard written English, and must be considered when making corrections to or improving sentences on the PSAT. Following is a short list of common idiomatic phrases as they might be used in a sentence:

Correct	Incorrect
Please *look up* that word in the dictionary.	Please *look on* that word in the dictionary.
My sister *listens to* many types of music.	My sister *listens with* many types of music.
That is a very *eye-catching* bracelet.	That is a very *eyeball-catching* bracelet.
The figurine should be placed *on top of* the cake.	The figurine should be placed *at top of* the cake.
He is often *singled out from* a crowd.	He is often *singled out with* a crowd.
I captured a caterpillar that *turned into* a butterfly.	I captured a caterpillar that *turned out of* a butterfly.
I sat *across from* my best friend on the bus today.	I sat *across with* my best friend on the bus today.

Rhetoric

Rhetoric refers to the effective and persuasive use of language. Rhetorical skills, then, refer to your ability to make choices about the effectiveness and clarity of a word, phrase, sentence, or paragraph. The Writing Skills Section of the PSAT tests your rhetorical skills by asking you to improve both sentences and paragraphs. Good writing involves effective word choice as well as clear and unambiguous expression. The best-written sentences will be relevant based on the context of the paragraph, will avoid redundancy, and will clearly and simply express the intended idea.

Identifying Sentence Errors, Improving Sentences, and Improving Paragraphs

Following are some strategies on how best to approach each of the areas tested on the PSAT Writing Skills section. Apply your knowledge of standard written English and the basic rules of grammar along with these strategies to maximize your PSAT score.

Identifying Sentence Errors

As you write more in high school and college, the ability to recognize mistakes in sentences will become very important. Good writers can express ideas clearly by correctly applying the rules of grammar and selecting the most appropriate words and phrases.

 When you encounter a possible error, mentally "rewrite" the sentence and correct the underlined portion that contains the error. If you can't find an error, the correct answer may be E, which is No Error. This answer choice is correct nearly as often as any of the other answer choices.

The Identifying Sentence Errors section of the PSAT is tricky, in that you must select the answer choice that contains a mistake. Following are some simple strategies to apply as you work through this type of question:

➤ Read each sentence carefully. Many errors are obvious, and if you can spot them right away, you will be able to move quickly through this section.

➤ Read aloud as you practice, and learn to "sub-vocalize," or read to yourself. Remember that if your brain can "hear" an error, it is more likely to recognize it.

➤ Learn to look for common mistakes, and correct them automatically as you read the sentence. This chapter includes a list of words that are commonly misused. Review the list so that you can avoid making these mistakes, and recognize them when you see them.

➤ Look over the answer choices (A–D) as you read the sentence to see if something in the sentence needs to be changed. Remember to trust what you know about basic grammar. If you struggle with one of the underlined portions as you read the sentence, that portion is most likely the one that contains the error.

➤ If the sentence seems correct as it is, mark E on your answer sheet. The test is designed to assess your ability to recognize mistakes, which also includes recognizing when there is *not* a mistake.

When you get to the Improving Sentences section, carefully read each of the sentences so that you don't miss any potential problems. Answer choice A will always be a repeat of the initial underlined portion, so if the sentence is best as it is written, mark A on your answer sheet.

Improving Sentences

This section tests your ability to write clear, effective sentences, which is another important skill to develop as you write at the high school and college levels. Follow these strategies to select the best answers on the Improving Sentences section of the PSAT:

➤ The portion of the sentence that is underlined might need to be revised. When reading the sentence, pay attention to the underlined portion. If the underlined portion makes the sentence awkward, or contains errors in standard written English, it will need to be revised.

➤ If the underlined portion seems correct within the sentence as it is, mark A on your answer sheet. The test is designed to assess your ability to improve sentences, which also includes recognizing when a sentence is best as it is written.

➤ If the underlined portion does not seem correct, try to predict the correct answer. If an answer choice matches your predicted answer, it is most likely correct.

➤ If your predicted answer does not match any of the answer choices, determine which of the selections is the most clear and simple. Read the sentence again, replacing the underlined portion with the answer choices in order from B–E. (Remember that answer choice A will always be a repeat of the original underlined portion.)

➤ Sub-vocalize (read "aloud silently" to yourself) to allow your brain to "hear" the sentence with each of the answer choices inserted. Your brain might automatically make the necessary improvement, or recognize the best version of the sentence.

➤ Look for common problems, such as redundancy, misplaced modifiers, faulty parallelism, ambiguous pronouns, and disagreement between the subject and the verb. Be sure that the answer choice you select does not contain any of these errors.

Improving Paragraphs

The Improving Paragraphs section of the PSAT requires you to use all of your skills in writing and revising, as you will be asked to read a rough draft of a student essay and make improvements to the writing style and writing strategies. It will be necessary to recognize and eliminate redundant material, understand the tone of the essay, and make sure that the ideas are expressed clearly and succinctly. This section is also designed to test issues related to the organization of ideas within an essay, the most logical order of sentences and paragraphs, and the relevance of statements made within the context of the essay. Following are some simple strategies to apply as you work through the Improving Paragraph questions:

Effective practice for this section of the PSAT will include writing rough drafts of essays and revising the structure and placement of sentences within the essays until the essays are in their final form. Apply the rules of standard written English to your writing. Be certain that your essays are logical and organized so that the purpose and message are clear to the reader.

➤ Quickly read over the entire essay, focusing on its general meaning. You will need to have a feel for the essay's organization and style to correctly answer many of the questions.

➤ The purpose of this section is for you to revise the given essay. Because the essay is a rough draft, expect to notice several errors as you are reading. The questions will not address every error, so don't linger on these mistakes as you read the essay.

➤ Make sure that all of your answer choices fit within the overall context of the essay. If a statement is not relevant to the main idea of the essay or a particular paragraph, it should not be added.

➤ It is your job to select the best choice; other options might be satisfactory, but one will always be better than the others. Focus on the style, organization, and tone of the essay when making your selections. Eliminate the answer choices that will definitely not work, and select the best from those that remain.

➤ Typically, the best way to improve your writing is to simplify it. An awkwardly constructed or wordy sentence will not clearly express an idea. It's a good idea to select the answer choice that is the most simple.

Commonly Misused Words

Certain words in the English language are often misused, and you might be tested on them in the PSAT Writing Skills Sections. We've included a list of some of these words here, along with definitions and examples of the proper use of the words.

Accept, Except

➤ **Accept** is a verb that means "to agree to receive something."

Example: I could not pay for my purchases with a credit card because the store would only *accept* cash.

➤ **Except** is either a preposition that means "other than, or but," or a verb meaning "to omit or leave out."

Example: *Except* for a B+ in history, Kate received all A's on her report card.

Affect, Effect

➤ **Affect** is usually a verb meaning "to influence."

Example: Fortunately, Kylie's sore ankle did not *affect* her performance in the game.

➤ **Effect** is usually a noun used to "indicate or achieve a result." Effect is also sometimes used as a transitive verb meaning "to bring into existence," but it is generally not used in this way on the PSAT.

Example: Studies have shown that too much exercise can have a negative *effect* on a person's health.

Among, Between

➤ **Among** is used with more than two items.

Example: Jackie's performance last night was the best *among* all of the actors in the play.

➤ **Between** is usually used with two items.

Example: Simon could not decide *between* the two puppies at the pound, so he adopted them both.

Assure, Insure, Ensure

➤ **Assure** means "to convince" or "to guarantee" and usually takes a direct object.

Example: If we leave two hours early, I *assure* you that we will arrive at the concert on time.

➤ **Insure** means "to guard against loss."

Example: Before he could leave for his trip, Steve had to *insure* his car against theft.

➤ **Ensure** means "to make certain."

Example: Our company goes to great lengths to *ensure* that every product that leaves the warehouse is of the highest quality.

Compare to, Compare with

➤ **Compare to** means "assert a likeness."

Example: The only way to describe her eyes is to *compare* them *to* the color of the sky.

➤ **Compare with** means "analyze for similarities and differences."

Example: For her final project, Susan had to *compare* bike riding *with* other aerobic activities and report her findings.

Complement, Compliment

➤ **Complement** implies "something that completes or adds to" something else.

Example: My favorite place to dine is on the terrace; the breathtaking views are the ideal *complement* to a romantic dinner.

➤ A **compliment** is "flattery or praise."

Example: Larry was thrilled when the award-winning author *complimented* him on his writing style.

Farther, Further

➤ **Farther** refers to distance.

Example: At baseball camp, Jack learned that with the correct stance and technique, he could throw the ball *farther* this year than he could last year.

➤ **Further** indicates "additional degree, time, or quantity."

Example: I enjoyed the book to a certain degree, but I felt that the author should have provided *further* details about the characters.

Fewer, Less

➤ **Fewer** refers to units or individuals that can be counted.

Example: Trish received all the credit, even though she worked *fewer* hours on the project than did the other members of the group.

➤ **Less** refers to mass or bulk that can't be counted.

Example: When it comes to reading, Mike is *less* inclined to read for pleasure than is Stephanie.

Imply, Infer

➤ **Imply** means "to suggest."

Example: His sister did not mean to *imply* that he was incorrect.

➤ **Infer** means "to deduce," "to guess," or "to conclude."

Example: The professor's *inference* was correct concerning the identity of the student.

Its, It's

➤ **Its** is the possessive form of "it."

Example: In the summer, my family enjoys drinking white tea for *its* refreshing, light flavor.

➤ **It's** is the contraction of "it is."

Example: Fortunately for the runners, *it's* a sunny day.

Lay, Lie

➤ **Lay** means "to put" or "to place," and requires a direct object to complete its meaning.

Example: To protect your floor or carpet, you should always *lay* newspaper or a sheet on the ground before you begin to paint a room.

➤ **Lie** means "to recline, rest, or stay," or "to take a position of rest." This verb cannot take a direct object. The past tense of lie is lay, so use extra caution if you see these words on the PSAT.

Example: On sunny days, our lazy cat will *lie* on the porch and bask in the warmth of the sunlight.

Example: Yesterday, our lazy cat *lay* in the sun for most of the afternoon.

Precede, Proceed

➤ **Precede** means "to go before."

Example: When I go to an expensive restaurant, I expect a salad course to *precede* the main course.

➤ **Proceed** means "to move forward."

Example: As a result of failed negotiations, the labor union announced its plan to *proceed* with a nationwide strike.

Principal, Principle

➤ **Principal** is a noun meaning "the head of a school or an organization."

Example: A high school *principal* is responsible not only for the educational progress of his students, but also for their emotional well-being.

➤ **Principal** can also mean "a sum of money."

Example: I hope to see a 30% return on my *principal* investment within the first two years.

➤ **Principal** can also be used as an adjective to mean "first" or "leading."

Example: Our *principal* concern is the welfare of our customers, not the generation of profits.

➤ **Principle** is a noun meaning "a basic truth or law."

Example: A study of basic physics will include Newton's *principle* that every action has an opposite and equal reaction.

Set, Sit

➤ The verb **set** takes an object.

Example: I *set* the bowl of pretzels in the middle of the table so that everyone could reach it.

➤ The verb **sit** does not take an object.

Example: When I dine alone, I always *sit* by the window so that I can watch all the people who pass by the restaurant.

Than, Then

➤ **Than** is a conjunction used in comparison.

Example: Rana made fewer mistakes during her presentation *than* she thought she would make.

➤ **Then** is an adverb denoting time.

Example: Mandy updated her resume, *then* applied for the job.

That, Which

➤ **That** is used to introduce an essential clause in a sentence. Commas are not required before the word "that."

Example: I usually take the long route because the main highway *that* runs through town is always so busy.

➤ **Which** is best used to introduce a clause containing nonessential and descriptive information. Commas are required before the word "which" if is used in this way. "Which" can also be used to introduce an essential clause in order to avoid repeating the word "that" in the sentence.

Example: The purpose of the Civil Rights Act of 1991, *which* amended the original Civil Rights Act of 1964, was to strengthen and improve Federal civil rights laws.

Example: I gave Mandy that book *which* I thought she might like.

There, Their, They're

➤ **There** is an adverb specifying location.

Example: Many people love to visit a big city, but few of them could ever live *there*.

➤ **Their** is a possessive pronoun.

Example: More employers are offering new benefits to *their* employees, such as daycare services and flexible scheduling.

➤ **They're** is a contraction of "they are."

Example: *They're* hoping to reach a decision by the end of the day.

To, Too

➤ **To** has many different uses in the English language, including the indication of direction and comparison. It is also used as an infinitive in verb phrases.

Example: Mary is driving *to* the beach tomorrow.

Example: Jill's painting is superior *to* Alan's painting.

Example: I try *to* run three miles every day.

➤ **Too** generally means "in addition," or "more than enough."

Example: It is important that we consider Kara's opinion *too*.

Example: Yesterday, I ran *too* far and injured my foot.

Your, You're

➤ **Your** is a possessive pronoun.

Example: Sunscreen protects *your* skin from sun damage.

➤ **You're** is a contraction of "you are."

Example: When *you're* at the beach, always remember to wear sunscreen.

Now that you've got a good feel for how to approach the questions found in the PSAT Writing Skills section, try these sample questions. Be sure to read the explanations to help you gain a better understanding of why the correct answer is correct.

This is a simulated PSAT Writing Section in format. Time yourself strictly on these practice questions so that you can begin to learn how to pace yourself. Read the directions carefully, and tear out the accompanying answer sheet on page 61before you begin answering the questions. Mark the answer sheet with your choices. Make educated guesses as necessary.

Practice Questions

Time—30 Minutes
39 Questions

> **Directions:** For each question, select the best answer from among the choices listed. Fill in the corresponding circle on your answer sheet.
>
> The following questions test your ability to recognize grammar and usage errors in standard written English. Each sentence contains either a single error or no error at all. Refer to the underlined, lettered portions of each sentence. If the sentence contains no error, select answer choice E. If the sentence contains an error, select the one underlined and lettered portion (A, B, C, or D) that is incorrect.

1. <u>Before</u> she learned how to prepare <u>healthful</u> foods, most of the
      A   B

   meals Katie <u>eats</u> came from fast food restaurants <u>or</u> pizza parlors.
                     C   D

   <u>No error</u>
     E

2. <u>Thus far</u> in the ceremony, <u>only</u> the actors in the movie, not the
      A   B

   director, <u>has received</u> any awards for <u>their</u> accomplishments. <u>No error</u>
             C   D   E

3. Most Italians <u>who disliked</u> composer Antonio Vivaldi <u>were</u>
                   A   B

   uncomfortable with an ordained priest composing operas; others
   <u>who were</u> fond <u>of his</u> music admired him for the very same reason.
     C   D

   <u>No error</u>
     E

4. Because of <u>its</u> steep drop-offs and narrow passes, the hiking trails
             A

   in Zion National Park <u>are recommended</u> for experts only, <u>and are</u>
                     B   C

   considered <u>some of the most</u> dangerous hiking trails in Utah. <u>No error</u>
              D   E

5. To earn a black belt in Tae Kwon Do, Tyler first <u>has to</u> earn his
                                                    A
novice belts, then his intermediate belts, and <u>finally has to earn</u> his
                                                         B
advanced belts <u>before</u> <u>he can</u> fight in a tournament for his black belt.
                    C   D
<u>No error</u>
    E

6. <u>Whereas</u> most students value <u>their</u> education and <u>work diligently</u> to
       A   B   C
earn their grades, others <u>attempting to</u> cheat because they simply do
                              D
not care. <u>No error</u>
               E

7. <u>Although</u> the wilderness preserve <u>continues</u> to exist because of money
       A   B
<u>generated with</u> tourists, the <u>increasing amount</u> of foot traffic in the
    C   D
preserve worries some conservation experts. <u>No error</u>
                                                  E

8. The <u>popularity of</u> her new album, <u>which</u> earned the pop star a gold
           A   B
record, <u>are proof</u> that with the right sound and image, an unknown
           C
artist <u>can become</u> a worldwide success overnight. <u>No error</u>
           D   E

9. The suspect <u>claimed that</u> the statement he made to the first detective
                    A
<u>was</u> neither accurate, <u>nor</u> <u>could it be</u> interpreted as an admission of
    B   C   D
guilt. <u>No error</u>
          E

10. Surprisingly, <u>since</u> the opening of the museum, <u>less than</u> ten
                      A   B
collectors <u>have</u> inquired <u>about</u> our collection of ancient Roman
              C   D
marble and terracotta artifacts. <u>No error</u>
                                      E

11. People who admire horses <u>often praise</u> them for <u>their</u> strength and
                                          A   B
<u>power; people</u> who fear horses often condemn them for the same
      C
<u>reasons</u>. <u>No error</u>
      D   E

12. <u>Although</u> a popular and prodigious composer, Mozart <u>has not lived</u> to
      A   B
see his final composition <u>performed</u>, and died penniless at
                                C
<u>an early age</u>. <u>No error</u>
      D   E

13. <u>Arguably,</u> Mark Twain's greatest work of fiction <u>was, in fact,</u>
      A   B
Mark Twain; the image that Samuel Clemens <u>conjured up</u> with the
                                                  C
creation of his alter ego <u>will have continued</u> to live in the hearts and
                                D
minds of Americans to this day. <u>No error</u>
                                      E

14. Professor Evans is always <u>in high demand</u> as a public speaker; <u>in fact,</u>
                                    A   B
he <u>has</u> never been <u>more busier</u> than he is this semester. <u>No error</u>
      C   D   E

Directions: The following questions test the correct and effective use of standard written English in expressing an idea. Part of each sentence (or the entire sentence) is underlined. Beneath each sentence are five different ways of phrasing the underlined portion. Answer choice A repeats the original phrasing. If you think that the original phrasing is best, select answer choice A. Otherwise, select from the remaining four choices. Your selection should result in the most effective, clear sentence, free from awkwardness or ambiguity.

15. Jenny wondered if she <u>had chosen</u> wisely when selecting her classes for the next term.

    (A) had chosen

    (B) chooses

    (C) has chosen

    (D) will choose

    (E) would have been choosing

16. <u>The fire, it was fanned by the high winds,</u> threatened the entire forest.

    (A) The fire, it was fanned by the high winds,

    (B) Fanned by the high winds, it

    (C) The fire, fanned by the high winds,

    (D) It was fanned by the high winds, and the fire

    (E) The high winds fanned the fire so that they

17. In order to effectively audit the class, <u>it is necessary to be there and attend every session</u>.

    (A) it is necessary to be there and attend every session

    (B) it is necessary to attend every session

    (C) attendance and to be there at every session is necessary

    (D) the necessity is to be there and attend every session

    (E) necessarily attend every session

18. In my letter of recommendation, <u>I stated that</u> Mike had been a punctual employee.

    (A) I stated that

    (B) it was stated that

    (C) there was a statement that

    (D) I made a statement about that

    (E) I gave a statement that

19. <u>The debate is going on about whether Mr. Smith's final exam is fair in its assessment of student's abilities or not</u>.

    (A) The debate is going on about whether Mr. Smith's final exam is fair in its assessment of student's abilities or not

    (B) There is an ongoing debate about whether or not Mr. Smith's final exam fairly assesses students' abilities

    (C) There is an ongoing debate about whether Mr. Smith's final exam is fairly assessing of students' abilities or not

    (D) There is a debate ongoing about whether the final exam given by Mr. Smith fairly assesses students' abilities or not

    (E) Whether or not Mr. Smith's final exam is a fair assessing of students' abilities is an ongoing debate

20. Many people enjoy visiting national monuments, touring capital cities, and <u>to see historic buildings</u>.

    (A) to see historic buildings

    (B) they see historic buildings

    (C) in seeing historic buildings

    (D) will see historic buildings

    (E) seeing historic buildings

21. As sales continue to go up, the company managers <u>predicting that the first quarter numbers this year will be higher</u> than during the first quarter of last year.

    (A) predicting that the first quarter numbers this year will be higher

    (B) predicting that, the higher first quarter numbers this year will be

    (C) predict that it will be higher first quarter numbers this year

    (D) predict that the first quarter numbers this year will be higher

    (E) predicts that this year's first quarter numbers, to be higher

22. Having carefully prepared for her debate, <u>the failure of the audience in understanding her argument's main points frustrated Mary Ellen</u>.

    (A) the failure of the audience in understanding her argument's main points frustrated Mary Ellen

    (B) the audience's failure to understand the main points of her argument was a frustration to Mary Ellen

    (C) Mary Ellen's frustration at the audience's failure to understand her argument's main points

    (D) Mary Ellen was frustrated by the audience's failure in understanding the main points of her argument

    (E) Mary Ellen was frustrated by the audience's failure to understand the main points of her argument

23. In a recent food marketing survey, the main reasons <u>most consumers' gave for choosing to regularly dine out was</u> convenience and time.

    (A) most consumers' gave for choosing to regularly dine out was

    (B) most consumers had given for choosing to regularly dine out was

    (C) given by most consumers for regularly choosing to dine out were

    (D) given by most consumer's for regularly dining out were

    (E) consumers would give for the regular choice of dining out is

24. The process of building a model train track in my basement <u>was tedious and intricate, but a success</u>.

    (A) was tedious and intricate, but a success

    (B) was tedious, intricate, but a success

    (C) was tedious, intricate, successful

    (D) was tedious and intricate, but successful

    (E) was tedious and intricate, and a success

25. <u>A hiker must carefully make plans before you can begin a backpacking trip into the canyon.</u>

    (A) A hiker must carefully make plans before you can begin a backpacking trip into the canyon

    (B) A hiker must make careful plans before beginning a backpacking trip into the canyon

    (C) Careful plans must be made by a hiker before you can begin a backpacking trip into the canyon

    (D) Before you can begin a backpacking trip into the canyon, a hiker must make careful plans

    (E) A hiker must make carefully made plans before beginning a backpacking trip into the canyon

26. <u>Following the election, the winning candidates stood before the crowd of students, making their acceptance speeches</u>.

    (A) Following the election, the winning candidates stood before the crowd of students, making their acceptance speeches

    (B) The winning candidates, following the election, stood before the crowd of students as they made their acceptance speeches

    (C) Standing before the crowd of students following the election, the winning candidates made their acceptance speeches

    (D) Following the election, the winning candidates stood before the crowd of students and made their acceptance speeches

    (E) The winning candidates stood before the crowd of students following the election, making their acceptance speeches

27. At the conclusion of the experiment, the <u>scientists discovered that the results were unexpected</u>.
    - (A) scientists discovered that the results were unexpected
    - (B) results discovered by the scientists were unexpected
    - (C) results were unexpectedly discovered by the scientists
    - (D) scientists unexpectedly discovered the results
    - (E) scientists discovered unexpected results

28. Mammals appeared on the earth long before the extinction of the dinosaurs; <u>in fact, they originated in the early Jurassic Period about 200 million years ago</u>.
    - (A) in fact, they originated in the early Jurassic Period about 200 million years ago
    - (B) originating in the early Jurassic about 200 million years ago
    - (C) in fact, in the early Jurassic Period they originated, about 200 million years ago
    - (D) about 200 million years ago, they originated in the early Jurassic Period
    - (E) in fact, originating in the early Jurassic about 200 million years ago

29. <u>It has long been known that, throughout the first several months of life, the human brain grows</u> at a rapid and dramatic pace, producing millions of brain cells.
    - (A) It has long been known that, throughout the first several months of life, the human brain grows
    - (B) The human brain grows throughout the first several months of life, it has long been known,
    - (C) Throughout the first several months of life, it has long been known that the human brain grows
    - (D) The human brain grows, it has long been known, throughout the first several months of life
    - (E) It has long been known that the human brain, growing throughout the first several months of life

30. Some people might be surprised to learn that *To Kill a Mockingbird* was <u>the only published novel of Harper Lee</u>.
    - (A) the only published novel of Harper Lee
    - (B) Harper Lee's only novel that was published
    - (C) Harper Lee's only published novel
    - (D) the novel that was the only one of Harper Lee
    - (E) the only novel published by Harper Lee

31. Due to the delay of the game, the coach, as well as his players, <u>were expecting the fans to go home</u>.

    (A) were expecting the fans to go home

    (B) was expecting the fans to go home

    (C) expecting the fans to go home

    (D) were to be expecting the fans to go home

    (E) are expecting the fans to go home

32. When the school board needs to make an important decision, <u>a committee is selected, and they assist in the process</u>.

    (A) a committee is selected, and they assist in the process

    (B) they select a committee and they assist in the process

    (C) they assist in the process by electing a committee to decide

    (D) a committee it selects to assist in the process

    (E) it selects a committee to assist in the process

33. <u>Even when the teachers and the principal agreed</u>, the decision to expel a student is never easy.

    (A) Even when the teachers and the principal agreed

    (B) Even when the teachers and the principal agree

    (C) Even when the teachers and the principal were in agreement

    (D) When the teachers and the principal agree, even

    (E) Even when there is an agreement with the teachers and the principal

34. My comments are first, that the decision is unfair, and second, <u>the timing of it is unfortunate</u>.

    (A) the timing of it is unfortunate

    (B) that the timing is unfortunate of it

    (C) the unfortunate timing

    (D) that its timing is unfortunate

    (E) unfortunately for the timing

> **Directions:** The following passage is a rough draft of a student essay. Some parts of the passage need to be rewritten in order to improve the essay. Read the passage and select the best answer for each question that follows. Some questions ask you to improve the structure or word choice of specific sentences or parts of sentences, whereas others ask you to consider the organization and development of the essay. Follow the requirements of standard written English.

(1) Our society creates leaders and followers and many people give directions while some people are constantly following orders. (2) Once you become a follower you lose your sense of identity and take upon the personality that people want you to take on. (3) Voice is one of the most important representations of who you are and what you stand for. (4) Ben strips his partner Gus of his identity, controlling the actions and thought of Gus. (5) In Harold Pinter's *The Dumb Waiter*, Gus is a representation of the dumb waiter, he is constantly being manipulated by others to carry out directions and has no real voice of his own. (6) A dumb waiter is controlled by people pulling the string at either end controlling the movements of it. (7) This system of control is mirrored in society as people of higher power are always telling us what to do. (8) It has become so powerful that many do not know they are being controlled.

(9) Gus, the antagonist, makes the audience feel sorry for him because Gus is taken advantage of by his partner, Ben. (10) The audience is most likely sympathizing with themselves. (11) We all play the pawn at some time in our life, we follow orders to please others. (12) No questions asked or at least none answered.

35. Which of the following revisions would create a more concise version of sentence 1 (reproduced below) while best retaining the sentence's original meaning?

    Our society creates leaders and followers and many people give directions while some people are constantly following orders.

    (A) Delete the word "people" after "some."
    (B) Change "some people are constantly following orders" to "some people follow orders."
    (C) Change "many people give directions" to "many people are giving directions."
    (D) Change "while some people are constantly following orders" to "while some people constantly follow."
    (E) Change the word "leaders" to "masters."

36. In context, which is the best version of sentence 3 (reproduced below)?

Voice is one of the most important representations of who you are and what you stand for.

    (A) As it is now.

    (B) A person's voice is one of their most important representations of who they are and what they stand for.

    (C) A person's voice is one of the most important representations of his or her own ideals and identity.

    (D) Voice is one of people's most important representations of who he or she is and what they stand for.

    (E) Voice is one of the most important representations of who one is and their ideals.

37. In context, which of the following most logically replaces "it" in sentence 8 (reproduced below)?

It has become so powerful that many do not know they are being controlled.

    (A) society

    (B) people of higher power

    (C) the system of control

    (D) being told what to do

    (E) being controlled

38. What should be done with sentence 11 (reproduced below)?

We all play the pawn at some time in our life, we follow orders to please others.

    (A) Leave it as it is.

    (B) Delete it.

    (C) Delete the comma.

    (D) Add "consequently" at the beginning of the sentence.

    (E) Add a period after "life" and capitalize the "we" that follows.

39. Which is the best way to deal with sentence 12 (reproduced below)?

No questions asked or at least none answered.

    (A) Leave it as it is.

    (B) Delete it.

    (C) Change the "or" to "and."

    (D) Delete "or at least."

    (E) Rearrange the sentence to read "None are answered no questions asked."

Answer Explanations

Identifying Sentence Errors (Questions 1–14)

1. **The best answer is C.** The portion of the sentence after the comma describes an event that occurred before; therefore, the present tense verb "eats" should be the past tense verb "ate." The preposition "before" effectively introduces the connection between the two events in the sentence. The adjective "healthful" is properly used to describe the foods. "Or" is an effective coordinating conjunction of the phrases "fast food restaurants" and "pizza parlors."

2. **The best answer is C.** In this sentence, "has received" should be "have received" because the plural subject of the sentence, "the actors," requires a plural verb. "Thus far" is an appropriate way to refer to the amount of time that has elapsed, "only" correctly indicates to whom the sentence is referring, and "their" matches the plural noun "the actors."

3. **The best answer is E.** There are no errors in this sentence. The phrases "who disliked," "were," and "who were" correctly agree with the plural noun "Italians" and the verb tense of the sentence. "Of" is an appropriate preposition to follow "fond," and "his" clearly refers to "Antonio Vivaldi."

4. **The best answer is A.** "Its" is a possessive pronoun that modifies a singular noun. In this sentence, the noun "trails" is plural, so the possessive pronoun should be "their." "Are recommended," "and are," and "some of the most" correctly refer to the plural noun "trails."

5. **The best answer is B.** To maintain parallel construction, only "finally" is necessary to effectively complete the sentence; in fact, "has to earn" is redundant. The verb phrase "has to" is properly used, as is the preposition "before" and the verb phrase "he can."

6. **The best answer is D.** The progressive verb "attempting" suggests an ongoing action. The context of this sentence requires that all verbs be in present tense and refer to the plural noun "students"; therefore, "attempting to" should be "attempt to." "Whereas" is effective in introducing the direct contrast within the sentence, the possessive pronoun "their" agrees with the plural noun "the students," and "diligently" correctly modifies the verb "work."

7. The best answer is C. In this sentence, the money comes *from* the tourists, so it would be correct to use "from," or "by," rather than "with." The adverb "although" is appropriate for introducing the contrast within the sentence. The form of the verb "continues" agrees with the singular noun "preserve." The word "increasing" is used correctly to describe how the "amount of foot traffic" is changing.

8. The best answer is C. The subject of this sentence is the singular noun "popularity," which requires the singular verb "is" instead of the plural verb "are." "Of" is an appropriate preposition to use after "popularity." The use of "which" properly introduces the non-essential clause "earned the pop star a gold record." The verb phrase "can become" agrees with the singular noun "unknown artist" and is in the correct tense.

9. The best answer is E. There are no errors in this sentence. "Claimed" agrees with the verb tense of rest of the sentence, and "that" correctly introduces an essential clause of the sentence. "Was" agrees with the singular noun "statement" and is also in the proper verb tense. "Nor" is the correct coordinating conjunction to use with "neither." The pronoun "it" in the phrase "could it be" correctly refers to the suspect's "statement." The phrase also maintains parallelism within the sentence.

10. The best answer is B. "Less than" refers to mass or bulk, not units or individuals that can be counted, such as "ten collectors." In this case, the proper phrase is "fewer than." "Since" is an appropriate way to refer to an event that has occurred between one point in time and another. The verb "have" correctly refers to the plural noun "collectors," and "about" is an appropriate preposition to follow "inquired."

11. The best answer is E. There are no errors in this sentence. The phrase "often praise" is correct because "often" correctly modifies the verb "praise." The possessive pronoun "their" agrees with the plural noun "horses." A semicolon is necessary between "power" and "people" because it separates two main clauses. "Power" is an appropriate noun used to describe "horses," and "people" correctly precedes the pronoun "who." The plural form of the noun "reasons" agrees with "strength and power," which are the multiple reasons referred to in the first portion of the sentence.

12. The best answer is B. The phrase "has not lived" is in present tense. This sentence describes events that occurred in the past and requires the past tense of the phrase "did not live." The adverb "although" is appropriate for introducing the contrast within the sentence.

"Performed" agrees with the verb tense of the sentence, and the phrase "an early age" is correctly used.

13. **The best answer is D.** This sentence requires two different verb tenses: The first portion of the sentence describes events that occurred in the past, and the second portion of the sentence describes events that are ongoing and currently taking place. "Will have continued" should be changed to "continues," which implies that the event is still occurring. The word "arguably" is an appropriate introduction to the sentence. The phrase "was, in fact," contains correct punctuation and effectively conveys the meaning of the first part of the sentence. The phrase "conjured up" correctly refers to a past event.

14. **The best answer is D.** The comparative "more" must be followed by the verb "busy." It would also be correct to simply say "busier." "In" is an appropriate preposition to precede "high demand." "In fact" effectively introduces the descriptive information in the rest of the sentence. "Has" agrees with the singular subject of the sentence, "he," or "Professor Evans," and is also in the correct verb tense; "has never been" implies that the event began at some point in the past, is occurring in the present, and will continue to occur until some point in the future.

Improving Sentences (Questions 15–34)

15. **The best answer is A.** This sentence is best as it is written. The past participle form of a verb is used with words such as "has," "had," and "have." The past participle form of "chose" is "chosen"; the past tense verb "had" agrees with the verb tense of the rest of the sentence. "Chooses" refers to the present tense, "has chosen" refers to the past but includes the present, "will choose" refers to the future, and "would have been choosing" refers to events in the past that might have occurred.

16. **The best answer is C.** The answer choice that correctly places the modifier "fanned by the high winds" is: "The fire, fanned by the high winds, threatened the entire forest." As written, the underlined portion includes the unnecessary phrase "it was." Answer choice B is incorrect because the pronoun "it" is redundant. In answer choices C and D, it is unclear as to what the pronoun "it" is referring.

17. **The best answer is B.** The phrases "to be there" and "attend every session" have the same meaning. The sentence only requires one of the phrases to be clear and effective, so answer choices A, C, and D are incorrect. Answer choice E includes the incorrect form of the word "necessary."

18. **The best answer is A.** This sentence is best as it is written. The first person pronoun "I" agrees with "my," the past tense verb "stated" is used correctly, and "that" correctly introduces an essential clause of the sentence. Answer choices B and C are incorrect because they use passive voice. In answer choice D, "about" is unnecessary. In both answer choices D and E, "I made a statement" and "I gave a statement" are better expressed simply as "I stated."

19. **The best answer is B.** This sentence, as it is written, is awkward and unclear. Answer choice B is correct because it clearly indicates both that the "debate is ongoing," and what the debate is about. Answer choices A, C, D, and E are awkward and include grammatical errors.

20. **The best answer is E.** To maintain parallel construction, the parts of the list separated by commas must agree. The answer choice that properly matches the verbs in the list is: "seeing historic buildings." "To see…" does not agree with "visiting" and "touring." Likewise, "they see…" does not agree with the other verbs in the list. Although "in seeing historic buildings" uses the proper form of the verb "see," "in" is not an appropriate preposition. "Will see…" does not agree with the other verbs in the sentence.

21. **The best answer is D.** The progressive verb "predicting" suggests an ongoing action. The context of this sentence requires that all verbs be in the present tense and refer to the plural noun "managers"; therefore, "predicting that" should be "predict that." The rest of the underlined portion is acceptable, so answer choice D is correct. Answer choice B uses the progressive verb "predicting." In answer choice C, it is unclear to what the pronoun "it" is referring. In answer choice E, "predicts" incorrectly refers to a singular noun.

22. **The best answer is E.** The clause "having carefully prepared for her debate" modifies "Mary Ellen." Therefore, "Mary Ellen" should directly follow that descriptive clause. Answer choices A and B suggest that the "audience's failure" carefully prepared for her debate, which doesn't make sense. Answer choices C and D are awkward and do not express the idea as clearly as does answer choice E.

23. **The best answer is C.** This sentence requires the present perfect verb "given," which implies that an event began in the past and leads up to the present, instead of the past tense verb "gave." In addition, the verb "were" should be used instead of "was" in order to agree with the plural noun "reasons." Finally, "consumers" does not require any apostrophes to show possession because it is just a plural noun. Answer choice C meets these requirements and best states the idea presented in the underlined portion. Answer choice B uses the verb "was" instead of "were." Answer choice D includes "consumers'," which is the plural possessive form. Answer choice E not only uses the incorrect verb phrase "would give," but also the present tense verb "is."

24. **The best answer is D.** The words "tedious" and "intricate" are adverbs that describe the process of building a model train track. As the sentence is written, the phrase "but a success" is a noun phrase. Therefore, this sentence lacks parallelism. Answer choice D correctly uses the word "successful" as an adverb to describe the train-building process. Answer choice C creates an incomplete sentence. Answer choices A, B, and E do not maintain parallel construction within the sentence.

25. **The best answer is B.** This sentence describes an activity that must be done before another activity can occur in the future; therefore, the present tense verb "begin" should be changed to "beginning." The definite pronoun "you" cannot replace the noun "hiker." Answer choice B is correct because it uses the correct verb form and eliminates "you can." Answer choices A, C, and D include the definite pronoun "you," which is incorrect. The phrase "make carefully made plans" in answer choice E is awkward.

26. **The best answer is D.** As it is written, the sentence, as well as the options in answer choices B and E, suggest that the "crowd of students" made the "acceptance speeches," which doesn't make sense. Since the "winning candidates" made the "acceptance speeches," the best written sentence will place the elements of the sentence in the correct order. Answer choice D is best because it clearly indicates when the speeches were made and who made them. Answer choice C is awkward and does not clearly express the idea.

27. **The best answer is E.** It is usually better to use the active voice rather than the passive voice. Therefore, the best answer choice will state that the scientists discovered the results, not that the results were discovered by the scientists. Answer choice E is best because it uses

the active voice, and it clearly indicates what happened. Answer choices B and C include passive language. Answer choice A is wordy and awkward. Answer choice D indicates that the discovery of the results was unexpected, which doesn't make sense.

28. **The best answer is A.** This sentence is best as it is written. Answer choices B and E create incomplete sentences. Answer choices C and D are awkward.

29. **The best answer is A.** This sentence is best as it is written. The phrase "it has long been known" is a good introduction to the sentence. Answer choices B, C, and D are awkward, and answer choice E creates an incomplete sentence.

30. **The best answer is C.** The phrase "Harper Lee's only published novel" most clearly and simply expresses the idea. Answer choice A is incorrect because the novel is "by" Harper Lee, not "of" Harper Lee. Answer choice E is incorrect because Harper Lee wrote the novel, but a publisher most likely published it. Answer choices B and D are awkward and unclear.

31. **The best answer is B.** The singular subject of this sentence is "the coach," so a singular verb is necessary. Answer choices A, D, and E contain plural verbs. Answer choice C creates an incomplete sentence.

32. **The best answer is E.** Answer choice E is best because it uses the active voice, and it makes clear who selects the committee and what the committee does. Answer choices A, B, and C contain the ambiguous pronoun "they," which makes it unclear who is doing what in the sentence. Answer choice D contains the correct pronoun "it," but it is awkwardly constructed.

33. **The best answer is B.** The portion of the sentence that is not underlined contains the present tense verb "is." Therefore, the underlined portion must be in the present tense. Answer choice B is best because it is in the present tense, and it clearly expresses the idea. Answer choices A and C are in the past tense. Answer choices D and E are awkward; the phrase "when there is agreement with" is inappropriate. Because two groups are being discussed, the agreement should be "between" the parties, not "with" the parties.

34. **The best answer is D.** Answer choice D is best because the possessive pronoun "its" clearly refers to the decision and maintains parallelism within the sentence. Answer choice C creates an incomplete sentence. The sentence, as it is written, does not include parallel construction. Answer choices B and E are awkward.

Improving Paragraphs (Questions 35–39)

35. **The best answer is A.** In this sentence, it is clear that "many" and "some" both refer to people. Therefore, it is redundant to use "people" after both words. Answer choice B might have appeared to be correct. However, changing the sentence in this way would also change its tone. The author wants to emphasize that some people *constantly* follow orders.

36. **The best answer is A.** Answer choice A is simple and clear, and closely follows the tone of the paragraph. Answer choices B, D, and E all contain grammatical errors. Answer choice C is somewhat wordy and awkward, and does not present the idea as clearly as does answer choice A.

37. **The best answer is C.** Answer choice C is correct because it clearly identifies what "has become so powerful." The sentence, as it is written, contains an ambiguous pronoun. Answer choice B might have appeared to be correct. However, the word "it" would not be used to refer to "people of higher power."

38. **The best answer is E.** The original sentence contains a comma splice. The sentence contains two separate ideas that cannot be connected with only a comma. The sentence contains information relevant to the essay, so answer choice B is not correct. Answer choice C might have appeared to be correct. However, deleting the comma would create a run-on sentence.

39. **The best answer is B.** This sentence is awkwardly constructed and does not flow well after sentence 11, nor does it add any valuable information to the paragraph. None of the other answer choices would have corrected these problems. Therefore, deleting sentence 12 is the best choice.

CHAPTER 2
PRACTICE QUESTIONS
ANSWER SHEET

Begin with number 1. There may be fewer than 40 questions-
leave the rest of the answer spaces blank.
Completely erase any unnecessary marks.

SECTION 1			
1 Ⓐ Ⓑ Ⓒ Ⓓ Ⓔ	11 Ⓐ Ⓑ Ⓒ Ⓓ Ⓔ	21 Ⓐ Ⓑ Ⓒ Ⓓ Ⓔ	31 Ⓐ Ⓑ Ⓒ Ⓓ Ⓔ
2 Ⓐ Ⓑ Ⓒ Ⓓ Ⓔ	12 Ⓐ Ⓑ Ⓒ Ⓓ Ⓔ	22 Ⓐ Ⓑ Ⓒ Ⓓ Ⓔ	32 Ⓐ Ⓑ Ⓒ Ⓓ Ⓔ
3 Ⓐ Ⓑ Ⓒ Ⓓ Ⓔ	13 Ⓐ Ⓑ Ⓒ Ⓓ Ⓔ	23 Ⓐ Ⓑ Ⓒ Ⓓ Ⓔ	33 Ⓐ Ⓑ Ⓒ Ⓓ Ⓔ
4 Ⓐ Ⓑ Ⓒ Ⓓ Ⓔ	14 Ⓐ Ⓑ Ⓒ Ⓓ Ⓔ	24 Ⓐ Ⓑ Ⓒ Ⓓ Ⓔ	34 Ⓐ Ⓑ Ⓒ Ⓓ Ⓔ
5 Ⓐ Ⓑ Ⓒ Ⓓ Ⓔ	15 Ⓐ Ⓑ Ⓒ Ⓓ Ⓔ	25 Ⓐ Ⓑ Ⓒ Ⓓ Ⓔ	35 Ⓐ Ⓑ Ⓒ Ⓓ Ⓔ
6 Ⓐ Ⓑ Ⓒ Ⓓ Ⓔ	16 Ⓐ Ⓑ Ⓒ Ⓓ Ⓔ	26 Ⓐ Ⓑ Ⓒ Ⓓ Ⓔ	36 Ⓐ Ⓑ Ⓒ Ⓓ Ⓔ
7 Ⓐ Ⓑ Ⓒ Ⓓ Ⓔ	17 Ⓐ Ⓑ Ⓒ Ⓓ Ⓔ	27 Ⓐ Ⓑ Ⓒ Ⓓ Ⓔ	37 Ⓐ Ⓑ Ⓒ Ⓓ Ⓔ
8 Ⓐ Ⓑ Ⓒ Ⓓ Ⓔ	18 Ⓐ Ⓑ Ⓒ Ⓓ Ⓔ	28 Ⓐ Ⓑ Ⓒ Ⓓ Ⓔ	38 Ⓐ Ⓑ Ⓒ Ⓓ Ⓔ
9 Ⓐ Ⓑ Ⓒ Ⓓ Ⓔ	19 Ⓐ Ⓑ Ⓒ Ⓓ Ⓔ	29 Ⓐ Ⓑ Ⓒ Ⓓ Ⓔ	39 Ⓐ Ⓑ Ⓒ Ⓓ Ⓔ
10 Ⓐ Ⓑ Ⓒ Ⓓ Ⓔ	20 Ⓐ Ⓑ Ⓒ Ⓓ Ⓔ	30 Ⓐ Ⓑ Ⓒ Ⓓ Ⓔ	40 Ⓐ Ⓑ Ⓒ Ⓓ Ⓔ

Math Section

Terms You'll Need to Understand

- ✓ Absolute value
- ✓ Acute angle
- ✓ Adjacent angle
- ✓ Arc
- ✓ Area
- ✓ Associative Property
- ✓ Average
- ✓ Base of a triangle
- ✓ Circumference
- ✓ Commutative Property
- ✓ Complementary angle
- ✓ Congruent
- ✓ Coordinate Plane
- ✓ Denominator
- ✓ Diameter
- ✓ Distributive Property
- ✓ Divisible
- ✓ Domain
- ✓ Equilateral triangle
- ✓ Exponent
- ✓ Factor
- ✓ Function
- ✓ Greatest Common Factor (GCF)
- ✓ Hypotenuse
- ✓ Improper fractions
- ✓ Inequality
- ✓ Integer
- ✓ Intersection
- ✓ Isosceles triangle
- ✓ Least Common Multiple (LCM)
- ✓ Line
- ✓ Line segment
- ✓ Median
- ✓ Midpoint
- ✓ Mixed numbers
- ✓ Mode
- ✓ Numerator
- ✓ Obtuse angle
- ✓ Parallel
- ✓ Perimeter
- ✓ Percent
- ✓ Point
- ✓ Prime number
- ✓ Proportion
- ✓ Pythagorean Theorem
- ✓ Quadrilateral
- ✓ Radius
- ✓ Range
- ✓ Ratio
- ✓ Reciprocal
- ✓ Right angle
- ✓ Sequence
- ✓ Set
- ✓ Similar triangles
- ✓ Slope
- ✓ Square root
- ✓ System of equations
- ✓ Tangent
- ✓ Transversal
- ✓ Vertical angle
- ✓ Volume

Concepts You'll Need to Master

✓ Basic arithmetic operations on real numbers, including integers and fractions
✓ Properties of integers
✓ Calculating averages and determining median and mode
✓ Translating word problems
✓ Simplifying algebraic expressions
✓ Factoring polynomials
✓ Solving algebraic equations and inequalities

✓ Working with number sets and sequences
✓ Properties of parallel and perpendicular lines
✓ Relationships between angles in geometric figures
✓ Properties of triangles, polygons, and circles, including perimeter, area, and circumference
✓ Simple coordinate geometry, including using slope and midpoint formulas

The PSAT Math Test is designed to test your ability to reason mathematically, to understand basic math terminology, and to recall basic mathematic formulas and principles. You should be able to solve problems and apply relevant mathematics concepts in arithmetic, algebra, and geometry.

Remember these general strategies when approaching PSAT math questions.

Draw Pictures

It really helps sometimes to visualize the problem. This strategy should not take a lot of time, and can prevent careless errors. Sometimes you are given a figure or a table; sometimes you just have to make your own. Use the blank space that is available in the math section of the test booklet.

Apply Logic

Most of the calculations are fairly simple and actually will not require the use of a calculator. In fact, the PSAT test writers are just as likely to test your logical reasoning ability or your ability to follow directions as they are to test your ability to plug numbers into your calculator. If you do use your calculator, be sure that you have an estimate of what your answer should look like ahead of time. If the answer you get from your calculator is not what you expected, try again.

Answer the Question That They Ask You

If the problem requires three steps to reach a solution and you only completed two of the steps, it is likely that the answer you arrived at will be one of the choices. However, it will not be the correct choice! Don't quit early—reason your way through the problem so that it makes sense. Keep in mind, though, that these questions do not usually involve intensive calculations or complicated manipulations.

Check the Choices

Take a quick look at the answer choices as you read the problem for the first time. They can provide valuable clues about how to proceed. For example, many answer choices will be in either ascending or descending order. If the question asks you for the least possible value, try the smallest answer choice first. If it does not correctly answer the question, work through the rest of the answer choices from smallest to largest. Remember that one of them is the correct choice.

Pick Numbers for the Variables

You can sometimes simplify your work on a given problem by using actual numbers as "stand-ins" for variables. This strategy works when you have variables in the question and some of the same variables in the answer choices. You can simplify the answer choices by substituting actual numbers for the variables. Pick numbers that are easy to work with. If you use this strategy, remember that numbers on the PSAT can be either positive or negative and are sometimes whole numbers and sometimes fractions. You should also be careful not to use 1 or 0 as your "stand-ins" because they can create "identities," which can lead to more than one seemingly correct answer choice.

Skip Around

There are bound to be a few questions that you will get wrong on any given testing day. The questions are each weighted the same as one another. In other words, you don't get any extra points for answering the harder questions. So, you would be foolish to waste time on a question when you aren't making any progress. Move on to questions that are easier for you, mark the tougher ones in your test booklet and come back to them only if you have time. Remember that you should never guess at random. If you simply don't know the answer, it might be best to leave the circle on your answer sheet empty.

Read the Questions Carefully

When you are looking at ratio problems, for example, note whether the question is giving a part-to-part ratio or a part-to-whole ratio. The ratio of girls to boys in a class is a part-to-part ratio. The ratio of girls to students in a class is a part-to-whole ratio.

Look for "New Operations"

Some of the questions on the math section will involve new, artificial operations that you have never seen. If you take a moment to read the entire question, you'll find that the new "operation" is defined for you. This means that these questions are usually straightforward substitution questions. Just apply the definition given in the question, and the actual math is typically easy.

 Familiarize yourself with the basic mathematical concepts included in this chapter and be able to apply them to a variety of math problems. Remember that you will not be required to perform any elaborate computations.

Arithmetic

This book assumes a basic understanding of arithmetic. Our focus will be on reviewing some general concepts and applying those concepts to questions that might appear on the PSAT math sections.

Understanding Operations Using Whole Numbers, Decimals, and Fractions

 The PSAT math sections will require you to add, subtract, multiply, and divide whole numbers, fractions, and decimals. When performing these operations, be sure to keep track of negative signs and line up decimal points in order to eliminate careless mistakes.

Following are some simple rules to keep in mind regarding whole numbers, fractions, and decimals:

1. Ordering is the process of arranging numbers from smallest to greatest or from greatest to smallest. The symbol > is used to represent

"greater than," and the symbol < is used to represent "less than." To represent "greater than and equal to," use the symbol ≥; to represent "less than and equal to," use the symbol ≤.

2. The Commutative Property of Multiplication can be expressed as $a \times b = b \times a$, or $ab = ba$. When two numbers are multiplied together, the order they are in doesn't matter. For example: $2 \times 3 = 6$, and $3 \times 2 = 6$.

3. The Distributive Property of Multiplication can be expressed as $a(b + c) = ab + ac$. Multiply each element within the parentheses by the element outside of the parentheses. For example: $2(2x + 4) = 4x + 8$.

4. The Associative Property of Multiplication can be expressed as $(a \times b) \times c = a \times (b \times c)$. It doesn't matter in which order the numbers are multiplied. For example: $(2 \times 3) \times 4 = 6 \times 4$, or 24; $2 \times (3 \times 4) = 2 \times 12$, or 24.

5. The Order of Operations for whole numbers can be remembered by using the acronym **PEMDAS**:

   P: First, do the operations within the *parentheses*, if any.

   E: Next, do the *exponents*, if any.

   M: Next, do the *multiplication*, in order from left to right.

   D: Next, do the *division*, in order from left to right.

   A: Next, do the *addition*, in order from left to right.

   S: Finally, do the *subtraction*, in order from left to right.

6. When a number is expressed as the product of two or more numbers, it is in factored form. Factors are all the numbers that will divide evenly into one number. For example, 1, 3, and 9 are factors of 9: $9 \div 1 = 9; 9 \div 3 = 3; 9 \div 9 = 1$.

7. A number is called a multiple of another number if it can be expressed as the product of that number and a second number. For example, the multiples of 4 are 4, 8, 12, 16, and so on, because $4 \times 1 = 4, 4 \times 2 = 8, 4 \times 3 = 12, 4 \times 4 = 16$, and so on.

8. The Greatest Common Factor (GCF) is the largest number that will divide evenly into any two or more numbers. The Least Common Multiple (LCM) is the smallest number that any two or more numbers will divide evenly into. For example, the GCF of 24 and 36 is 12 because 12 is the largest number that will divide evenly into both 24 and 36. The LCM of 24 and 36 is 72 because 72 is the smallest number that both 24 and 36 will divide evenly into.

9. Multiplying and dividing both the numerator and the denominator of a fraction by the same non-zero number will result in an equivalent fraction. For example, $\frac{1}{4} \times \frac{3}{3} = \frac{3}{12}$, which can be reduced to $\frac{1}{4}$. This works because any non-zero number divided by itself is always equal to 1.

10. When multiplying fractions, multiply the numerators to get the numerator of the product, and multiply the denominators to get the denominator of the product. For example, $\frac{1}{4} \times \frac{5}{6} = \frac{5}{24}$.

11. To divide fractions, multiply the first fraction by the reciprocal of the second fraction. In mathematics, the reciprocal of any number is the number that, when multiplied by the first number, will yield a product of 1. For example: The reciprocal of $\frac{1}{4}$ is $\frac{4}{1}$ because $\frac{1}{4} \times \frac{4}{1} = 1$. So, $\frac{1}{3} \div \frac{1}{4} = \frac{1}{3} \times \frac{4}{1}$, which equals $\frac{4}{3}$.

12. When adding and subtracting like fractions (fractions with the same denominator), add or subtract the numerators and write the sum or difference over the denominator. So, $\frac{1}{8} + \frac{2}{8} = \frac{3}{8}$, and $\frac{4}{7} - \frac{2}{7} = \frac{2}{7}$.

13. When adding or subtracting unlike fractions, first find the Lowest (or Least) Common Denominator (LCD). The LCD is the smallest number that all the denominators will divide evenly into. For example, to add $\frac{3}{4}$ and $\frac{5}{6}$, find the smallest number that both 4 and 6 will divide evenly into. That number is 12, so the LCD of 4 and 6 is 12. Multiply $\frac{3}{4}$ by $\frac{3}{3}$ to get $\frac{9}{12}$, and multiply $\frac{5}{6}$ by $\frac{2}{2}$ to get $\frac{10}{12}$. Now you can add the fractions, as follows: $\frac{9}{12} + \frac{10}{12} = \frac{19}{12}$, which can be simplified to $1\frac{7}{12}$.

14. To convert a mixed number into an improper fraction, first multiply the whole number by the denominator, add the result to the numerator, and place that quantity over the denominator. For example, $1\frac{7}{12} = \frac{(1 \times 12)}{12} + \frac{7}{12}$, or $\frac{19}{12}$. To convert an improper fraction into a mixed number, first determine how many times the denominator will divide evenly into the numerator. Then, place the remainder over the denominator, as follows: In the improper fraction $\frac{21}{8}$, 8 divides evenly into 21 twice ($8 \times 2 = 16$), with a remainder of 5 ($21 - 16 = 5$). Therefore, $\frac{21}{8}$ is equal to $2\frac{5}{8}$.

15. When converting a fraction to a decimal, divide the numerator by the denominator. For example, $\frac{3}{4}$ = 3 ÷ 4, or .75.

16. Place value refers to the value of a digit in a number relative to its position. Starting from the left of the decimal point, the values of the digits are ones, tens, hundreds, and so on. Starting to the right of the decimal point, the values of the digits are tenths, hundredths, thousandths, and so on.

Understanding Squares and Square Roots

In mathematics, a square is the product of any number multiplied by itself, and is expressed as $a^2 = n$. A square root is written as $\sqrt{n}$, and is the non-negative value a that fulfills the expression $a^2 = n$. For example, the square root of 25 would be written as $\sqrt{25}$. The square root of 25 is 5, and 5-squared, or 5^2, equals 5 × 5, or 25. A number is considered a perfect square when the square root of that number is a whole number. So, 25 is a perfect square because the square root of 25 is 5, which is a whole number.

When you square a fraction, simply calculate the square of both the numerator and the denominator.

➤ $\left(\frac{3}{5}\right)^2 =$

➤ $\frac{3}{5} \times \frac{3}{5} = \frac{9}{25}$

Understanding Exponents

When a whole number is multiplied by itself, the number of times it is multiplied is referred to as the exponent. As shown above with square roots, the exponent of 5^2 is 2 and it signifies 5 × 5. Any number can be raised to any exponential value.

➤$7^6 = 7 \times 7 \times 7 \times 7 \times 7 \times 7 = 117,649.$

Remember that when you multiply a negative number by a negative number, the result will be a positive number. When you multiply a negative number by a positive number, the result will be a negative number. These rules should be applied when working with exponents, too.

➤ $-3^2 = -3 \times -3$

➤ $-3 \times -3 = 9$

➤ $-3^3 = -3 \times -3 \times -3$

➤ $(-3 \times -3) = 9$

➤ $9 \times -3 = -27$

 Remember the Order of Operations mentioned previously, especially when you are working with negative numbers. For example, $-4^2 = 16$, but $-(4^2) = -16$ because you must perform the operation within the parentheses first.

The basic rules of exponents follow:

➤ $a^m \times a^n = a^{(m+n)}$

➤ $(a^m)^n = a^{mn}$

➤ $(ab)^m = a^m \times b^m$

➤ $\left[\dfrac{a}{b}\right]^m = \dfrac{a^m}{b^m}$

➤ $a^0 = 1$, when $a \neq 0$

➤ $a^{-m} = \dfrac{1}{am}$, when $a \neq 0$

➤ $\dfrac{a}{b^{-m}} = ab^m$, when $b \neq 0$

Understanding Ratios and Proportions

A ratio is the relationship between two quantities expressed as one divided by the other.

For example: Kate works 2 hours for every 3 hours that Darleen works. This can be expressed as $\dfrac{2}{3}$ or 2:3, and is known as a part-to-part ratio. If you compared the number of hours that Kate works in one week to the total number of hours that every employee works in one week, that would be a part-to-whole ratio.

A proportion is an equation in which two ratios are set equal to each other.

For example: Kate worked 30 hours in one week and earned \$480. If she received the same hourly rate the next week, how much would she earn for working 25 hours that week?

➤ $\dfrac{480}{30} = \dfrac{x}{25}$;solve for x

➤ $30x = 12,000$

➤ $x = 400$

Kate would earn $400 that week.

Understanding Percent and Percentages

A percent is a fraction whose denominator is 100. The fraction $\frac{55}{100}$ is equal to 55%.

Percentage problems often deal with calculating an increase or a decrease in number or price.

For example: A jacket that originally sells for $90 is on sale for 35% off. What is the sale price of the jacket (not including tax)?

➤ 35% of $90 =

➤ $\frac{35}{100} \times \$90 =$

➤ $.35 \times \$90 = \$31.50$

The discount is equal to $31.50, but the question asked for the sale price. Therefore, you must subtract $31.50 from $90.

➤ $\$90.00 - \$31.50 = \$58.50$

You could also more quickly solve a problem like this by recognizing that, if the jacket is 35% off of the regular price, the sale price must be equal to 100% – 35%, or 65% of the original price.

➤ 65% of $90 =

➤ $\frac{65}{100} \times \$90 =$

➤ $.65 \times \$90 = \$58.50.$

Remember to answer the question that is asked. It might help to underline relevant information within the questions to help you to stay on track. You can be certain that $31.50 would have been an answer choice if the above problem had appeared on your test, but it is not the correct answer!

Understanding Simple Probability

Probability is used to measure how likely an event is to occur. It is always between 0 and 1; an event that will definitely not occur has a probability of 0, whereas an event that will certainly occur has a probability of 1. To determine probability, divide the number of outcomes that fit the conditions of an event by the total number of outcomes. For example, the chance of getting heads when flipping a coin is 1 out of 2, or $\frac{1}{2}$. There are 2 possible outcomes (heads or tails) but only 1 outcome (heads) that fits the conditions of the event. Therefore, the probability of the coin toss resulting in heads is $\frac{1}{2}$ or .5.

When two events are independent, meaning the outcome of one event does not affect the other, you can calculate the probability of both occurring by multiplying the probabilities of each of the events together. For example, the probability of flipping 3 heads in a row would be $\frac{1}{2} \times \frac{1}{2} \times \frac{1}{2}$, or $\frac{1}{8}$.

Understanding Number Lines and Sequences

A number line is a geometric representation of the relationships between numbers, including integers, fractions, and decimals. The numbers on a number line always increase as you move to the right and decrease when you move to the left. Number line questions typically require you to determine the relationships among certain numbers on the line.

 Remember that the distance between points on the number line does not always have to be measured in whole units. Sometimes the distance between points is a fraction. For example: The distance on the number line between 1 and 1.5 is .5, or $\frac{1}{2}$.

An arithmetic sequence is one in which the difference between consecutive terms is the same. For example, 2, 4, 6, 8..., is an arithmetic sequence where 2 is the constant difference. In an arithmetic sequence, the nth term can be found using the formula $a_n = a_1 + (n - 1)d$, where d is the common difference. A geometric sequence is one in which the ratio between two terms is constant. For example, $\frac{1}{2}$, 1, 2, 4, 8..., is a geometric sequence where 2 is the constant ratio. With geometric sequences, you can find the nth term using the formula $a_n = a_1(r)^{n-1}$, where r is the constant ratio.

Typically, if you can identify the pattern or the relationship between the numbers, you will be able to answer the question. Following is an example of a sequence question similar to one you might find on the PSAT:

0,1,2,0,1,2,...

The numbers 0, 1, and 2 repeat in a sequence, as shown above. If this pattern continues, what will be the sum of the ninth and twelfth numbers in the sequence?

➤ To solve this problem, simply recognize that the third number in the sequence is 2, which means that both the ninth number and the twelfth number in the sequence will also be 2. Therefore, the sum of the ninth and twelfth numbers is 4.

Understanding Absolute Value

The absolute value of a number is indicated by placing that number inside two vertical lines. For example, the absolute value of 10 is written as follows: | 10 |. Absolute value can be defined as the numerical value of a real number without regard to its sign. This means that the absolute value of 10, | 10 |, is the same as the absolute value of -10, | -10 |, in that they both equal 10. Think of it as the distance from -10 to 0 on the number line, and the distance from 0 to 10 on the number line…both distances equal 10 units, as shown below:

Following is an example of how to solve an absolute value question:

➤ | 3 – 5 | =

➤ | –2 | = 2

Understanding Mean, Median, and Mode

The arithmetic mean refers to the average of a set of values. For example, if a student received grades of 80%, 90%, and 95% on three tests, the average test grade is $80 + 90 + 95 \div 3$. The median is the middle value of an ordered list. If the list contains an even number of values, the median is simply the average of the two middle values. It is important to put the values in either ascending or descending order before selecting the median. The mode is the value or values that appear the greatest number of times in a list of values.

Algebra

This book assumes a basic understanding of algebra. Our focus will be on reviewing some general concepts and applying those concepts to questions that might appear on the PSAT math sections.

Understanding Linear Equations with One Variable

In a linear equation with one variable, the variable cannot have an exponent or be in the denominator of a fraction. An example of a linear equation is $2x + 13 = 43$. The PSAT will most likely require you to solve for x in that equation. Do this by isolating x on the left side of the equation, as follows:

➤ $2x + 13 = 43$

➤ $2x = 43 - 13$

➤ $2x = 30$

➤ $x = \dfrac{30}{2}$, or 15

 Some PSAT questions involving simple equations might at first look like they can't be solved. For example,

If $b + c = 8$, what is the value of $2b + 2c$?

You won't be able to solve the first equation, but you can determine the value of the quantity $2b + 2c$ by factoring, as follows:

$2b + 2c = 2(b + c)$. Because you are given that $b + c = 8$, you know that $2b + 2c$ must equal $2(8)$, or 16.

Understanding Systems of Equations

A system of equations is a set of equations that is satisfied by the same set of values of the variables. On the PSAT, a system of equations will generally take the form of two linear equations with two variables. Following is an example of a system of equations, and the steps necessary to solve it:

➤ $4x + 5y = 21$

➤ $5x + 10y = 30$

The first step will be to make either the x-values or the y-values cancel each other out. In the above system, it will be easier to work with the y-values, since 5 is a factor of 10. Multiply each element in the first equation by -2:

➤ $-2(4x) + -2(5y) = -2(21)$

➤ $-8x - 10y = -42$

Now, you can add the like terms in each equation:

➤ $(-8x + 5x) = -3x$

➤ $(-10y + 10y) = 0$

➤ -42 + 30 = -12

➤ -3x = -12

Therefore, notice that the two y-terms cancel each other out. Solving for x, you get $x = 4$. Now, choose one of the original two equations, plug 4 in for x, and solve for y:

➤ 4(4) + 5y = 21

➤ 16 + 5y =21

➤ 5y = 5

➤ y = 1

The solutions for the system of equations are $x = 4$ and $y = 1$.

Understanding Polynomial Operations and Factoring Simple Quadratic Expressions

A polynomial is the sum or difference of expressions like $2x^2$ and $14x$. The most common polynomial takes the form of a simple quadratic expression, such as: $2x^2 + 14x + 8$, with the terms in decreasing order. The standard form of a simple quadratic expression is $ax^2 + bx + c$, where a, b, and c are whole numbers. When the terms include both a number and a variable, such as x, the number is called the coefficient. For example, in the expression $2x$, 2 is the coefficient of x.

The PSAT will often require you to evaluate or solve a polynomial by substituting a given value for the variable.

For example: If $x = -2$, what is the value of $2x^2 + 14x + 8 = ?$

➤ $2(-2)^2 + 14(-2) + 8 =$

➤ $2(4) + (-28) + 8 =$

➤ $8 - 28 + 8 = -12$

You will also be required to add, subtract, multiply, and divide polynomials. To add or subtract polynomials, simply combine like terms, as in the following examples:

➤ $(2x^2 + 14x + 8) + (3x^2 + 5x + 32) = 5x^2 + 19x + 40$

➤ $(8x^2 + 11x + 23) - (7x^2 + 3x + 13) = x^2 + 8x + 10$

To multiply polynomials, use the Distributive Property to multiply each term of one polynomial by each term of the other polynomial. Following are some examples:

➤ $(3x)(x^2 + 4x - 2) = (3x^3 + 12x^2 - 6x)$

Remember the *FOIL* Method to help solve some polynomial problems: multiply the *F*irst terms, then the *O*utside terms, then the *I*nside terms, then the *L*ast terms.

For example: If $(2x + 5)(x - 3) = ax^2 + bx + c$ for all values of x, what is the value of b?

➤ *First* terms: $(2x)(x) = 2x^2$

➤ *Outside* terms: $(2x)(-3) = -6x$

➤ *Inside* terms: $(5)(x) = 5x$

➤ *Last* terms: $(5)(-3) = -15$

Now put the terms in decreasing order:

➤ $2x^2 + (-6x) + 5x + (-15) =$

➤ $2x - x - 15$

Therefore, the value of b is 1, because the coefficient of x is 1.

You might also be asked to find the factors or solution sets of certain simple quadratic expressions. A factor or solution set takes the form, $(x \pm$ some number$)$. Simple quadratic expressions will usually have 2 of these factors or solution sets. The PSAT might require you to calculate the values of the solution sets.

For example: If $(2x + 5)(x - 3) = 0$, what are all the possible values of x?

Set both elements of the equation equal to 0.

➤ $(2x + 5) = 0$

➤ $(x - 3) = 0$

Now solve for x:

➤ $2x + 5 =$

➤ $2x = -5$

➤ $x = -\dfrac{5}{2}$

➤ $x - 3 =$

➤ $x = 3$

The possible values of x are $-\dfrac{5}{2}$ and 3.

Following are some general factoring rules that might prove useful for answering PSAT math questions:

➤ Finding the difference between two squares: $a^2 - b^2 = (a + b)(a - b)$

➤ Finding common factors, such as: $x^2 - 2x = x(x + 2)$

➤ Factoring quadratic equations, such as: $x^2 + 2x - 8 = (x + 4)(x - 2)$

The PSAT might ask you to solve one variable in terms of another variable. You might not be able to find a specific numerical value for the variables, but generally you won't need to. Your job will be to manipulate the given expression so that you can isolate one variable on one side of the equation.

Understanding Linear Inequalities with One Variable

Linear inequalities with one variable are solved in almost the same manner as linear equations with one variable: by isolating the variable on one side of the inequality. Remember, though, that when multiplying both sides of an inequality by a negative number, the direction of the sign must be reversed.

For example: If $3x + 4 > 5x + 1$, then $x =$

First, isolate x on one side of the inequality.

➤ $3x - 5x > 1 - 4$

➤ $-2x > -3$

Now, since you have to divide both sides by -2, remember to reverse the inequality sign.

➤ $x < \dfrac{3}{2}$

Understanding Inequalities and Absolute Value Equations

An inequality with an absolute value will be in the form of $|ax + b| > c$, or $|ax + b| < c$. To solve $|ax + b| > c$, first drop the absolute value and create two separate inequalities with the word OR between them. To solve $|ax + b| < c$, first drop the absolute value and create two separate inequalities with the word AND between them. The first inequality will look just like the original inequality without the absolute value. For the second inequality, you must switch the inequality sign and change the sign of c. For example,

To solve $|x + 3| > 5$, first drop the absolute value sign and create two separate inequalities with the word OR between them.

➤ $x + 3 > 5$ OR $x + 3 < -5$

Solve for x:

➤$x > 2$ OR $x < -8$

To solve $|x + 3| < 5$, first drop the absolute value sign and create two separate inequalities with the word AND between them:

➤$x + 3 < 5$ AND $x + 3 > -5$

Solve for x:

➤$x < 2$ AND $x > -8$

 Remember that when you multiply or divide both sides of an inequality by a negative number, you must reverse the direction of the inequality. This applies to operations involving the greater than or equal to symbol ($\geq$) and the less than or equal to symbol ($\leq$) as well.

Understanding Functions

A function is a set of ordered pairs in which no two of the ordered pairs has the same x-value. In a function, each input (x-value) has exactly one output (y-value). An example of this relationship would be $y = x^2$. Here, y is a function of x because for any value of x, there is exactly one value of y. However, x is not a function of y because for certain values of y, there is more than one value of x. The domain of a function refers to the x-values, whereas the range of a function refers to the y-values. If the values in the domain correspond to more than one value in the range, the relation is not a function.

For example: Let the function *f* be defined by $f(x) = 2(3x)$. What is the value of $f(5)$?

Solve this problem by substituting 5 for *x* wherever *x* appears in the function:

➤ $f(x) = x^2 - 3x$

➤ $f(5) = (5)^2 - (3)(5)$

➤ $f(5) = 25 - 15$

➤ $f(5) = 10$

Geometry

This book assumes a basic understanding of both coordinate geometry and plane geometry. The focus will be on reviewing some general concepts and applying those concepts to questions that might appear on the PSAT math sections.

Understanding the Coordinate Plane

The *xy*-coordinate plane has four separate quadrants, as shown in Figure 3.1.

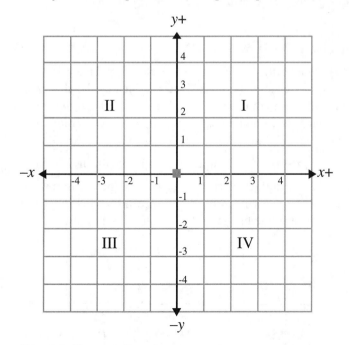

Figure 3.1   The *xy*-coordinate plane.

The x-coordinates in Quadrants I and IV will be positive, and the x-coordinates in Quadrants II and III will be negative. The y-coordinates in Quadrants I and II will be positive, and the y-coordinates in Quadrants III and IV will be negative.

Understanding the Equation of a Line

The PSAT will include questions concerning the slope-intercept form of a line, which is expressed as $y = mx + b$, where m is the slope of the line and b is the y-intercept (that is, the point at which the graph of the line crosses the y-axis). You might be required to put the equation of a line into the slope-intercept form to determine either the slope or the y-intercept of a line.

For example: In the xy-plane, a line has the equation $3x + 7y - 16 = 0$. What is the slope of the line?

The first step is to isolate y on the left side of the equation.

➤ $3x + 7y - 16 = 0$

➤ $7y = -3x + 16$

➤ $y = -\dfrac{3}{7}x + \dfrac{16}{7}$

According to the slope-intercept formula, the slope of the line is $-\dfrac{3}{7}$.

Understanding Slope

The slope of a line is commonly defined as "rise over run," and is a value that is calculated by taking the change in y-coordinates divided by the change in x-coordinates from two given points on a line. The formula for slope is $m = (y_2 - y_1) / (x_2 - x_1)$ where (x_1, y_1) and (x_2, y_2) are the two given points. For example, if you are given $(3,2)$ and $(5,6)$ as two points on a line, the slope would be $m = (6 - 2) / (5 - 3) = \dfrac{4}{2} = 2$. A positive slope will mean that the graph of the line will go up and to the right. A negative slope will mean that the graph of the line will go down and to the right. A horizontal line has a slope of 0, whereas a vertical line has an undefined slope (see Figure 3.2).

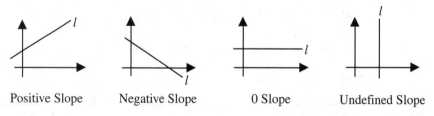

| Positive Slope | Negative Slope | 0 Slope | Undefined Slope |

Figure 3.2 Slopes of a line.

Understanding Parallel and Perpendicular Lines

Two lines are parallel if and only if they have the same slope. Two lines are perpendicular if and only if the slope of one of the lines is the negative reciprocal of the slope of the other line. If the slope of line a is 5, then the slope of line b must be $-\frac{1}{5}$ for the lines to be perpendicular (see Figure 3.3).

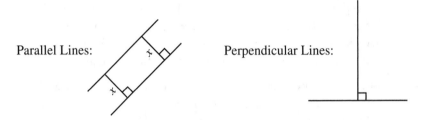

Parallel Lines: Perpendicular Lines:

Figure 3.3   Parallel and perpendicular lines.

Understanding Distance and Midpoint Formulas

To find the distance between two points on a coordinate graph, use the formula $\sqrt{\left([x_2 - x_1]^2 + [y_2 - y_1]^2\right)}$, where (x_1, y_1) and (x_2, y_2) are the two given points. For instance, the distance between (3,2) and (7,6) is calculated as follows:

➤ $\sqrt{\left([7 - 3]^2 + [6 - 2]^2\right)} =$

➤ $\sqrt{(16 + 16)} = \sqrt{32}$

➤ $\sqrt{(4)(8)} = 2\sqrt{8}$

To find the midpoint of a line given two points on the line, use the formula $\left(\frac{x_1 + x_2}{2}, \frac{y_1 + y_2}{2}\right)$. For example, the midpoint between (5,4) and (9,2) is $\left(\frac{(5 + 9)}{2}, \frac{4 + 2}{2}\right)$, or (7,3).

Understanding Properties and Relations of Plane Figures

Plane figures include circles, triangles, rectangles, squares, and other parallelograms. This book assumes a basic understanding of the properties of plane figures.

Triangles

A triangle is a polygon with three sides and three angles. If the measure of all three angles in the triangle are the same and all three sides of the triangle are the same length, then the triangle is an *equilateral* triangle. If the measure of two of the angles and two of the sides of the triangle are the same, then the triangle is an *isosceles* triangle. A *scalene* triangle has three unequal sides.

The sum of the interior angles in a triangle is always 180°. If the measure of one of the angles in the triangle is 90° (a right angle), then the triangle is a right triangle, as shown in Figure 3.4.

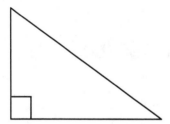

Figure 3.4   Right triangle.

Some right triangles have unique relationships between the angles and the lengths of the sides. These are called "Special Right Triangles." It might be helpful to remember the information shown in Figure 3.5.

The perimeter of a triangle is the sum of the lengths of the sides. The area of a triangle is calculate by using the formula $A = \frac{1}{2}$ (base)(height). For any right triangle, the Pythagorean theorem states that $a^2 + b^2 = c^2$, where a and b are legs (sides) and c is the hypotenuse.

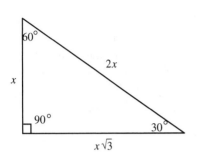 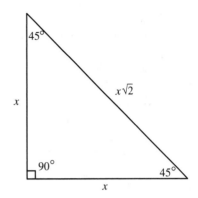

Figure 3.5 Special right triangles.

 Similar triangles always have the same shape, and each corresponding pair of angles has the same measure. The lengths of the pairs of corresponding sides that form the angles are proportional.

Circles

The equation of a circle centered at the point (h,k) is $(x - h)^2 + (y - k)^2 = r^2$, where r is the radius of the circle. The radius of a circle is the distance from the center of the circle to any point on the circle. The diameter of a circle is twice the radius. The formula for the circumference of a circle is $C = 2\pi r$, or πd, while the formula for the area of a circle is $A = \pi r^2$. A circle contains 360°.

Rectangle

A rectangle, as shown in Figure 3.6, is a polygon with four sides (two sets of congruent, or equal sides) and four right angles. The sum of the angles in a rectangle is always 360°. The perimeter of a rectangle is $P = 2l + 2w$, where l is the length and w is the width. The area of a rectangle is $A = lw$. The lengths of the diagonals of a rectangle are congruent, or equal. A square is a special rectangle where all four sides are of equal length.

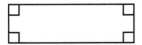

Figure 3.6 Rectangle.

Parallelograms

A parallelogram, shown in Figure 3.7, is a polygon with four sides and four angles, which are not right angles. A parallelogram has two sets of congruent sides and two sets of congruent angles. The sum of the angles of a parallelogram is 360°. The perimeter of a parallelogram is $P = 2l + 2w$. The area of a parallelogram is A = (base)(height). The height is the distance from top to bottom. A rhombus is a special parallelogram with four congruent sides.

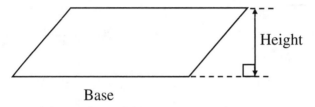

Base

Figure 3.7   Parallelogram.

Trapezoids

A trapezoid, as shown in Figure 3.8, is a polygon with four sides and four angles. The bases of the trapezoids (top and bottom) are never the same length. The sides of the trapezoid can be the same length (isosceles trapezoid), or they might not be. The perimeter of the trapezoid is the sum of the lengths of the sides. The area of a trapezoid is $A = \frac{1}{2}(\text{base}_1 + \text{base}_2)(\text{height})$.

The height is the distance between the bases. The diagonals of a trapezoid have a unique feature. When the diagonals of a trapezoid intersect, the ratio of the top of the diagonals to the bottom of the diagonals is the same as the ratio of the top base to the bottom base.

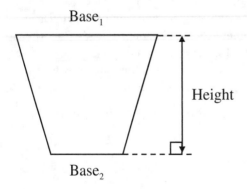

Figure 3.8   Trapezoid.

Understanding Angles

Angles can be classified as acute, obtuse, or right. An acute angle is any angle less than 90°. An obtuse angle is any angle greater than 90° and less than 180°. A right angle is a 90° angle.

When two parallel lines are cut by a perpendicular line, right angles are created, as shown in Figure 3.9.

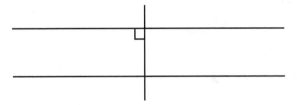

Figure 3.9 Parallel lines cut by a perpendicular line.

When two parallel lines are cut by a transversal, or intersecting line, the angles created have special properties. Each of the parallel lines cut by the transversal has four angles surrounding the intersection, that are matched in measure and position with a counterpart at the other parallel line. The vertical (opposite) angles are congruent, and the adjacent angles are supplementary; that is, the sum of the two supplementary angles is 180°. Figure 3.10 shows these special relationships.

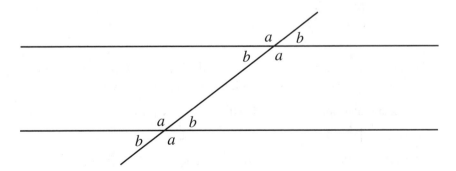

Figure 3.10 Parallel lines cut by a transversal.

Understanding Perimeter, Area, and Volume

The area, perimeter, and volume of geometric figures involve the size and amount of space taken up by a particular figure. Several of these formulas are included in reference information that is printed in the directions on the PSAT math sections, but we will review the basic formulas here.

Perimeter

The formulas for calculating the perimeter of shapes that might appear on the PSAT math sections are as follows:

1. Triangle: sum of the sides

2. Rectangle and parallelogram: $2l + 2w$

3. Square: $4s$ (s is the length of each side)

4. Trapezoid: sum of the sides

5. Circle (Circumference): $2\pi r$, or πd.

Area

The formulas for calculating the area of shapes that might appear on the PSAT math sections are as follows:

1. Triangle: $\frac{1}{2}$(base)(height)

2. Rectangle and square: (length)(width)

3. Parallelogram: (base)(height)

4. Trapezoid: $\frac{1}{2}$(base 1 + base 2)(height)

5. Circle: πr^2

Volume

The formulas for calculating the volume of basic three-dimensional shapes that might appear on the PSAT math sections are as follows:

1. Rectangular box and cube: (length)(width)(height)

2. Sphere: $\left(\frac{4}{3}\right)\pi r^3$

3. Right circular cylinder: $\pi r^2 h$ (h is the height)

Understanding Word Problems

Many PSAT math questions are presented as word problems that require you to apply math skills to everyday situations. It is important that you carefully read the questions and understand what is being asked. Some of the information given might not be relevant to answering the question. To stay on track, you can cross out any information that is not necessary to solve the problem. The table shown in Figure 3.11 represents the relationship between some words and their mathematical counterparts.

Description	Mathematical Translation
5 more than n	$n + 5$
5 less than n	$n - 5$
2 times the quantity $(x + 3)$	$2(x + 3)$
the sum of a and b	$a + b$
the difference between a and b	$a - b$
the product of a and b	$a \times b$
the quotient of a and b	$a \div b$
50 miles per hour	50 miles/60 minutes, or 50 miles/1 hour
3 more than twice n	$2n + 3$
3 less than twice n	$2n - 3$
The average of a and b	$\dfrac{a + b}{2}$
20 percent of n	$n(.2)$

Figure 3.11   Word problem translations.

It is a good idea to actually set up tables or equations based on the relevant information in word problems. Do not try to solve these problems in your head. Visualizing the situation presented in the problem will help you to keep track of the important information and prevent you from making silly mistakes.

Understanding Data Interpretation Problems

These questions require you to interpret information that is presented in charts, graphs, or tables, compare quantities, recognize trends and changes in the data, and perform basic calculations based on the information contained in the figures.

Get a general understanding of the charts, graphs, or tables before you look at the questions. If you can determine the relationships between the data elements, the questions will be much easier to answer.

Pie Charts

Information can be presented in the form of a pie chart. Figure 3.12 is an example of a pie chart like one that you might see on the PSAT.

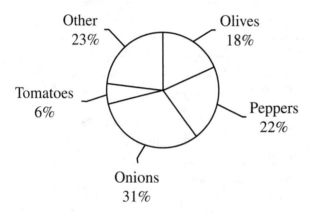

**FAVORITE PIZZA TOPPINGS
OF REGULAR CUSTOMERS**

Figure 3.12 Sample pie chart.

Line Graphs

Line graphs can also be used to display information. Figure 3.13 shows an example of a line graph like one that you might see on the PSAT.

**COMPARISON OF UNITS SOLD
PER QUARTER**

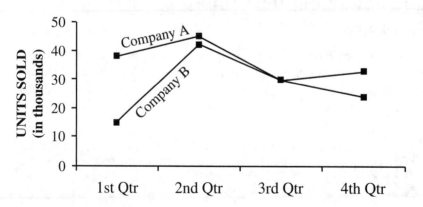

Figure 3.13 Sample line graph.

Bar Graphs

Data can also be represented on a bar graph. Figure 3.14 is an example of a bar graph like one that you might see on the PSAT.

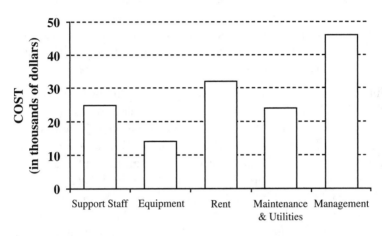

COMPANY OVERHEAD COSTS

Figure 3.14 Sample bar graph.

Pictographs

A pictograph displays statistical information using pictures or symbols. Figure 3.15 shows an example of a pictograph like one that you might see on the PSAT.

Class	Number of Students Registered
Beginner Ballet	🚹 🚹 🚹
Intermediate Ballet	🚹 🚹 🚹 🚹 🚹
Advanced Ballet	🚹
Beginner Tap	🚹 🚹
Intermediate Tap	🚹 🚹 🚹
Advanced Tap	🚹
Jazz 1	🚹 🚹 🚹 🚹
Jazz 2	🚹 🚹

🚹 = 12 students

Figure 3.15 Sample pictograph.

Multiple Choice Versus Student-Produced Response

The PSAT math sections include a total of 28 multiple choice questions, each with five answer choices (A–E). The answer choices correspond to the circles on your answer sheet. The multiple choice questions cover the content previously discussed in this chapter. You may use a calculator to assist you in answering any of the multiple choice questions, but none of the questions actually require the use of a calculator.

You will not receive credit for anything that you write in your test booklet, but you should work through the problems in the available space so that you can check your work. Be sure to do enough practice to determine just how much space you will need to solve various problems. You can use whatever space is available in the section on which you are working, but you cannot move to another section in search of blank space to solve your math problems. As mentioned earlier, if you don't know the answer to a question, mark it in your test booklet and come back to it later if you have time. If you are able to eliminate answer choices, cross them off in your test booklet. Make an educated guess if you are able to eliminate at least one answer choice. Remember that you get one point for each correct answer and zero points for answers that are left blank. If you answer a question incorrectly, you will lose an additional $\frac{1}{4}$ of a point.

Multiple Choice questions will include answer choices in the Roman Numeral format. Always take each Roman Numeral as a true or false statement: Does it answer the question or not? As you evaluate each of the Roman Numerals, eliminate answer choices based on whether the answer choices include the Roman Numeral. This process may allow you to arrive at the correct answer without looking at every Roman Numeral statement.

The PSAT math sections include a total of 10 student-produced response, or grid-in questions. These questions also cover the content previously discussed in this chapter. The only real difference between multiple choice questions and grid-in questions is that the latter do not include any answer choices. You must work out the problems in the space provided in your test booklet and fill in the circles on a special part of the answer sheet. You may use a calculator to assist you in answering any of the math questions, but none of the questions actually require the use of a calculator.

You will not receive credit for anything that you write in your test booklet, but you should work through the problems in the available space so that you can check your work. As mentioned earlier, if you don't know the answer to a question, mark it in your test booklet and come back to it later if you have time. Each correct answer is worth one point; you will not penalized for marking an incorrect answer in this section, so it is to your advantage to fill in an answer, even if you're not sure it's correct.

It is a good idea to practice with the answer sheet, or grid. We have included an answer sheet at the end of this chapter. Tear it out and use it as you work through the student-produced response questions that follow. Only the answers that you actually put in the grid will be scored. The grid has four places and can only accommodate positive numbers and zero. As long as your answer is filled in completely, you can start in any column on the grid. The grid includes both decimal points and fraction lines, so you can grid your answer as either a decimal or a fraction. If your answer is zero, be sure to grid it in column 2, 3, or 4.

We've included the directions for the student-produced response questions here (see Figure 3.16).

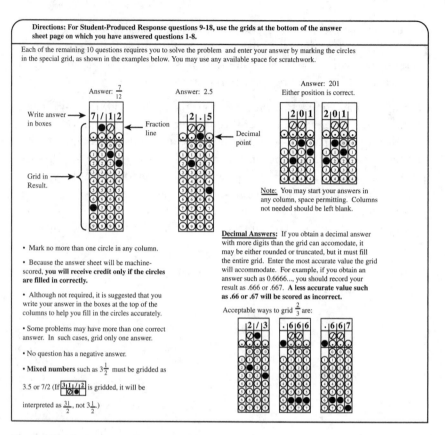

Figure 3.16   Student produced response directions.

 Some student-produced response questions ask you for more than one answer. These questions might ask something like, "What is one possible value of x?" You can fill in any one of the possible correct answers to the question.

Now that you've got a good feel for how to approach the questions found in the PSAT Math sections, try these sample questions. Be sure to read the explanations to help you gain a better understanding of why the correct answer is correct.

Practice Questions

Time—25 minutes
18 Questions

> **Directions:** Solve each problem and determine which is the best of the answer choices given. Fill in the corresponding circle on your answer sheet. Use any available space to solve the problems.

Notes

1. The use of a calculator is permitted.
2. All numbers are real numbers.
3. Figures that accompany problems in this test are intended to provide information useful in solving the problems. They are drawn as accurately as possible EXCEPT when it is stated in a specific problem that the figure is not drawn to scale. All figures lie in a plane unless otherwise indicated.
4. Unless otherwise specified, the domain of any function f is assumed to be the set of all real numbers x for which $f(x)$ is real number.

Reference Information

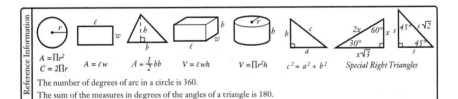

$A = \Pi r^2$
$C = 2\Pi r$ $A = \ell w$ $A = \frac{1}{2}bh$ $V = \ell wh$ $V = \Pi r^2 h$ $c^2 = a^2 + b^2$ *Special Right Triangles*

The number of degrees of arc in a circle is 360.
The sum of the measures in degrees of the angles of a triangle is 180.

Set P = {14, 15, 16, 17, 18, 19, 20}
Set Q = {16, 17, 18, 19, 20, 21, 22}

1. Sets P and Q are shown above. How many numbers in Set P are also in Set Q?

    (A) Three
    (B) Four
    (C) Five
    (D) Six
    (E) Seven

2. If John traveled 30 miles in 6 hours and Seth traveled three times as far in half the time, what was Seth's average speed, in miles per hour?

    (A) 5
    (B) 15
    (C) 30
    (D) 45
    (E) 90

3. If $r = -2$ and $p < 0$, which of the following has the least value?

(A) $4pr^2$
(B) $2pr^3$
(C) $-2pr^4$
(D) $-4pr^5$
(E) $-6pr^6$

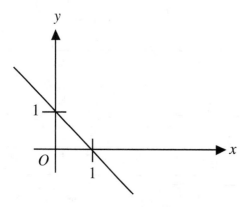

4. The figure above shows the graph of the line $y = ax + b$, where a and b are constants. Which of the following best represents the graph of the line $y = \frac{1}{2} ax + b$?

(A)

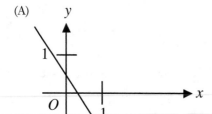

(B)

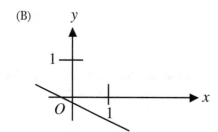

(C)

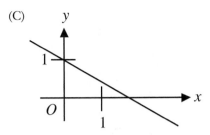

(D)

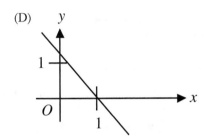

(E)

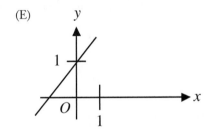

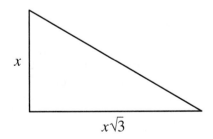

5. In the figure above, the perimeter of the triangle is $12 + 4\sqrt{3}$. What is the value of x?

  (A) 2
  (B) 4
  (C) 6
  (D) 8
  (E) 12

COIN COLLECTIONS	
Number of Coins	Number of Coin Collectors
100	1
95	3
90	3
85	4
80	2
75	1
70	2
65	0
60	2

6. At a recent coin collection exhibit, 18 coin collectors brought their collections for viewing. The number of coins each collector brought is shown in the table above. Mike, who was the only collector not able to attend the exhibit, would have brought 75 coins. Had he been able to attend, what would have been the median number of coins?

(A) 90

(B) 87.5

(C) 85

(D) 82.5

(E) 80

7. If 4 more than twice n is a negative number and 6 more than n is a positive number, which of the following could be the value of n?

(A) -8

(B) -6

(C) -4

(D) -2

(E) 4

8. Rectangle *PQRS* lies in the *xy*-coordinate plane so that its sides are *not* parallel to the axes. What is the product of the slopes of all four sides of rectangle *PQRS*?

(A) -2

(B) -1

(C) 0

(D) 1

(E) 2

Directions: For Student-Produced Response questions 9-18, use the grids at the bottom of the answer sheet page on which you have answered questions 1-8.

Each of the remaining 10 questions requires you to solve the problem and enter your answer by marking the circles in the special grid, as shown in the examples below. You may use any available space for scratchwork.

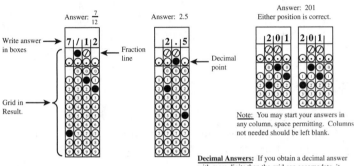

• Mark no more than one circle in any column.

• Because the answer sheet will be machine-scored, **you will receive credit only if the circles are filled in correctly.**

• Although not required, it is suggested that you write your answer in the boxes at the top of the columns to help you fill in the circles accurately.

• Some problems may have more than one correct answer. In such cases, grid only one answer.

• No question has a negative answer.

• **Mixed numbers** such as $3\frac{1}{2}$ must be gridded as 3.5 or 7/2 (If 3 1 / 1 2 is gridded, it will be interpreted as $\frac{31}{2}$, not $3\frac{1}{2}$.)

Note: You may start your answers in any column, space permitting. Columns not needed should be left blank.

Decimal Answers: If you obtain a decimal answer with more digits than the grid can accommodate, it may be either rounded or truncated, but it must fill the entire grid. Enter the most accurate value the grid will accommodate. For example, if you obtain an answer such as 0.6666..., you should record your result as .666 or .667. **A less accurate value such as .66 or .67 will be scored as incorrect.**

Acceptable ways to grid $\frac{2}{3}$ are:

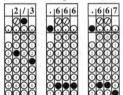

9. A $2\frac{1}{2}$ hour-long television movie included 30 minutes of commercials. What fraction of the $2\frac{1}{2}$ hour-long movie was not commercials?

10. If the product of 0.75 and a number is equal to 2, what is the number?

11. If $8s = 96$ and $sp = 4$, what is the value of p?

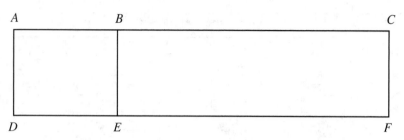

Note: Figure not drawn to scale.

12. In the figure above, *ACFD* is a rectangle and *ABED* is a square. *BC* = 8 and *AB* is a positive integer. If the area of *ACFD* must be more than 14 but less than 35, what is one possible value of *AB*?

13. A company sells boxes of napkins in which the napkins are red, white, and blue. Betty purchased a box of napkins in which $\frac{1}{2}$ were blue. If there were twice as many white napkins as blue ones and 25 napkins were red, how many napkins were in the box?

14. The four distinct points *T*, *U*, *V*, and *W* lie on a line *l*; the five distinct points *J*, *K*, *L*, *M*, and *N* lie on a different line that is parallel to *l*. What is the total number of different lines that can be drawn so that each line contains exactly two of the nine points?

15. If $4^{2x} + 4^{2x} + 4^{2x} + 4^{2x} = 4^9$, what is the value of *x*?

16. Each of 9 people had a blank card on which they wrote a positive integer. If the average (arithmetic mean) of these integers is 56, what is the greatest possible integer that could be on one of the cards?

17. Jeff and Scott stand back to back. They each take 12 steps in opposite directions away from each other and stop. Jeff then turns around, walks toward Scott, and reaches him in 16 steps. The length of one of Jeff's steps is how many times the length of one of Scott's steps? (All of Jeff's steps are the same length as each other, and all of Scott's steps are the same length as each other.)

18. If *rs* = 13 and 3*r* + 2*s* = 10, then $3r^2s + 2rs^2 = ?$

Answer Explanations

Multiple Choice (Questions 1–8)

1. **The correct answer is C.** To solve this problem, simply count the numbers that appear both in set P and in set Q. Sets P and Q share the following numbers: 16, 17, 18, 19, and 20. Therefore, five numbers in set P are also in Set Q.

2. **The correct answer is C.** You are given that John traveled 30 miles in 6 hours and that Seth traveled three times as far in half the time. This means that Seth traveled 30(3), or 90 miles in $6(\frac{1}{2})$, or 3 hours. Therefore, Seth traveled $\frac{90}{3}$, or 30 miles per hour.

3. **The correct answer is D.** You are given that $r = -2$. Therefore, the best approach to solving this problem is to replace r with -2 in each of the answer choices as follows:

   ➤ Answer choice A: $4pr^2 = 4p(-2)^2$, which equals $(4)(4)p$, or $16p$.

   ➤ Answer choice B: $2pr^3 = 2p(-2)^3$, which equals $(2)(-8)p$, or $-16p$.

   ➤ Answer choice C: $-2pr^4 = -2p(-2)^4$, which equals $(-2)(16)p$, or $-32p$.

   ➤ Answer choice D: $-4pr^5 = -4p(-2)^5$, which equals $(-4)(-32)p$, or $128p$.

   ➤ Answer choice E: $-6pr^6 = -6p(-2)^6$, which equals $(-6)(64)p$, or $-384p$.

   The question asks for the least value. You are given that $p < 0$, which means that p is a negative number. If you substitute any negative number into the results obtained above, only answer choices A and D will yield a negative value. Therefore, you can eliminate answer choices B, C, and E, because they will all be larger than either answer choice A or D. When $p < 0$, $128p$ will always be less than $16p$, so answer choice D is correct.

4. **The correct answer is C.** The equation of the line is given in the slope-intercept form ($y = mx + b$), where b is the y-intercept. The y-intercept is the point at which the line intersects the y-axis. Since the graph shown has the equation $y = ax + b$, and the new graph has the equation $y = \frac{1}{2}ax + b$, both graphs should have the same y-intercept. The graph shown has a y-intercept of 1. Eliminate answer choices A, B and D, since they do not have a y-intercept of 1. The slope of the graph shown is a, and the slope of the new graph (based on its equation) is $\frac{1}{2}a$. Because both slopes are positive, you can eliminate answer choice E, which has a negative slope. This leaves you with answer choice C.

5. **The correct answer is B.** To solve this problem, you must recognize that the triangle is a "special triangle." A right triangle in which the length of the longer leg is $\sqrt{3}$ times the length of the shorter leg is a $30°$–$60°$–$90°$ right triangle. Another property of this type of right triangle is that the hypotenuse is 2 times the length of the shorter leg. So, this right triangle has lengths x, $x\sqrt{3}$, and $2x$. The perimeter is the sum of the lengths of the sides. You are given that the perimeter equals $12 + 4\sqrt{3}$. Plug this value into the formula for the perimeter of a triangle, as follows:

➤ $12 + 4\sqrt{3} = x + x\sqrt{3} + 2x$
➤ $12 + 4\sqrt{3} = 3x + x\sqrt{3}$

For the right side of the equation to equal the left side of the equation, x must be equal to 4.

6. **The correct answer is C.** The median of a list of values is the middle value when the list is in chronological order and there are an odd number of values. In this case, if we include Mike and his 75 coins, there will be 19 coin collectors. List the number of coins for each collector in chronological order as follows:

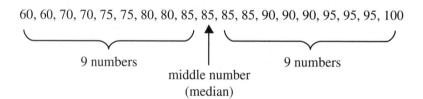

As you can see, the middle number is 85, so that is the median.

7. **The correct answer is C**. To solve, first translate the words into their mathematical equivalents:

➤ 4 more than twice n translates to $4 + 2n$. You are given that this quantity is a negative number, which translates to $4 + 2n < 0$.

➤ 6 more than n translates to $6 + n$. You are given that this quantity is a positive number, which translates to $6 + n > 0$.

Solve each inequality as follows:

➤ $4 + 2n < 0$

➤ $n < -2$

➤ $6 + n > 0$

➤ $n > -6$

So, n could be any number less than -2 and greater than -6. Only -4, answer choice C, is greater than -6 and less than -2.

8. **The correct answer is D**. Since the figure is a rectangle, the adjacent sides are perpendicular. Perpendicular lines have slopes that are negative reciprocals of each other, meaning that the product of their slopes is -1. Since there are four lines and four perpendicular angles, the product of the slopes is $(-1)(-1)(-1)(-1)$, or 1.

Student-Produced Response (Questions 9–18)

9. **Answer:** $\frac{4}{5}$. To solve this problem, convert hours into minutes. $2\frac{1}{2}$ hours is equivalent to 150 minutes. You are given that the movie included 30 minutes of commercials; therefore, the movie included 120 minutes that were not commercials. The fraction of the movie that was not commercials is $\frac{120}{150}$, or $\frac{4}{5}$.

10. **Answer: 2.66, 2.67, or $\frac{8}{3}$.**

    To solve this problem, set up an equation based on the information given:

    ➤ $0.75x = 2$

    Solve for x.

    ➤ $x = 2 \div 0.75$

    ➤ $x = 2.66666$ (This is a repeating decimal.)

    For the purposes of the PSAT, the answer can be simplified to either 2.66 or 2.67. If you first converted .75 to $\frac{3}{4}$, you would arrive at $\frac{8}{3}$ as your answer, which is also correct.

11. **Answer: $\frac{1}{3}$.** You are given that $8s = 96$. Therefore, $s = \frac{96}{8}$, or 12. You are given that $sp = 4$, and you now know that $s = 12$. Therefore, $12p = 4$ and $p = \frac{4}{12}$, or $\frac{1}{3}$.

12. **Answer: 2 or 3**. The formula for the area of a rectangle is A = $(l)(w)$. Therefore, the area of $ACFD$ will be $(AC)(AD)$. Because you must solve for the value of AB, let $AB = x$. Since $ABED$ is a square, it follows that $AB = AD = x$. Therefore, since $BC = 8$, the area of $ACFD$ will be $(8 + x)x$, or $x^2 + 8x$. Since, according to the question, the area must be between 14 and 35, set up the inequality $14 < x^2 + 8x < 35$. Now, pick some easy numbers to work with to replace x in the inequality. Because x is a positive value and 14 and 35 are not particularly large numbers, start with $x = 1$. If $x = 1$, then the area is $x^2 + 8x$, or $(1)^2 + 8(1)$, or 9. This value is not between 14 and 35, so x cannot be 1. If $x = 2$, then the area is $x^2 + 8x$, or $(2)^2 + 8(2)$, or 20. This value is between 14 and 35, so $x = 2$ is a possible solution. If $x = 3$, then the area is $x^2 + 8x$, or $(3)^2 + 8(3)$, or 33. This value is between 14 and 35, so $x = 3$ is another possible solution. If $x = 4$, then the area is $x^2 + 8x$, or $(4)^2 + 8(4)$ or 48. This value is not between 14 and 35, so x cannot be 4, or any number greater than 4. Therefore, x, or AB, can be either 2 or 3.

13. **Answer: 100.** To solve this problem, let the total number of napkins in the box equal x. According to information in the problem, there are 25 red napkins in the box. One quarter of the total number of napkins is blue, so there are $(\frac{1}{4})x$ blue napkins in the box. There are twice as many white napkins as blue napkins, so there are $2(\frac{1}{4})x$, or $(\frac{1}{2})x$ white napkins in the box. To calculate the total number of napkins in the box, set up an equation and solve for x.

➤ $x = 25 + \frac{1}{4}x + \frac{1}{2}x$

➤ $x = 25 + \frac{3}{4}x$

➤ $\frac{1}{4}x = 25$

➤ $x = 100$

14. **Answer: 20.** You are given that there are 4 points on line l, and 5 points on the line parallel to line l. Therefore, from each of the 4 points on line l, T, U, V, and W, you can draw one line to each of the 5 points on the second line. This means that there can be (4)(5), or 20 different lines containing exactly 2 of the 9 points.

15. **Answer: 4.** To solve this problem, rewrite $4^{2x} + 4^{2x} + 4^{2x} + 4^{2x}$ as $4(4^{2x})$. Now you have $4(4^{2x}) = 4^9$. When you multiply numbers with the same base, you add the exponents. The number 4 is equivalent to 4^1. Therefore, $4(4^{2x}) = 4^{2x+1}$. Now, because $4^{2x+1} = 4^9$, set the exponents equal to each other, and solve for x.

➤ $2x + 1 = 9$

➤ $2x = 8$

➤ $x = 4$

16. **Answer: 496.** If the average of the 9 numbers is 56, then the total value of the 9 numbers is (9)(56), or 504. The question asks for the greatest possible integer on one card, so set the values of the other cards at the lowest possible integer, which is 1. If there are 8 cards with a value of 1, then the value of the ninth card must be $504 - 8(1)$, or 496.

17. **Answer: 3.** Let j be the length of one of Jeff's steps, and let s be the length of one of Scott's steps. If they each take 12 steps away from each other, the distance between them is $12j + 12s$. Since it takes Jeff 16 steps to reach Scott, then $12j + 12s = 16j$. Subtract $12j$ from both sides to get $12s = 4j$. Divide both sides by 4 to get $3s = j$. The length of one of Jeff's steps (j) is 3 times the length of one of Scott's steps (s).

18. **Answer: 130.** To solve this problem, you should recognize that rs is a factor of $3r^2s + 2rs^2$. Rewrite $3r^2s + 2rs^2$ as $rs(3r + 2s)$. You are given that $rs = 13$ and $3r + 2s = 10$. Substitute those values into $rs(3r + 2s)$ to get $13(10)$, which equals 130.

Begin with number 1. There may be fewer than 40 questions-leave the rest of the answer spaces blank. Completely erase any unnecessary marks.

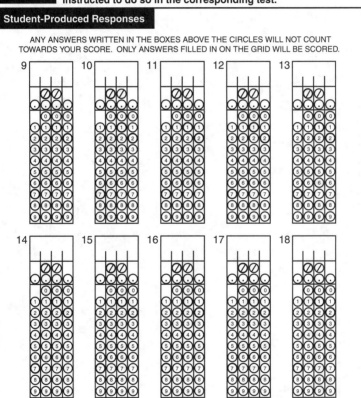

CHAPTER 3 SAMPLE QUESTIONS

1 Ⓐ Ⓑ Ⓒ Ⓓ Ⓔ   11 Ⓐ Ⓑ Ⓒ Ⓓ Ⓔ   21 Ⓐ Ⓑ Ⓒ Ⓓ Ⓔ   31 Ⓐ Ⓑ Ⓒ Ⓓ Ⓔ
2 Ⓐ Ⓑ Ⓒ Ⓓ Ⓔ   12 Ⓐ Ⓑ Ⓒ Ⓓ Ⓔ   22 Ⓐ Ⓑ Ⓒ Ⓓ Ⓔ   32 Ⓐ Ⓑ Ⓒ Ⓓ Ⓔ
3 Ⓐ Ⓑ Ⓒ Ⓓ Ⓔ   13 Ⓐ Ⓑ Ⓒ Ⓓ Ⓔ   23 Ⓐ Ⓑ Ⓒ Ⓓ Ⓔ   33 Ⓐ Ⓑ Ⓒ Ⓓ Ⓔ
4 Ⓐ Ⓑ Ⓒ Ⓓ Ⓔ   14 Ⓐ Ⓑ Ⓒ Ⓓ Ⓔ   24 Ⓐ Ⓑ Ⓒ Ⓓ Ⓔ   34 Ⓐ Ⓑ Ⓒ Ⓓ Ⓔ
5 Ⓐ Ⓑ Ⓒ Ⓓ Ⓔ   15 Ⓐ Ⓑ Ⓒ Ⓓ Ⓔ   25 Ⓐ Ⓑ Ⓒ Ⓓ Ⓔ   35 Ⓐ Ⓑ Ⓒ Ⓓ Ⓔ
6 Ⓐ Ⓑ Ⓒ Ⓓ Ⓔ   16 Ⓐ Ⓑ Ⓒ Ⓓ Ⓔ   26 Ⓐ Ⓑ Ⓒ Ⓓ Ⓔ   36 Ⓐ Ⓑ Ⓒ Ⓓ Ⓔ
7 Ⓐ Ⓑ Ⓒ Ⓓ Ⓔ   17 Ⓐ Ⓑ Ⓒ Ⓓ Ⓔ   27 Ⓐ Ⓑ Ⓒ Ⓓ Ⓔ   37 Ⓐ Ⓑ Ⓒ Ⓓ Ⓔ
8 Ⓐ Ⓑ Ⓒ Ⓓ Ⓔ   18 Ⓐ Ⓑ Ⓒ Ⓓ Ⓔ   28 Ⓐ Ⓑ Ⓒ Ⓓ Ⓔ   38 Ⓐ Ⓑ Ⓒ Ⓓ Ⓔ
9 Ⓐ Ⓑ Ⓒ Ⓓ Ⓔ   19 Ⓐ Ⓑ Ⓒ Ⓓ Ⓔ   29 Ⓐ Ⓑ Ⓒ Ⓓ Ⓔ   39 Ⓐ Ⓑ Ⓒ Ⓓ Ⓔ
10 Ⓐ Ⓑ Ⓒ Ⓓ Ⓔ   20 Ⓐ Ⓑ Ⓒ Ⓓ Ⓔ   30 Ⓐ Ⓑ Ⓒ Ⓓ Ⓔ   40 Ⓐ Ⓑ Ⓒ Ⓓ Ⓔ

CAUTION   Only use the answer grids below for Section 4 if you are instructed to do so in the corresponding test.

Student-Produced Responses

ANY ANSWERS WRITTEN IN THE BOXES ABOVE THE CIRCLES WILL NOT COUNT TOWARDS YOUR SCORE. ONLY ANSWERS FILLED IN ON THE GRID WILL BE SCORED.

Practice Exam 1

This practice PSAT consists of 125 questions, divided into five sections. To achieve the best results, time yourself strictly on each section. Use the Answer Sheet at the end of the chapter to mark your answers. Read the directions carefully, and remember not to guess at random. A scoring guide is included in Appendix D that should be used to calculate an approximate test score. Your score on the actual PSAT will be dependant on many factors, including your level of preparedness and your fatigue level on test day.

We suggest that you make this practice test as much like the real test as possible. Find a quiet location, free from distractions, and make sure that you have pencils, a calculator, and a timepiece. You should read the chapters for each specific section of the PSAT prior to taking this practice test.

SECTION 1

Time—25 Minutes

23 Questions

Directions: For each question, select the best answer from among the choices listed. Fill in the corresponding circle on your answer sheet.

Each sentence below has either one or two blanks. Each blank indicates that a word has been omitted from the sentence. Beneath each sentence are five words or sets of words. Select the word or set of words that, when inserted into the sentence in place of the blank(s), best fits the context of the sentence as a whole.

---

1. Despite her best efforts to please her boss, Melissa's _____ employer always found something wrong with her work.
   - (A) encouraging
   - (B) critical
   - (C) taciturn
   - (D) approving
   - (E) appreciative

2. Jordan spoke in such a _____ tone that it was clear he expected people to follow his instructions without question.
   - (A) submissive
   - (B) forceless
   - (C) controversial
   - (D) peremptory
   - (E) deliberate

3. After numerous rejections, the actress was _____, certain that she would never act in a Broadway play.
   - (A) speculative
   - (B) optimistic
   - (C) despondent
   - (D) resilient
   - (E) insipid

4. The _____ waitress was unusually _____ tonight; normally, her tiresome chatter kept diners from enjoying their meals.

 (A) apprehensive . . loud

 (B) garrulous . . silent

 (C) inane . . diligent

 (D) scurrilous . . problematic

 (E) industrious . . prompt

5. I could barely keep up with the _____ storyline; the numerous twists and turns in the plot made it extremely hard to follow.

 (A) convoluted

 (B) unambiguous

 (C) conventional

 (D) resolute

 (E) dependable

6. The demand for trained guards at the warehouse began to _____ as computers and motion-detection equipment _____ the midnight security guard position.

 (A) escalate . . undermined

 (B) improve . . devalued

 (C) wane . . created

 (D) decline . . supplanted

 (E) increase . . sabotaged

7. The interior designer chose a gauzy, _____ window curtain that allowed natural sunlight to pour into the room.

 (A) translucent

 (B) ominous

 (C) dismal

 (D) impenetrable

 (E) opaque

Each passage below is followed by several questions based on the content of the passage. Answer the questions based on what is either stated or implied in each passage. Be sure to read any introductory material that is provided.

Questions 8–14 are based on the following passage.

We had been anticipating this maiden voyage for a full nine months, since the initial purchase of 109 acres of northern, forested property. The property included a large pond that we were eager to investigate. In late April, the wait for decent weather was over, even
5 though the sky still held intermittent steel gray clouds and the thermometer registered a mere 54° F. We could wait no longer; Buck's Pond was begging to be explored.

Four adults and a precocious golden retriever gingerly climbed into the oversized five person canoe and, surprisingly, remained dry as
10 the helmsman shoved us off the sandy launch. A bit of wind created ripples on the surface of the water, but we could only remark that this same breeze would be aiding us on our way back to shore; there was no room for any negative thoughts to mar our excitement and enthusiasm for this long-awaited adventure.

15 After five minutes of steady but fairly effortless paddling, we found ourselves floating amid dozens of fresh green lily pads. The lone fisherman in the group marveled at the prospect of summer bass fishing that these lily pads promised, as the rest of us imagined dozens of bullfrogs sitting atop these leafy, green thrones. Suddenly, the cloud-
20 filled sky opened into an incredible blue, and the sun poured down on us, glistening over the water and spotlighting the shiny shells of several basking wood turtles atop water-bound tree trunks. It didn't take long for the creatures to silently slip off their resting places and into the water, disappearing silently into the murky depths of the pond.

25 A black-headed loon honked its disgust at our intrusion, and furtively began swimming in the opposite direction, no doubt attempting to steer us away from its nesting site. Within seconds, a line of mallard ducklings appeared, carefully following their mother as she made her way through the thick mass of lily pads. We were
30 determined to cause as little interruption as possible among the pond's wildlife, and began to feel like nosy neighbors touring a new home under construction.

Spotting what looked like a hilly island up ahead, we began a more direct course with a plan to disembark and check out the view from
35 the top of the hill. Just as we were nearing the chosen patch of beach, a pair of downy white trumpeter swans was spotted, regally swimming

along the pristine shoreline. But, wait! There were not just two
swans, but four... six... eight! Four matched sets were now swimming
in a row, chattering among themselves, growing louder and more agi-
40 tated as we hesitated in our movement. Suddenly, the closest pair of
swans made a 180° turn and began swimming directly toward us.
Clearly, this pair had taken on the responsibility of distracting us
while the other swans returned to their nesting areas to stand guard.

    We quickly but quietly switched our paddles to the other side of
45 the canoe, slowly paddling ourselves away from the angry cacophony.
Apparently, this was not sufficient for the eight swans, as they suddenly propelled themselves off the surface of the water, taking flight
one beautiful pair at a time. The sight of these giant, snow-white aviators taking to the air, swooping in front of us and ultimately landing
50 on the other side of the pond, left us awed and speechless. We had
indeed seen what we had come for. This view into the private world
of the magnificent wild creatures inhabiting the pond was well worth
the long wait, and provided a solid affirmation of our decision to purchase the property nine long months ago.

"Those who contemplate the beauty of the earth find reserves of strength that
will endure as long as life lasts."

-Rachel Carson

8. The primary purpose of the passage is to

(A) compare the natural habitats of various aquatic animals

(B) analyze the psychology of anticipating a new experience

(C) defend man's right to explore nature

(D) describe a personal experience involving man and nature

(E) demonstrate the different interests among people

9. In line 1, "maiden voyage" primarily refers to

(A) the first use of a new watercraft

(B) the first time the group had explored Buck's Pond

(C) the author's first canoe trip

(D) the pristine wilderness surrounding Buck's Pond

(E) the purchase of 109 acres of northern, forested property

10. It can be inferred from the passage that the author would most appreciate which of the following events?

(A) A bass-fishing tournament

(B) A trip to the zoo

(C) A visit to a nature preserve

(D) A ride on a large motorboat

(E) An interview with a pilot

11. In line 17, "marveled" most nearly means

    (A) wondered

    (B) condemned

    (C) wished

    (D) prayed

    (E) shone

12. The author gives the most emphasis to which aspects of the exploration of Buck's Pond?

    (A) The size of the pond and the difficulty navigating to the other side

    (B) The natural state of the pond and the abundance of wildlife living there

    (C) The helmsman's adept handling of the canoe and expert guidance

    (D) The location of the pond on the property and the lack of modern conveniences

    (E) The inclement weather and poor traveling conditions

13. According to the passage, all of the following are examples of wildlife that the author actually saw at the pond EXCEPT

    (A) ducks

    (B) swans

    (C) turtles

    (D) loons

    (E) frogs

14. The author quotes Rachel Carson most probably in order to

    (A) inspire the reader to visit Buck's Pond

    (B) indicate the author's vast knowledge of natural history

    (C) dispute the validity of the final paragraph

    (D) enhance the reader's visual perception of nature

    (E) reflect the main thesis of the passage

Questions 15–23 are based on the following passage.

    In the early twentieth century, no other disease caused as much fear and anxiety in the United States as paralytic poliomyelitis. Paralytic poliomyelitis, more commonly known as polio, was a particularly devastating disease because of its effect on children. Many children stricken with polio became permanently confined to wheelchairs or died at a very early age.

    It was during the summer of 1916 that Americans first realized that polio was a threatening and deadly disease. As a virus, polio seemed to spread most quickly and easily during the summer months. Throughout that fateful summer, New York City experienced a polio epidemic that killed 9,000 people and left 27,000 paralyzed.

Even though polio was not a new disease, around the turn of the century medical experts were still uncertain about how to prevent it. While it is difficult to determine polio's first appearance in history, various accounts of lameness and paralysis suggest polio can be traced back to early Egypt. It was probably not until 1908, when two Austrian physicians identified the submicroscopic virus, that scientists began to have an accurate understanding of the disease. Until 1908, conditions like overheating, chilling, and even teething were thought to cause polio's afflictions. Some scientists and doctors even believed that diseases such as whooping cough and pneumonia were the cause of polio's symptoms.

For many decades, polio research centered on treating symptoms as well as developing a vaccine to prevent polio. There was no known cure for people already infected with polio, so doctors focused on managing the disease's debilitating effects. Scientists and doctors concentrated on making the polio patient more comfortable and preventing fatalities. During the 1920s, the *iron lung* became a common device used to assist polio patients in breathing. When using the iron lung, patients would lie in a metal, human-sized tank for long periods of time. Sometimes, polio patients would have to continue this treatment their entire lives. Serum therapy was also attempted. During this treatment, polio victims would receive doses of serum extracted from polio-recovered monkeys, humans, and even horses. After nearly 20 years of research and trials, serum therapy was finally abandoned and deemed unsuccessful.

In the medical field, other debates occurred regarding the proper treatment of polio patients. Initially, it was thought that diseased limbs should be immobilized and even placed in casts. In addition, polio patients were prescribed complete bed rest. However, other theories suggested that paralyzed arms and legs should be wrapped in hot compresses and exercised regularly to prevent muscle atrophy. This latter approach soon became typical protocol because it seemed to relieve some pain and discomfort.

During World War II, the effort to cure and prevent polio in the United States was stalled because medical researchers became more involved with military issues and diseases overseas. However, at the end of the War, as numerous troops returned home and polio epidemics once again increased, attention was turned back to this dreaded disease. Finally, a breakthrough occurred during the early 1950s when a medical researcher named Jonas Salk developed an effective vaccine using the tissue culture method. Salk discovered that injecting elements of the dead polio virus into healthy patients was effective because vaccinated patients would build antibodies against the dead virus. These acquired antibodies prevented any future infection.

Later, another medical researcher named Albert Sabin developed an even easier method of distributing the vaccine. Sabin's vaccine became known as the oral polio vaccine. This innovation eliminated the use of needles; the vaccine was administered by mouth. Children
60 had no difficulty tolerating the vaccine because it was infiltrated into a sugar cube. By 1955, the Salk vaccination trials were deemed successful. The government quickly established a program to administer vaccines to everyone in the country. By the early 1960s, the oral Sabin vaccine replaced the Salk injections. The Sabin vaccine was a
65 live, attenuated virus that provided longer-lasting effects. By 1964, only 121 cases of polio were reported. This was a dramatic decrease from the 58,000 cases reported in 1952.

While the scourge of polio is well under control in the United States, it is still a dangerous disease worldwide. Polio is especially a
70 threat in more remote and undeveloped countries. In addition, 500,000 Americans continue to live with the effects of childhood polio infections that occurred decades ago.

15. According to this passage, the most significant effects of the polio epidemic in America were on
   (A) the development of government programs
   (B) children stricken with the disease
   (C) soldiers returning home after World War II
   (D) the medical community that attempted to cure polio
   (E) public involvement in promoting the vaccine

16. As used in line 17, "submicroscopic" most nearly means
   (A) underneath the skin
   (B) incapable of being isolated
   (C) too minute to be seen with a microscope
   (D) able to be viewed only under water
   (E) discernible with the naked eye

17. Based on the passage, what would likely have happened if the iron lung (line 28) had not been invented?
   (A) Some polio patients would have perished more quickly.
   (B) Paralysis in children would have worsened.
   (C) Children would have survived more frequently.
   (D) Patients would not have received proper bed rest.
   (E) Muscle atrophy would not have been prevented.

18. According to the passage, why did medical research first focus on treatment of polio's symptoms?

   (A) Scientists and medical experts did not understand the symptoms.

   (B) There was no known cure for the debilitating disease.

   (C) Funds were not available from the government to develop a cure for polio.

   (D) Medical researchers were fearful of working with the polio virus.

   (E) Polio's symptoms were uncomplicated and easy to treat.

19. The phrase "became typical protocol" (line 43) suggests that

   (A) the most common practice for treating polio became widely accepted

   (B) medical experts debated with scientists regarding the proper treatment of polio

   (C) polio patients were dissatisfied with the iron lung and other treatments.

   (D) doctors and scientists had yet to discover effective polio treatment

   (E) there was no consistent or widespread treatment for those infected with polio

20. The author's discussion of the polio virus emphasizes the

   (A) consequential debate about dead versus live viruses for vaccines

   (B) competition among medical researchers to develop a cure

   (C) complexity of the disease and the difficulty in discovering a cure

   (D) lack of understanding in the medical community about curing diseases

   (E) vast amounts of money needed to conduct the necessary medical research

21. The information in the passage suggests that

   (A) the Salk vaccine was not truly successful

   (B) people were not willing to take the Salk vaccine

   (C) Salk and Sabin had strong disagreements over a polio cure

   (D) the Salk vaccine paved the way for the Sabin oral vaccine

   (E) the use of live virus is always better in developing a vaccine

22. Which of the following would the author probably consider to be most similar to the polio epidemic in the United States, as it is discussed in this passage?

   (A) Malnutrition and starvation in developing countries

   (B) Researching and developing a cure for cancer

   (C) The Chicago fire of 1871

   (D) Obesity in the United States

   (E) Social security deficits leading to poverty

23. Which statement best summarizes the author's perspective on the effects of the American polio epidemic of the early 1900s?

   (A) There is virtually no residual evidence of the epidemic today.

   (B) Polio continues to be a silent threat to American children.

   (C) Polio was never as devastating as modern diseases.

   (D) The cure for polio may be temporary and prove ineffective in the future.

   (E) Thousands of Americans continue to live with the effects of polio.

STOP

If you finish before your time is up, check your work on this section only. You may not turn to any other section in the test.

SECTION 2

Time—25 Minutes

20 Questions

Directions: Solve each problem and determine which is the best of the answer choices given. Fill in the corresponding circle on your answer sheet. Use any available space to solve the problems.

Reference Information

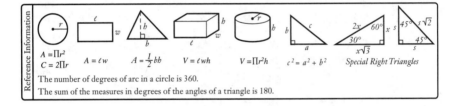

$A = \Pi r^2$
$C = 2\Pi r$

$A = \ell w$

$A = \frac{1}{2} bh$

$V = \ell wh$

$V = \Pi r^2 h$

$c^2 = a^2 + b^2$

Special Right Triangles

The number of degrees of arc in a circle is 360.

The sum of the measures in degrees of the angles of a triangle is 180.

---

1. When Mr. Smith arrived at the supermarket, there were 7 packages of hamburger buns left on the shelf. Two packages contained 8 buns and each of the others contained 12 buns. If Mr. Smith bought all 7 packages, how many hamburger buns did he purchase at the supermarket?

    (A) 20
    (B) 56
    (C) 68
    (D) 76
    (E) 84

2. A, B, and C are points on a line in that order. If $AB = 12$ and $BC = 13$ more than AB, what does AC equal?

    (A) 12
    (B) 25
    (C) 37
    (D) 40
    (E) 50

3. If $x + 7 = 12a$, then $3x + 21 =$
- (A) $12a$
- (B) $12a + 21$
- (C) $36a$
- (D) $36a + 7$
- (E) $48a$

Questions 4–5 refer to the following graph.

TEST SCORES OF FIVE STUDENTS

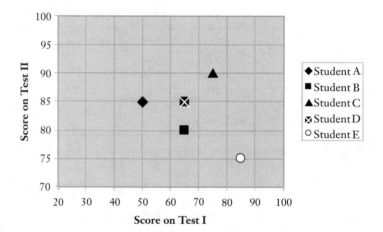

4. Which student scored fewer points on Test II than on Test I?
- (A) A
- (B) B
- (C) C
- (D) D
- (E) E

5. What was the average (arithmetic mean) of the scores of all of the students on Test I?
- (A) 68
- (B) 76
- (C) 83
- (D) 85
- (E) 90

6. On the number line above, t, u, v, w, x, y, and z are coordinates of the indicated points. Which of the following is closest in value to $|u + v|$?

    (A) t
    (B) w
    (C) x
    (D) y
    (E) z

7. If $x = \dfrac{1}{4}$, what is the value of $\dfrac{4+3}{x(x-1)}$?

    (A) -2
    (B) 0
    (C) 4
    (D) 12
    (E) 20

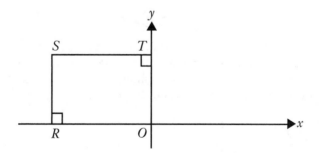

8. In the figure above, $RS = ST$ and the coordinates of S are $(k,4)$. What is the value of k?

    (A) -4
    (B) -2
    (C) 0
    (D) 2
    (E) 4

9. Which of the following represents the sum of positive integers a and b, divided by the product of a and b?

   (A) $\dfrac{ab + a}{b}$

   (B) $a + b(ab)$

   (C) $\dfrac{a + b}{ab}$

   (D) $\dfrac{ab}{a + b}$

   (E) $\dfrac{a + b}{a - b}$

10. How old was a person exactly 5 years ago if exactly $3x$ years ago the person was $2y$ years old?

    (A) $2y - 5$
    (B) $2y - 3x - 5$
    (C) $2y + 3x - 5$
    (D) $2y + 3x + 5$
    (E) $3x - 5$

D E A C B

11. The sequence above may be changed in either of two ways. Either two adjacent letters may be interchanged, or the entire sequence may be reversed. What is the <u>least</u> number of such changes needed to put the letters into alphabetical order from left to right?

    (A) 2
    (B) 3
    (C) 4
    (D) 5
    (E) 6

12. Set G consists of all multiples of 4 between 20 and 35. Set H consists of all multiples of 6 between 20 and 35. Which of the following is in Set H, but not in Set G?

    (A) 20
    (B) 24
    (C) 28
    (D) 30
    (E) 32

13. If $0 < n < 1$, which of the following gives the correct ordering of $4n$, n^2, $\sqrt{n}$, and n?

    (A) $4n < \sqrt{n} < n^2 < n$

    (B) $4n < n < n^2 < \sqrt{n}$

    (C) $n^2 < \sqrt{n} < n < 4n$

    (D) $n^2 < n < \sqrt{n} < 4n$

    (E) $n^2 < 4n < \sqrt{n} < n$

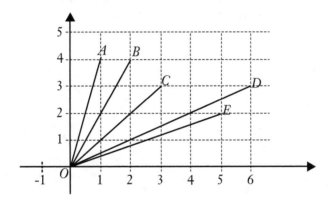

14. In the figure above, what is the median of the slopes of OA, OB, OC, OD, and OE?

    (A) $\dfrac{2}{5}$

    (B) $\dfrac{1}{2}$

    (C) 1

    (D) 2

    (E) 4

15. When it is 2:00 p.m. eastern standard time (EST) in Atlanta, it is 11:00 a.m. Pacific standard time in Los Angeles. A plane took off from Atlanta at 2:00 p.m. EST and arrived in Los Angeles at 4:00 p.m. PST. If a second plane left Los Angeles at 2:00 p.m. PST, what was the plane's arrival time (EST) in Atlanta?

    (A) 3:00 p.m. EST

    (B) 5:00 p.m. EST

    (C) 7:00 p.m. EST

    (D) 10:00 a.m. EST

    (E) 11:00 p.m. EST

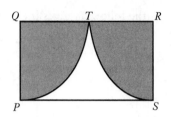

16. In rectangle *PQRS* above, arcs *PT* and *ST* are quarter circles with centers at *Q* and *R*, respectively. If the radius of each quarter circle is 2, what is the area of the non-shaded region?

(A) $4 - 4\pi$

(B) $4 - 2\pi$

(C) $8 - \pi$

(D) $8 - 2\pi$

(E) $8 - 4\pi$

17. $5^x + 5^x + 5^x + 5^x + 5^x =$

(A) 5^{x+1}

(B) 5^{x+2}

(C) 5^{x+5}

(D) 5^{5x}

(E) 5^{25x}

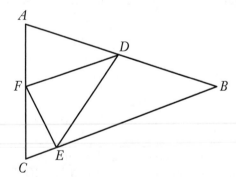

Note: Figure not drawn to scale.

18. In the figure above, $AB = BC$. If the measure of angle *ABC* is 40°, the measure of angle *BDE* is 95°, and the measure of angle *CFD* is 120°, what is the measure of angle *ADF*?

(A) 20°

(B) 30°

(C) 40°

(D) 50°

(E) 60°

19. If a, b, c, and d are four nonzero numbers, then all of the following proportions are equivalent EXCEPT

(A) $\dfrac{a}{b} = \dfrac{c}{d}$

(B) $\dfrac{a}{c} = \dfrac{b}{d}$

(C) $\dfrac{c}{a} = \dfrac{d}{b}$

(D) $\dfrac{bc}{ad} = \dfrac{1}{1}$

(E) $\dfrac{b}{c} = \dfrac{a}{d}$

20. For all numbers x and y, let the operation $\square$ be defined as $x \square y = 3xy - 3x$. If a and b are positive integers, which of the following can be equal to zero?

I. $a \square b$

II. $(a - b) \square b$

III. $b \square (a - b)$

(A) I only

(B) II only

(C) III only

(D) I and II only

(E) I, II, and III

STOP

If you finish before your time is up, check your work on this section only. You may not turn to any other section in the test.

SECTION 3

Time—30 Minutes

39 Questions

Directions: For each question, select the best answer from among the choices listed. Fill in the corresponding circle on your answer sheet.

The following questions test your ability to recognize grammar and usage errors in standard written English. Each sentence contains either a single error or no error at all. Refer to the underlined, lettered portions of each sentence. If the sentence contains no error, select answer choice E. If the sentence contains an error, select the one underlined and lettered portion (A, B, C, or D) that is incorrect.

1. After watching the presenter <u>stutter uncomfortably</u> and frantically
                                              A

   <u>search for</u> his <u>place in his</u> notes, Janelle realized the <u>important of</u>
        B   C   D

   being well prepared. <u>No error</u>
                              E

2. As usual, Jake <u>arrived at</u> the construction site several hours before
                        A

   either the roofing <u>and</u> the plumbing <u>contractors,</u> which
                         B   C

   <u>further increased</u> his frustration level. <u>No error</u>
          D   E

3. Rigorous preparation <u>is</u> considered <u>very necessary</u> <u>for</u> the amateur
                          A   B   C

   runner <u>who expects</u> to finish a full marathon. <u>No error</u>
              D   E

4. The veterinary clinic down the street never turns away <u>animals which</u>
                                                              A

   need help; <u>as a result,</u> the staff <u>has received</u> a special award for the
                    B   C

   <u>past</u> three years. <u>No error</u>
      D   E

5. As summer approached, the students <u>grew</u> <u>increasingly</u> unruly, forcing
                                          A   B
Miss Murray <u>to be</u> <u>more stricter</u> with her punishments. <u>No error</u>
                  C   D   E

6. The <u>applicant</u> we ultimately <u>choose</u> as our new art director
              A   B
<u>will probably</u> be selected <u>as much for</u> her personality as for her
       C   D
portfolio. <u>No error</u>
                E

7. Details <u>extracted from</u> eyewitness testimony, whether <u>contradictory to</u>
                  A   B
or in agreement with another account, often <u>provides</u> investigators
                                                  C
with <u>information necessary</u> to reconstruct the scene of a crime.
          D
<u>No error</u>
     E

8. Before the <u>construction of</u> the new highway was completed, Sheila
                        A
had a longer commute <u>because</u> she <u>must drive</u> an extra thirty minutes
                          B   C
everyday <u>to and from</u> work. <u>No error</u>
                D   E

9. Some actors, including Dave, <u>have</u> a genuine love for <u>their</u> trade,
                                      A   B
<u>but many others</u> appear to be driven by the possibility of either fame
       C
<u>or</u> wealth. <u>No error</u>
 D   E

10. Every year at my company's strategic planning meeting, no

matter how <u>patient</u> I <u>wait as others</u> share <u>their views</u>, someone
                A   B   C
<u>always interrupts</u> me as soon as I open my mouth. <u>No error</u>
        D   E

11. The dangers <u>of exposure to</u> ultraviolet radiation from the sun
                 A

    <u>has been</u> researched for many years, but only recently have experts
         B

    <u>strongly urged</u> the daily <u>use of</u> sunscreen or sun block. <u>No error</u>
           C   D   E

12. Because I <u>rarely watch</u> basketball, the conflicting predictions of the
                A

    announcers <u>make</u> it more difficult for me to decide which of the
               B

    teams <u>are</u> <u>most likely</u> to win the game. <u>No error</u>
          C   D   E

13. Dr. Adams, much admired for his unique and <u>highly effective</u>
                       A

    teaching style, is one of only a handful of college-level professors

    <u>who has</u> devoted his time to <u>ensuring</u> that no student <u>falls</u> through
         B   C   D

    the cracks. <u>No error</u>
             E

14. The tough job market <u>has forced</u> numerous college graduates
                  A

    <u>to make a decision</u> between <u>attempts to enter</u> the workforce <u>and</u>
            B   C   D

    attending graduate school. <u>No error</u>
                       E

The following questions test the correct and effective use of standard written English in expressing an idea. Part of each sentence (or the entire sentence) is underlined. Beneath each sentence are five different ways of phrasing the underlined portion. Answer choice A repeats the original phrasing. If you think that the original phrasing is best, select answer choice A. Otherwise, select from the remaining four choices. Your selection should result in the most effective, clear sentence, free from awkwardness or ambiguity.

15. Astronomers have recently discovered a black hole, <u>the origin of which is still largely unknown</u>.

    (A) the origin of which is still largely unknown

    (B) of which the origin is still largely unknown

    (C) still largely unknown as for the origin

    (D) the origin is still largely unknown of it

    (E) which the origin is still largely unknown of

16. In addition to being more rare than silver, <u>the price of gold is usually higher</u> and is in greater demand worldwide.

    (A) the price of gold is usually higher

    (B) gold usually has a higher price

    (C) the usually higher price of gold

    (D) gold has a usually higher price

    (E) gold's price is higher usually

17. <u>In 1942 *The Detroit Jewish News* was the first major Jewish newspaper in Michigan, it was published in Detroit</u>.

    (A) In 1942 The Detroit Jewish News was the first major Jewish newspaper in Michigan, it was published in Detroit

    (B) In 1942 the first major Jewish newspaper in Michigan, *The Detroit Jewish News*, was published in Detroit

    (C) In Detroit in 1942 *The Detroit Jewish News*, the first major Jewish newspaper in Michigan, was published

    (D) With its publication in Detroit in 1942, it was the first major Jewish newspaper in Michigan, *The Detroit Jewish News*

    (E) The first major Jewish newspaper in Michigan was when there was *The Detroit Jewish News* in Detroit in 1942

18. Jason passed the Michigan bar exam in 2003, and <u>he has since been practicing law in Michigan since that time</u>.

    (A) he has since been practicing law in Michigan since that time

    (B) has been practicing law in Michigan ever since

    (C) whereas he has been practicing law there ever since

    (D) since has been practicing law in Michigan

    (E) he, in Michigan, has been practicing law since then

19. Across the United States, one can encounter thousands of different healthcare plans, <u>each with its own premium</u>.
    (A) each with its own premium
    (B) each having their own premiums
    (C) when they have their own premiums
    (D) that has its own premium
    (E) they each have premiums of their own

20. Originally, diet soda products were popular not so much for their flavor or nutritional benefits, <u>but for their being low in sugar</u>.
    (A) but for their being low in sugar
    (B) the reason being their low sugar content
    (C) the reason was their low sugar content
    (D) but for their low sugar content
    (E) as for their being low in sugar

21. The responsibilities of a nurse are often as important <u>as a doctor's</u>.
    (A) as a doctor's
    (B) like a doctor's are
    (C) as much as a doctor
    (D) as that of doctor's
    (E) as those of a doctor

22. Participants in the student leadership conference expect to hear from prominent presenters <u>and gaining knowledge</u> about new opportunities for students.
    (A) and gaining knowledge
    (B) and also being knowledgeable
    (C) as well as being knowledgeable
    (D) and to gain knowledge
    (E) in addition they expect to gain knowledge

23. <u>The thoroughbred, one of the world's best-known horse breeds, whose origins arise from three distinct bloodlines</u>.
    (A) The thoroughbred, one of the world's best-known horse breeds, whose origins arise from three distinct bloodlines
    (B) The thoroughbred, has origins that arise from three distinct bloodlines, and it is one of the world's best-known horse breeds
    (C) The thoroughbred, one of the world's best-known horse breeds, originated from three distinct bloodlines
    (D) One of the world's best-known horse breeds, the thoroughbred, it originated from three distinct bloodlines
    (E) The origins of the thoroughbred, one of the world's best-known horse breeds, arising from three distinct bloodlines

24. Considered by many to be the most unique regional cuisine in the United States, <u>the Southwest is noted for such delicacies as</u> creamy enchiladas and flavored tequilas.

    (A) the Southwest is noted for such delicacies as

    (B) the Southwest includes among its notable delicacies as

    (C) the Southwest has such delicacies of note as

    (D) southwest cooking includes such notable delicacies as

    (E) southwest cooking is including such delicacies of note as

25. Vivaldi's *The Four Seasons* remains among the most popular pieces of <u>classical music; few people</u> realize that he wrote sonnets to accompany each of the four concertos.

    (A) classical music; few people

    (B) classical music, so few people

    (C) classical music but few people

    (D) classical music, few people

    (E) classical music; therefore, few people

26. Brian had the absolute support of his <u>family, this</u> wholehearted approval enabled him to succeed in college and beyond.

    (A) family, this

    (B) family: this

    (C) family; this

    (D) family; therefore

    (E) family, that

27. <u>Many opportunities exist for college graduates, and they often increase with advanced degrees</u>.

    (A) Many opportunities exist for college graduates, and they often increase with advanced degrees

    (B) Many opportunities exist for college graduates; these opportunities often increase for graduates with advanced degrees

    (C) Many opportunities exist for college graduates, who increase these with advanced degrees

    (D) Many opportunities exist for college graduates, which often increase with earning advanced degrees

    (E) Many opportunities exist for college graduates; these increase with the graduate's earning advanced degrees

28. If a person relies solely on audio tapes <u>to learn a foreign language, they</u> will never fully experience all that the language has to offer.

    (A) to learn a foreign language, they

    (B) while learning a foreign language, they

    (C) to learn a foreign language, he or she

    (D) in learning a foreign language, one

    (E) for to learn a foreign language, he or she

29. The high school football team <u>developed several activities to assess the stamina of potential players</u>, including an activity that required players to execute fifty pushups in less than sixty seconds.
    - (A) developed several activities to assess the stamina of potential players
    - (B) developing several activities assessing the stamina of potential players
    - (C) to assess the stamina of potential players, developed several activities
    - (D) developed several activities, which were assessing the stamina of potential players
    - (E) assessing the stamina of potential players, by developing several activities

30. The parents defending the suspended students declared <u>as to the rationality of their actions as prudent and responsible</u>.
    - (A) as to the rationality of their actions as prudent and responsible
    - (B) as to their actions and their rationality as prudent and responsible
    - (C) that their actions, that is to the students, are prudent and responsible
    - (D) that in regards to rationality their actions were prudent and responsible
    - (E) that the actions of the students were prudent and responsible

31. For weeks, one of the troupe's primary actors <u>were performing so badly that</u> audience members often left the theater during intermission.
    - (A) were performing so badly that
    - (B) when performing badly, were so that
    - (C) was performing so bad, that
    - (D) was performing so badly that
    - (E) was, when performing, so bad, in that

32. <u>Although Chinatown in New York City is better known than Chinatown in San Francisco, tourists familiar with both prefer Chinatown in San Francisco.</u>
    - (A) Although Chinatown in New York City is better known than Chinatown in San Francisco, tourists familiar with both prefer Chinatown in San Francisco
    - (B) Chinatown in New York City being better known than Chinatown in San Francisco, tourists familiar with both preferred the latter
    - (C) Although not as well known as Chinatown in New York City, tourists familiar with both preferred Chinatown in San Francisco
    - (D) Tourists familiar with both Chinatown in New York City better known than Chinatown in San Francisco, prefer Chinatown in San Francisco
    - (E) Although more people know about Chinatown in New York City than Chinatown in San Francisco: tourists who are familiar with both prefer Chinatown in San Francisco

33. <u>Unlike his predecessor, the new mayor was intent</u> on improving the city's cultural diversity.

    (A) Unlike his predecessor, the new mayor was intent

    (B) Unlike his predecessor, the new mayor was different and intended

    (C) The new mayor was intent, unlike his predecessor before him,

    (D) Unlike his predecessor before him, the new mayor was intent

    (E) The new mayor, unlike his predecessor, was different, and was intent

34. Annie, a great tennis player, could not continue her quest for a national title until she <u>can find a highly-skilled tennis coach</u>.

    (A) can find a highly-skilled tennis coach

    (B) found a highly-skilled tennis coach

    (C) would find a highly-skilled tennis coach

    (D) found a tennis coach that was highly-skilled

    (E) could, find a tennis coach, highly-skilled

Directions: The following passage is a rough draft of a student essay. Some parts of the passage need to be rewritten in order to improve the essay.

Read the passage and select the best answer for each question that follows. Some questions ask you to improve the structure or word choice of specific sentences or parts of sentences, whereas others ask you to consider the organization and development of the essay. Follow the requirements of standard written English.

---

(1) If someone were to tell you that a character from a book and a police detective were extremely similar, that person would be right. **(2)** Jim, an African American slave from the book *Huckleberry Finn*, and Virgil, the African American police detective from the movie *In the Heat of the Night*, are surprisingly alike. **(3)** They both lived during totally different eras of history, and the problems they faced were the same in many ways.

(4) During the time of the character Jim from *Huckleberry Finn*, he faced the problems of slavery and prejudice against African Americans. **(5)** People would treat him in a disrespectful way, which was the expected way of society. **(6)** Even young children such as Huck Finn himself were raised to be racist in many ways. **(7)** Even children in that time period were racist and had no respect for any other person of a different race. **(8)** Virgil, an African American police detective from the movie *In the Heat of the Night*, who was well respected in his hometown in Pennsylvania where he worked as a homicide expert, was faced with prejudice and racism when he visited the southern state of Mississippi. **(9)** Virgil was automatically suspect as the murderer of a well respected and high-class business owner in Sparta, Mississippi because of the color of his skin. **(10)** Even though about one hundred years had passed, prejudice and racism was still a part of society's ways.

35. Where is the most logical place to begin a new paragraph?
    (A) After sentence 2
    (B) After sentence 5
    (C) After sentence 7
    (D) After sentence 8
    (E) After sentence 9

36. In context, which is the best version of the underlined portion of sentence 4 (reproduced below)?

During the time of the character Jim from Huckleberry Finn, he faced the problems of slavery and prejudice against African Americans.

  (A) (As it is now)
  (B) *Huckleberry Finn,* during a time in which the character Jim
  (C) *Huckleberry Finn* was set during a time in which the character Jim
  (D) During the time of *Huckleberry Finn,* the character Jim, he
  (E) The character from *Huckleberry Finn,* Jim, during a time where he

37. In context, what is the best way to deal with sentence 7 (reproduced below)?

Even children in that time period were racist and had no respect for any other person with a different race.

  (A) Leave it as it is.
  (B) Place it immediately before sentence 6.
  (C) Use "and" to link sentence 7 to sentence 6.
  (D) Insert "On the contrary" at the beginning of the sentence.
  (E) Delete it because it contains ideas previously stated in the essay.

38. In context, which of the following changes should be made to sentence 10 (reproduced below)?

Even though about one hundred years had passed, prejudice and racism was still a part of society's ways.

  (A) Leave it as it is.
  (B) Delete "Even though" at the beginning of the sentence and replace it with "After all."
  (C) Delete the comma after "years" and insert a colon.
  (D) Change "was" to "were."
  (E) Delete the apostrophe in "society's ways."

39. Which of the following strategies are used by the writer of the passage?

  (A) compare and contrast
  (B) imaginative description
  (C) rhetorical questions
  (D) personal narration
  (E) direct quotation

STOP
If you finish before your time is up, check your work on this section only.
You may not turn to any other section in the test.

SECTION 4

Time—25 Minutes

18 Questions

Directions: This section includes two types of questions. For questions 1–8, solve each problem and determine which is the best of the answer choices given. Fill in the corresponding circle on your answer sheet. Use any available space to solve the problems. For questions 9–18, solve each problem and fill in your answer on the answer sheet.

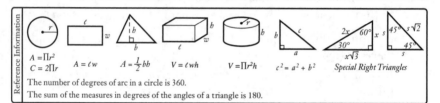

Reference Information

$A = \Pi r^2$ $A = \ell w$ $A = \frac{1}{2} bh$ $V = \ell wh$ $V = \Pi r^2 h$ $c^2 = a^2 + b^2$ *Special Right Triangles*

$C = 2\Pi r$

The number of degrees of arc in a circle is 360.

The sum of the measures in degrees of the angles of a triangle is 180.

1. If $3x + 6y = 24$, $y = 4z - 2$, and $z = 1$, what is the value of x?
   - (A) -12
   - (B) -4
   - (C) 4
   - (D) 12
   - (E) 20

2. Greg is younger than Daniel, but older than Henry. If g, d, and h represent the ages, in years, of Greg, Daniel, and Henry, respectively, which of the following is true?
   - (A) $h < d < g$
   - (B) $h < g < d$
   - (C) $d < h < g$
   - (D) $g < h < d$
   - (E) $d < g < h$

3. If the areas of four regions are all equal and the sum of the areas of the four regions is 25, what is the average (arithmetic mean) of the areas of the four regions?

(A) $\dfrac{25}{4}$

(B) $\dfrac{25}{2}$

(C) 25

(D) 50

(E) 100

4. Let S be the set of all integers that can be written as $3n^2 - 4n$, where n is a nonzero integer. Which of the following integers is in S?

(A) 4

(B) 6

(C) 13

(D) 30

(E) 54

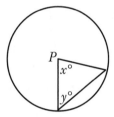

Note: Figure not drawn to scale.

5. In the figure above, point P is the center of the circle. If $x = 30°$, what is the value of y?

(A) 30°

(B) 45°

(C) 60°

(D) 75°

(E) 90°

6. A "simple square" is any integer greater than 1 that has only three positive integer factors—itself, its square root, and 1. Which of the following is a simple square?

    (A) 64

    (B) 81

    (C) 144

    (D) 196

    (E) 289

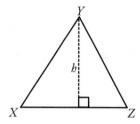

7. In $\triangle XYZ$ above, XZ is $\dfrac{5}{6}$ of b, the length of the altitude. What is the area of $\triangle XYZ$ in terms of b?

    (A) $\dfrac{5b}{12}$

    (B) $\dfrac{5b^2}{12}$

    (C) $\dfrac{5b}{6}$

    (D) $\dfrac{5b^2}{6}$

    (E) $\dfrac{5b^2}{3}$

8. If $cd = 35$, what is the value of the ratio of c to d?

    (A) 1 to 35

    (B) 3 to 5

    (C) 5 to 7

    (D) 35 to 1

    (E) It cannot be determined from the information given.

. . . .

Directions: For Student-Produced Response questions 9-18, use the grids at the bottom of the answer sheet page on which you have answered questions 1-8.

Each of the remaining 10 questions requires you to solve the problem and enter your answer by marking the circles in the special grid, as shown in the examples below. You may use any available space for scratchwork.

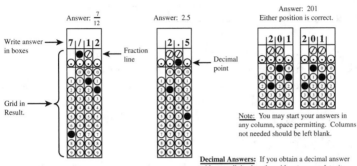

Answer: $\frac{7}{12}$

Write answer in boxes

Fraction line

Grid in Result.

Answer: 2.5

Decimal point

Answer: 201
Either position is correct.

Note: You may start your answers in any column, space permitting. Columns not needed should be left blank.

- Mark no more than one circle in any column.

- Because the answer sheet will be machine-scored, **you will receive credit only if the circles are filled in correctly.**

- Although not required, it is suggested that you write your answer in the boxes at the top of the columns to help you fill in the circles accurately.

- Some problems may have more than one correct answer. In such cases, grid only one answer.

- No question has a negative answer.

- **Mixed numbers** such as $3\frac{1}{2}$ must be gridded as

3.5 or 7/2 (If $3\frac{1}{2}$ is gridded, it will be

interpreted as $\frac{31}{2}$, not $3\frac{1}{2}$.)

Decimal Answers: If you obtain a decimal answer with more digits than the grid can accommodate, it may be either rounded or truncated, but it must fill the entire grid. Enter the most accurate value the grid will accommodate. For example, if you obtain an answer such as 0.6666..., you should record your result as .666 or .667. **A less accurate value such as .66 or .67 will be scored as incorrect.**

Acceptable ways to grid $\frac{2}{3}$ are:

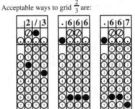

9. What is the greatest three-digit integer that has a factor of 16?

10. A recipe for chicken salad for 30 people requires 18 pounds of chicken. At this rate, how many people will 99 pounds of chicken feed?

11. When the positive <u>even</u> integer n is increased by 5 and then doubled, the result is between 20 and 30. What is one possible value of n?

12. The perimeter of a rectangular plot of land is 160 meters. If the length of one side of the plot is 35 meters, what is the area of the plot, in square meters?

13. In a mixture of sand and gravel, the ratio by weight of sand to gravel is 3 to 2. How many pounds of gravel will there be in 120 pounds of this mixture?

14. If $6(x - 2y)(2x + 3) = 324$ and $x - 2y = 6$, what is the value of $2x + y$?

15. In a rectangular coordinate system, the center of a circle has coordinates (3,9), and the circle touches the y-axis at one point only. What is the radius of the circle?

PARKERSVILLE VOTER REGISTRATION DATA

	Voting-Age Population	Number of Registered Voters
Men	3,500	2,700
Women	4,200	3,600

16. The table above gives the voter registration data for the town of Parkersville at the time of a recent election. In the election, 60% of the voting-age population actually voted. If the turnout for an election is defined to be the fraction (number who actually voted)/(number of registered voters), what was the turnout for this election?

17. If $3^x + 3^x + 3^x + 3^x = 3^{13}$, what is the value of x?

18. The number 0.0007 is equivalent to the ratio of 7 to what number?

STOP

If you finish before your time is up, check your work on this section only. You may not turn to any other section in the test.

SECTION 5

Time—25 Minutes

25 Questions

Directions: For each question, select the best answer from among the choices listed. Fill in the corresponding circle on your answer sheet.

Each sentence below has either one or two blanks. Each blank indicates that a word has been omitted from the sentence. Beneath each sentence are five words or sets of words. Select the word or set of words that, when inserted into the sentence in place of the blank(s), best fits the context of the sentence as a whole.

1. We were enchanted by the picturesque flower garden; it was full of _____ petunias, with colors ranging from bright yellow to a very deep blue.
   - (A) homogenous
   - (B) vibrant
   - (C) achromatic
   - (D) pallid
   - (E) sensitive

2. After a slump in sales, the board of directors decided to _____ with another corporation, forming one of the largest conglomerates in the country.
   - (A) disperse
   - (B) capitulate
   - (C) dissipate
   - (D) merge
   - (E) alternate

3. In an effort to _____ the friendship after an argument, Alan had to _____ that he was wrong and his friend was right.
   - (A) salvage . . concede
   - (B) resuscitate . . deny
   - (C) damage . . acknowledge
   - (D) squander . . comply
   - (E) secure . . refuse

4. The _____ speaker bellowed and provoked the protesters at the rally, _____ the intensity of the crowd until a riot ensued.

   (A) passionate . . placating

   (B) lethargic . . increasing

   (C) exhausted . . intensifying

   (D) fervent . . heightening

   (E) eloquent . . nurturing

5. Although she felt great _____ about flying in the airplane, Sofia was able to _____ her fear and successfully made it to her seat.

   (A) aberration . . lose

   (B) assurance. . oppose

   (C) trepidation . . overcome

   (D) confidence . . forget

   (E) apprehension . . define

6. Amid the commotion, the suspect was able to _____ from the crime scene and escape.

   (A) refrain

   (B) derive

   (C) permeate

   (D) abscond

   (E) abide

Each passage below is followed by several questions based on the content of the passage. Answer the questions based on what is either stated or implied in each passage. Be sure to read any introductory material that is provided.

Questions 7–13 are based on the following passages.

Below are two fictional accounts of modern-day refugees coming to America. The first describes a man and his son leaving Cuba, and the second describes two 'lost boys' of Sudan. Both are based on true accounts. Consider the relationship between the two situations.

Passage 1

Juan had heard his mother and father whispering each night now for over a week. He was sure they thought that he and his siblings were asleep, but in a two-room wooden shack it was difficult to keep voices quiet and unheard. As Juan drifted in and out of sleep, he occa-
5 sionally heard phrases like, "how many others?" and "what about the money?" In a quiet yet angry tone, he even heard his mother once harshly whisper, "But what will become of us?" As the oldest son, Juan always felt a strong sense of responsibility and duty to his family of seven. Now that he was 18, he felt somehow that he should be in on
10 whatever it was that his parents were so fervently discussing in secret.

Juan found out soon enough what the clandestine conversations were about when, the next evening, his parents put the other children to bed and took Juan outside to talk to him. The plan, explained to him in hushed voices, was that he and his father leave the next day for
15 a boat trip to America. It would be a long, arduous journey. They would never return to their homeland of Cuba. But this was their only chance to escape poverty and make a life for themselves. It would be nearly impossible to get permission to leave the country, so they would depart in 24 hours along with 15 other men on a small boat equipped
20 only with oars. A motor would be a dead giveaway to those looking for escapees. Anyone attempting to flee the country would be dealt with harshly by the authorities. Upon hearing the plan, Juan swallowed his fear, looked his father in the eye, and nodded.

If all went well, the group could reach American soil in about
25 three days. There was no way of knowing whether the attempted escape would be successful; the group would simply have to take their chances. Juan's Uncle Alfred had sent some money to help them pay for food and other supplies. He would open his home to them and help them to find jobs if they made it to Florida. These activities
30 would be conducted quietly and secretly, however, as the refugees could be threatened with deportation at any point.

Juan's father desperately hoped that, in a year or so, he would be able to send for the rest of the family and they could all live together in freedom. Juan had heard many horror stories of others in their small

35 town attempting similar escapes, but he knew that now was not the time to give voice to those fears.

Passage 2

James and Peter had been close friends for the past 12 years, since they were each about 8 years old. Their parents had been victims of a long and terrible civil war, and their sisters had been taken into cap-

40 tivity long ago. Only boys like James and Peter, who once lived quiet lives of tending their families' sheep, had been let go, to literally run from their war-torn country of Sudan in hopes of finding a new life somewhere else. In total, probably 10,000 boys and young men had left Sudan in this way, most of them without food and water, or shel-

45 ter from the elements. The boys had no idea where they were going, but many ended up crossing Sudan's border into neighboring Ethiopia. Unfortunately, many of them perished along the way.

For several years, Ethiopia provided crude camps for Peter and James and the others. While the conditions were far from ideal, the

50 boys at least had some food and limited water, and were free from the blasts of bombs and the constant fear that the explosions instilled in them. Peter and James managed to make the best of their internment in the camps, despite the bleakness of their situation. Unfortunately, the Ethiopian government shut down these camps for the 'lost boys'

55 in 1992, and once again Peter and James were let go on foot, to return to Sudan.

Although Peter and James had no real idea whether they were the oldest members of the 'lost boys'; they both had taken on leadership roles, perhaps because of their tremendous heights and deep voices.

60 One evening, as the group was resting for the night, a stranger approached the band of boys and asked to speak to one of the 'elder' boys. The younger boys directed the stranger to Peter and James, who were then told to head toward Kenya where help would be wait-ing.

65 After walking again for more than a year, the 'lost boys' entered Kenya, an African country that offered aid to thousands of refugees from the entire continent. James and Peter were two of the lucky ones; more than half of the 26,000 'lost boys' had succumbed to the harsh conditions they had been forced to endure during their long

70 trek. In Kenya, they once again found the basic necessities as well as protection from the many dangers and hardships they had faced over the years. One day, as Peter and James were settling into their new Kenyan life, they were called to a meeting of all the older boys. The announcement was made that several thousand boys would have the

75 opportunity to go to America where they would be assisted by many generous people in pursuing their education and finding a job. Though Peter and James were unsure of what the future would hold, they remained optimistic, knowing that, if chosen, they would go together to this new land of great opportunity.

7. Both passages are primarily concerned with the theme of

    (A) traveling to America to pursue an education

    (B) escaping difficult circumstances to have a better life

    (C) providing assistance to immigrants

    (D) denying freedom to young people in America

    (E) maintaining a strong family while enduring hardships

8. In Passage 2, the main characters could best be described as

    (A) secretive and angry

    (B) purposeful and weak

    (C) desolate and frightened

    (D) sullen and undeterred

    (E) determined and hopeful

9. How does the phrase "hushed voices" in line 14 support the author's tone?

    (A) It emphasizes the idea that the scene is taking place when people are sleeping.

    (B) It further describes the importance of secrecy in the activity being discussed.

    (C) It describes what Juan hears at night when he's trying to sleep.

    (D) It further demonstrates the small size of their house and the need to stay quiet.

    (E) It serves to accentuate the comfort of a large family living in a small house.

10. When Juan heard about the plan to go to America, he behaved most like someone who

    (A) enjoys taking risks and has little fear

    (B) wants his parents to be proud of him

    (C) has always wanted to leave his homeland

    (D) knows how to control fear and self-doubt

    (E) acts overly confident and boastful

11. The author of Passage 1 implies that the living quarters of the main character

    (A) left him sleepless and unable to concentrate on his duties

    (B) were much better than those of this family in America

    (C) reflected the impoverished conditions of many people in his country

    (D) created a sense of intimacy that others in his country did not have

    (E) were seen by others in the neighborhood as a status symbol

12. In line 48, "crude" most nearly means

    (A) ignorant and rude

    (B) rough and primitive

    (C) secretive

    (D) well organized

    (E) unnecessary

13. Which statement most accurately describes a difference between the two passages?

    (A) Passage 1 depicts a sense of hopelessness, whereas Passage 2 does not.

    (B) Passage 1 is more focused on the people in the story than is Passage 2.

    (C) Passage 1 does not emphasize the importance of education, whereas Passage 2 does.

    (D) Passage 1 does not center around the family unit, whereas Passage 2 does.

    (E) Passage 1 deals more with immigration policy than does Passage 2.

Questions 14–25 are based on the following passage.

As a little girl, I loved to help my mother in the kitchen. I especially enjoyed spending time with her while she was baking. While she rolled pie or cookie dough, my mother would always give me a small round ball of dough to make my own little pie or cookie. My
5 favorite creation was mud pie. My version of mud pie was a crudely patted piecrust baked in a miniature aluminum pie pan. The filling was a mixture of sugar and cinnamon and a few dribbles of milk. To create my masterpiece, I mixed all of the ingredients together and spread them on the crust with my stubby fingers. After five minutes
10 in the oven, my seemingly gruesome recipe would be transformed into a cinnamon and sugar confection that I would quickly devour. Afterward, the memory of my savory dessert assuaged my feelings of guilt—I had not saved even a bite for my older brother and sister to try when they returned home from school.

15 I can clearly recall the stories my mother would tell as we toiled over our baked goods. One of my mother's most vivid memories was having to share a single cookie with three of her siblings when she was a child. I am sure that my mother explained why they had so few cookies at the time, but I did not really grasp the importance of this
20 anecdote until I became an adult.

My mother's childhood began during the Great Depression, when the economy suffered and unemployment rates soared. While the Great Depression of the 1930s affected everyone, my grandfather always had a job as an automotive engineer. This enabled my moth-
25 er's family to purchase necessary food and staples. In fact, my mother told me stories about my grandmother feeding hobos who came to the back door. These same destitute people often came back repeat-

edly because they knew they could find succor at my grandmother's doorstep.

30   Later, during World War II, the government required rationing of a variety of food products and other goods. These items were rationed according to availability and need. Processed meats, lard, oils, sugar, and other nonperishable products were among the many items that were difficult to obtain. Attempts to purchase these items

35 were curbed because the products were needed for the troops overseas. Homemade baked goods became a special treat for those at home, and baked goods were often shipped out to loved ones fighting abroad. Many World War II soldiers delighted over the crumbly cookies and stale cakes that reminded them of the people they missed

40 and loved. My own father, who was a pilot during the war, often wrote home about having to hide his delicious homemade brownies from his comrades.

       Gasoline and fuel oil were also rationed during World War II. The government allowed those registered for fuel only a limited

45 quantity to purchase each month. The registrants would be allotted a certain number of points to use for an entire month because gasoline was needed for the many tanks, airplanes, and other military equipment. These points often allowed just enough gasoline to drive to and from work each day. The government even instituted 'war speeds' to

50 conserve fuel consumption. The supply of rubber tires was also limited. People who wanted new tires had to submit applications to a rationing board for approval. Often, consumers chose to have their tires repaired instead of replacing them to avoid all the paperwork. My mother never spoke very much about tire and gasoline rationing.

55 My grandfather worked for a major automobile company as a testing engineer, and I can imagine that he had access to gasoline and rubber tires when others did not.

       My mother did recall a shortage of nylon stockings. Nylon stockings were sacrificed in order to make parachutes for those who were

60 fighting overseas. It was considered a romantic notion that American ladies would give up their precious nylon stockings so their brothers, husbands, and boyfriends could return home safely.

       Americans were also asked to donate various metals to the war effort. Aluminum was the most sought after metal. Drives were held

65 across the country and people brought in any aluminum item they had. Pots and pans, kitchen items, hair curlers, and costume jewelry were all collected during these actions. On a radio show, one announcer would address the general public by saying, "I want to thank you, the people of Manhattan, for the way you have responded to the

70 appeal of our Mayor LaGuardia for aluminum for defense. This drive is a mighty important one. It's the first time that all of the people have

had an opportunity to take part in the defense program. And don't think that the results are not being carefully watched abroad."

Rationing was a sacrifice that most people gladly made during the war
75 because so many Americans had loved ones who were in constant peril fighting overseas. Almost everyone on the home front was willing to do his or her part to help in the war effort as they waited anxiously for the troops to come home and life to return to normal.

14. The passage as a whole can best be described as
    (A) recognition of the author's contributions during World War II
    (B) acknowledgment of the adversities endured during World War II
    (C) apprehension about the impact of the war on society
    (D) contemplation regarding firsthand memories of the war years
    (E) humor over the way people dealt with war rationing

15. In the first paragraph, the author suggests that
    (A) her bother and sister were angry with her for eating all of the pie
    (B) baking pies was her mother's favorite pastime
    (C) as a little girl, she was not very adept at baking
    (D) her mother did not encourage her to help in the kitchen
    (E) recalling memories of the war was troubling for her mother

16. The underlying sentiment in the sentence that begins "In fact, my mother told me stories..." (line 25) is the author's
    (A) apprehension for her mother's family
    (B) contentment and appreciation for her mother's security
    (C) pride in her grandmother's good deeds
    (D) regret for the poverty endured by her family
    (E) reverence for her grandfather's accomplishments

17. The author includes the sentence "Many World War II soldiers delighted over the crumbly cookies and stale cakes that reminded them of the people they missed and loved" (lines 38-40) to suggest that the soldiers abroad were
    (A) despondent
    (B) terrified
    (C) ravenous
    (D) pompous
    (E) lonesome

18. In line 35, "curbed" most nearly means
    (A) restricted
    (B) driven
    (C) increased
    (D) encouraged
    (E) desired

19. In lines 43-45 ("Gasoline and fuel oil were...each month"), the author suggests that

    (A) a procedure was required in order to buy gasoline

    (B) most people did not own a vehicle during World War II

    (C) many families lived together to conserve fuel oil

    (D) there were other ways, besides fuel oil, to heat a home

    (E) many families were able to find other means to obtain fuel

20. In line 49, "war speeds" most nearly means

    (A) the time period of World War II

    (B) the length of time it took for a soldier to receive a package from home

    (C) how long a soldier typically spent fighting overseas

    (D) special speed limits instituted by the government

    (E) government restrictions on gasoline sales and fuel prices

21. The author probably "can imagine" (line 56) because

    (A) the author has a vivid imagination as demonstrated in the passage

    (B) her mother had told her many facts about World War II while they were baking

    (C) she was an avid reader and discovered facts about the War in books

    (D) the author wants to believe that something is true

    (E) she is conjecturing and was never directly given this information

22. The phrase "romantic notion" in line 60 emphasizes the author's belief that

    (A) many women were happy to make sacrifices for the soldiers overseas

    (B) most American women were waiting to form relationships or get married

    (C) nylon stockings were not significant to the women on the home front

    (D) many romances started from people sending packages from home

    (E) war rationing was a hardship that everyone endured

23. The quotation about the aluminum program (lines 68-73) most likely served as a notice about

    (A) the scarcity of aluminum and other precious metals

    (B) the importance of showing support for the war

    (C) the lack of necessary equipment overseas

    (D) the consequences of not participating in the war effort

    (E) the threat of having army equipment that was not made of aluminum

24. Which of the following best describes the author's knowledge of war rationing during World War II?

    (A) She had experienced war rationing as a young girl.

    (B) Her grandparents told her many anecdotes about the war years.

    (C) She interviewed many people who were living during World War II.

    (D) Her mother told her various stories about growing up during the war.

    (E) Her father was a World War II pilot and aviation expert.

25. In the last sentence (lines 76-78), the author implies that

    (A) people believed that rationing would cease as soon as the war ended

    (B) no one thought there would be a Great Depression following World War II

    (C) life would not return to normal even after the troops came home

    (D) few Americans supported World War II at its conception

    (E) the majority of World War II soldiers never returned from overseas

---

STOP

If you finish before your time is up, check your work on this section only. You may not turn to any other section in the test.

PSAT PRACTICE TEST 1
ANSWER SHEET

Begin with number 1. There may be fewer than 40 questions-leave the rest of the answer spaces blank. Completely erase any unnecessary marks.

SECTION 1

1 Ⓐ Ⓑ Ⓒ Ⓓ Ⓔ	11 Ⓐ Ⓑ Ⓒ Ⓓ Ⓔ	21 Ⓐ Ⓑ Ⓒ Ⓓ Ⓔ	31 Ⓐ Ⓑ Ⓒ Ⓓ Ⓔ
2 Ⓐ Ⓑ Ⓒ Ⓓ Ⓔ	12 Ⓐ Ⓑ Ⓒ Ⓓ Ⓔ	22 Ⓐ Ⓑ Ⓒ Ⓓ Ⓔ	32 Ⓐ Ⓑ Ⓒ Ⓓ Ⓔ
3 Ⓐ Ⓑ Ⓒ Ⓓ Ⓔ	13 Ⓐ Ⓑ Ⓒ Ⓓ Ⓔ	23 Ⓐ Ⓑ Ⓒ Ⓓ Ⓔ	33 Ⓐ Ⓑ Ⓒ Ⓓ Ⓔ
4 Ⓐ Ⓑ Ⓒ Ⓓ Ⓔ	14 Ⓐ Ⓑ Ⓒ Ⓓ Ⓔ	24 Ⓐ Ⓑ Ⓒ Ⓓ Ⓔ	34 Ⓐ Ⓑ Ⓒ Ⓓ Ⓔ
5 Ⓐ Ⓑ Ⓒ Ⓓ Ⓔ	15 Ⓐ Ⓑ Ⓒ Ⓓ Ⓔ	25 Ⓐ Ⓑ Ⓒ Ⓓ Ⓔ	35 Ⓐ Ⓑ Ⓒ Ⓓ Ⓔ
6 Ⓐ Ⓑ Ⓒ Ⓓ Ⓔ	16 Ⓐ Ⓑ Ⓒ Ⓓ Ⓔ	26 Ⓐ Ⓑ Ⓒ Ⓓ Ⓔ	36 Ⓐ Ⓑ Ⓒ Ⓓ Ⓔ
7 Ⓐ Ⓑ Ⓒ Ⓓ Ⓔ	17 Ⓐ Ⓑ Ⓒ Ⓓ Ⓔ	27 Ⓐ Ⓑ Ⓒ Ⓓ Ⓔ	37 Ⓐ Ⓑ Ⓒ Ⓓ Ⓔ
8 Ⓐ Ⓑ Ⓒ Ⓓ Ⓔ	18 Ⓐ Ⓑ Ⓒ Ⓓ Ⓔ	28 Ⓐ Ⓑ Ⓒ Ⓓ Ⓔ	38 Ⓐ Ⓑ Ⓒ Ⓓ Ⓔ
9 Ⓐ Ⓑ Ⓒ Ⓓ Ⓔ	19 Ⓐ Ⓑ Ⓒ Ⓓ Ⓔ	29 Ⓐ Ⓑ Ⓒ Ⓓ Ⓔ	39 Ⓐ Ⓑ Ⓒ Ⓓ Ⓔ
10 Ⓐ Ⓑ Ⓒ Ⓓ Ⓔ	20 Ⓐ Ⓑ Ⓒ Ⓓ Ⓔ	30 Ⓐ Ⓑ Ⓒ Ⓓ Ⓔ	40 Ⓐ Ⓑ Ⓒ Ⓓ Ⓔ

SECTION 2

1 Ⓐ Ⓑ Ⓒ Ⓓ Ⓔ	11 Ⓐ Ⓑ Ⓒ Ⓓ Ⓔ	21 Ⓐ Ⓑ Ⓒ Ⓓ Ⓔ	31 Ⓐ Ⓑ Ⓒ Ⓓ Ⓔ
2 Ⓐ Ⓑ Ⓒ Ⓓ Ⓔ	12 Ⓐ Ⓑ Ⓒ Ⓓ Ⓔ	22 Ⓐ Ⓑ Ⓒ Ⓓ Ⓔ	32 Ⓐ Ⓑ Ⓒ Ⓓ Ⓔ
3 Ⓐ Ⓑ Ⓒ Ⓓ Ⓔ	13 Ⓐ Ⓑ Ⓒ Ⓓ Ⓔ	23 Ⓐ Ⓑ Ⓒ Ⓓ Ⓔ	33 Ⓐ Ⓑ Ⓒ Ⓓ Ⓔ
4 Ⓐ Ⓑ Ⓒ Ⓓ Ⓔ	14 Ⓐ Ⓑ Ⓒ Ⓓ Ⓔ	24 Ⓐ Ⓑ Ⓒ Ⓓ Ⓔ	34 Ⓐ Ⓑ Ⓒ Ⓓ Ⓔ
5 Ⓐ Ⓑ Ⓒ Ⓓ Ⓔ	15 Ⓐ Ⓑ Ⓒ Ⓓ Ⓔ	25 Ⓐ Ⓑ Ⓒ Ⓓ Ⓔ	35 Ⓐ Ⓑ Ⓒ Ⓓ Ⓔ
6 Ⓐ Ⓑ Ⓒ Ⓓ Ⓔ	16 Ⓐ Ⓑ Ⓒ Ⓓ Ⓔ	26 Ⓐ Ⓑ Ⓒ Ⓓ Ⓔ	36 Ⓐ Ⓑ Ⓒ Ⓓ Ⓔ
7 Ⓐ Ⓑ Ⓒ Ⓓ Ⓔ	17 Ⓐ Ⓑ Ⓒ Ⓓ Ⓔ	27 Ⓐ Ⓑ Ⓒ Ⓓ Ⓔ	37 Ⓐ Ⓑ Ⓒ Ⓓ Ⓔ
8 Ⓐ Ⓑ Ⓒ Ⓓ Ⓔ	18 Ⓐ Ⓑ Ⓒ Ⓓ Ⓔ	28 Ⓐ Ⓑ Ⓒ Ⓓ Ⓔ	38 Ⓐ Ⓑ Ⓒ Ⓓ Ⓔ
9 Ⓐ Ⓑ Ⓒ Ⓓ Ⓔ	19 Ⓐ Ⓑ Ⓒ Ⓓ Ⓔ	29 Ⓐ Ⓑ Ⓒ Ⓓ Ⓔ	39 Ⓐ Ⓑ Ⓒ Ⓓ Ⓔ
10 Ⓐ Ⓑ Ⓒ Ⓓ Ⓔ	20 Ⓐ Ⓑ Ⓒ Ⓓ Ⓔ	30 Ⓐ Ⓑ Ⓒ Ⓓ Ⓔ	40 Ⓐ Ⓑ Ⓒ Ⓓ Ⓔ

SECTION 3

1 Ⓐ Ⓑ Ⓒ Ⓓ Ⓔ	11 Ⓐ Ⓑ Ⓒ Ⓓ Ⓔ	21 Ⓐ Ⓑ Ⓒ Ⓓ Ⓔ	31 Ⓐ Ⓑ Ⓒ Ⓓ Ⓔ
2 Ⓐ Ⓑ Ⓒ Ⓓ Ⓔ	12 Ⓐ Ⓑ Ⓒ Ⓓ Ⓔ	22 Ⓐ Ⓑ Ⓒ Ⓓ Ⓔ	32 Ⓐ Ⓑ Ⓒ Ⓓ Ⓔ
3 Ⓐ Ⓑ Ⓒ Ⓓ Ⓔ	13 Ⓐ Ⓑ Ⓒ Ⓓ Ⓔ	23 Ⓐ Ⓑ Ⓒ Ⓓ Ⓔ	33 Ⓐ Ⓑ Ⓒ Ⓓ Ⓔ
4 Ⓐ Ⓑ Ⓒ Ⓓ Ⓔ	14 Ⓐ Ⓑ Ⓒ Ⓓ Ⓔ	24 Ⓐ Ⓑ Ⓒ Ⓓ Ⓔ	34 Ⓐ Ⓑ Ⓒ Ⓓ Ⓔ
5 Ⓐ Ⓑ Ⓒ Ⓓ Ⓔ	15 Ⓐ Ⓑ Ⓒ Ⓓ Ⓔ	25 Ⓐ Ⓑ Ⓒ Ⓓ Ⓔ	35 Ⓐ Ⓑ Ⓒ Ⓓ Ⓔ
6 Ⓐ Ⓑ Ⓒ Ⓓ Ⓔ	16 Ⓐ Ⓑ Ⓒ Ⓓ Ⓔ	26 Ⓐ Ⓑ Ⓒ Ⓓ Ⓔ	36 Ⓐ Ⓑ Ⓒ Ⓓ Ⓔ
7 Ⓐ Ⓑ Ⓒ Ⓓ Ⓔ	17 Ⓐ Ⓑ Ⓒ Ⓓ Ⓔ	27 Ⓐ Ⓑ Ⓒ Ⓓ Ⓔ	37 Ⓐ Ⓑ Ⓒ Ⓓ Ⓔ
8 Ⓐ Ⓑ Ⓒ Ⓓ Ⓔ	18 Ⓐ Ⓑ Ⓒ Ⓓ Ⓔ	28 Ⓐ Ⓑ Ⓒ Ⓓ Ⓔ	38 Ⓐ Ⓑ Ⓒ Ⓓ Ⓔ
9 Ⓐ Ⓑ Ⓒ Ⓓ Ⓔ	19 Ⓐ Ⓑ Ⓒ Ⓓ Ⓔ	29 Ⓐ Ⓑ Ⓒ Ⓓ Ⓔ	39 Ⓐ Ⓑ Ⓒ Ⓓ Ⓔ
10 Ⓐ Ⓑ Ⓒ Ⓓ Ⓔ	20 Ⓐ Ⓑ Ⓒ Ⓓ Ⓔ	30 Ⓐ Ⓑ Ⓒ Ⓓ Ⓔ	40 Ⓐ Ⓑ Ⓒ Ⓓ Ⓔ

Begin with number 1. There may be fewer than 40 questions-leave the rest of the answer spaces blank. Completely erase any unnecessary marks.

SECTION 4

1 Ⓐ Ⓑ Ⓒ Ⓓ Ⓔ	11 Ⓐ Ⓑ Ⓒ Ⓓ Ⓔ	21 Ⓐ Ⓑ Ⓒ Ⓓ Ⓔ	31 Ⓐ Ⓑ Ⓒ Ⓓ Ⓔ
2 Ⓐ Ⓑ Ⓒ Ⓓ Ⓔ	12 Ⓐ Ⓑ Ⓒ Ⓓ Ⓔ	22 Ⓐ Ⓑ Ⓒ Ⓓ Ⓔ	32 Ⓐ Ⓑ Ⓒ Ⓓ Ⓔ
3 Ⓐ Ⓑ Ⓒ Ⓓ Ⓔ	13 Ⓐ Ⓑ Ⓒ Ⓓ Ⓔ	23 Ⓐ Ⓑ Ⓒ Ⓓ Ⓔ	33 Ⓐ Ⓑ Ⓒ Ⓓ Ⓔ
4 Ⓐ Ⓑ Ⓒ Ⓓ Ⓔ	14 Ⓐ Ⓑ Ⓒ Ⓓ Ⓔ	24 Ⓐ Ⓑ Ⓒ Ⓓ Ⓔ	34 Ⓐ Ⓑ Ⓒ Ⓓ Ⓔ
5 Ⓐ Ⓑ Ⓒ Ⓓ Ⓔ	15 Ⓐ Ⓑ Ⓒ Ⓓ Ⓔ	25 Ⓐ Ⓑ Ⓒ Ⓓ Ⓔ	35 Ⓐ Ⓑ Ⓒ Ⓓ Ⓔ
6 Ⓐ Ⓑ Ⓒ Ⓓ Ⓔ	16 Ⓐ Ⓑ Ⓒ Ⓓ Ⓔ	26 Ⓐ Ⓑ Ⓒ Ⓓ Ⓔ	36 Ⓐ Ⓑ Ⓒ Ⓓ Ⓔ
7 Ⓐ Ⓑ Ⓒ Ⓓ Ⓔ	17 Ⓐ Ⓑ Ⓒ Ⓓ Ⓔ	27 Ⓐ Ⓑ Ⓒ Ⓓ Ⓔ	37 Ⓐ Ⓑ Ⓒ Ⓓ Ⓔ
8 Ⓐ Ⓑ Ⓒ Ⓓ Ⓔ	18 Ⓐ Ⓑ Ⓒ Ⓓ Ⓔ	28 Ⓐ Ⓑ Ⓒ Ⓓ Ⓔ	38 Ⓐ Ⓑ Ⓒ Ⓓ Ⓔ
9 Ⓐ Ⓑ Ⓒ Ⓓ Ⓔ	19 Ⓐ Ⓑ Ⓒ Ⓓ Ⓔ	29 Ⓐ Ⓑ Ⓒ Ⓓ Ⓔ	39 Ⓐ Ⓑ Ⓒ Ⓓ Ⓔ
10 Ⓐ Ⓑ Ⓒ Ⓓ Ⓔ	20 Ⓐ Ⓑ Ⓒ Ⓓ Ⓔ	30 Ⓐ Ⓑ Ⓒ Ⓓ Ⓔ	40 Ⓐ Ⓑ Ⓒ Ⓓ Ⓔ

CAUTION Only use the answer grids below for Section 4 if you are instructed to do so in the corresponding test.

Student-Produced Responses

ANY ANSWERS WRITTEN IN THE BOXES ABOVE THE CIRCLES WILL NOT COUNT TOWARDS YOUR SCORE. ONLY ANSWERS FILLED IN ON THE GRID WILL BE SCORED.

Begin with number 1. There may be fewer than 40 questions-leave the rest of the answer spaces blank. Completely erase any unnecessary marks.

SECTION 5

1 Ⓐ Ⓑ Ⓒ Ⓓ Ⓔ	11 Ⓐ Ⓑ Ⓒ Ⓓ Ⓔ	21 Ⓐ Ⓑ Ⓒ Ⓓ Ⓔ	31 Ⓐ Ⓑ Ⓒ Ⓓ Ⓔ
2 Ⓐ Ⓑ Ⓒ Ⓓ Ⓔ	12 Ⓐ Ⓑ Ⓒ Ⓓ Ⓔ	22 Ⓐ Ⓑ Ⓒ Ⓓ Ⓔ	32 Ⓐ Ⓑ Ⓒ Ⓓ Ⓔ
3 Ⓐ Ⓑ Ⓒ Ⓓ Ⓔ	13 Ⓐ Ⓑ Ⓒ Ⓓ Ⓔ	23 Ⓐ Ⓑ Ⓒ Ⓓ Ⓔ	33 Ⓐ Ⓑ Ⓒ Ⓓ Ⓔ
4 Ⓐ Ⓑ Ⓒ Ⓓ Ⓔ	14 Ⓐ Ⓑ Ⓒ Ⓓ Ⓔ	24 Ⓐ Ⓑ Ⓒ Ⓓ Ⓔ	34 Ⓐ Ⓑ Ⓒ Ⓓ Ⓔ
5 Ⓐ Ⓑ Ⓒ Ⓓ Ⓔ	15 Ⓐ Ⓑ Ⓒ Ⓓ Ⓔ	25 Ⓐ Ⓑ Ⓒ Ⓓ Ⓔ	35 Ⓐ Ⓑ Ⓒ Ⓓ Ⓔ
6 Ⓐ Ⓑ Ⓒ Ⓓ Ⓔ	16 Ⓐ Ⓑ Ⓒ Ⓓ Ⓔ	26 Ⓐ Ⓑ Ⓒ Ⓓ Ⓔ	36 Ⓐ Ⓑ Ⓒ Ⓓ Ⓔ
7 Ⓐ Ⓑ Ⓒ Ⓓ Ⓔ	17 Ⓐ Ⓑ Ⓒ Ⓓ Ⓔ	27 Ⓐ Ⓑ Ⓒ Ⓓ Ⓔ	37 Ⓐ Ⓑ Ⓒ Ⓓ Ⓔ
8 Ⓐ Ⓑ Ⓒ Ⓓ Ⓔ	18 Ⓐ Ⓑ Ⓒ Ⓓ Ⓔ	28 Ⓐ Ⓑ Ⓒ Ⓓ Ⓔ	38 Ⓐ Ⓑ Ⓒ Ⓓ Ⓔ
9 Ⓐ Ⓑ Ⓒ Ⓓ Ⓔ	19 Ⓐ Ⓑ Ⓒ Ⓓ Ⓔ	29 Ⓐ Ⓑ Ⓒ Ⓓ Ⓔ	39 Ⓐ Ⓑ Ⓒ Ⓓ Ⓔ
10 Ⓐ Ⓑ Ⓒ Ⓓ Ⓔ	20 Ⓐ Ⓑ Ⓒ Ⓓ Ⓔ	30 Ⓐ Ⓑ Ⓒ Ⓓ Ⓔ	40 Ⓐ Ⓑ Ⓒ Ⓓ Ⓔ

Answer Key 1

The Scoring Guide included in Appendix D should only be used to approximate your test score. Your focus should be on reading the explanations for each of the questions that you missed, and working toward strengthening your weak areas.

PRACTICE TEST 1 ANSWER KEY

<table>
<tr><td colspan="2" align="center">SECTION 1
Critical Reading</td><td colspan="2" align="center">SECTION 2
Math</td></tr>
<tr><td>1. B</td><td>13. E</td><td>1. D</td><td>11. C</td></tr>
<tr><td>2. D</td><td>14. E</td><td>2. C</td><td>12. D</td></tr>
<tr><td>3. C</td><td>15. B</td><td>3. C</td><td>13. D</td></tr>
<tr><td>4. B</td><td>16. C</td><td>4. E</td><td>14. C</td></tr>
<tr><td>5. A</td><td>17. A</td><td>5. A</td><td>15. C</td></tr>
<tr><td>6. D</td><td>18. B</td><td>6. B</td><td>16. D</td></tr>
<tr><td>7. A</td><td>19. A</td><td>7. D</td><td>17. A</td></tr>
<tr><td>8. D</td><td>20. C</td><td>8. A</td><td>18. D</td></tr>
<tr><td>9. B</td><td>21. D</td><td>9. C</td><td>19. E</td></tr>
<tr><td>10. C</td><td>22. B</td><td>10. C</td><td>20. E</td></tr>
<tr><td>11. A</td><td>23. E</td><td></td><td></td></tr>
<tr><td>12. B</td><td></td><td></td><td></td></tr>
</table>

SECTION 3
Writing Skills

1. D	21. E
2. B	22. D
3. E	23. C
4. A	24. D
5. D	25. A
6. E	26. C
7. C	27. B
8. C	28. C
9. E	29. A
10. A	30. E
11. B	31. D
12. C	32. A
13. E	33. A
14. C	34. B
15. A	35. C
16. B	36. C
17. B	37. E
18. B	38. D
19. A	39. A
20. D	

SECTION 4
Math

1. C
2. B
3. A
4. A
5. D
6. E
7. B
8. E
9. 992
10. 165
11. 6 or 8
12. 1,575
13. 48
14. $\frac{9}{2}$ or 4.5
15. 3
16. 73.3%
17. $\frac{13}{4}$ or 3.25
18. 10,000

SECTION 5
Critical Reading

1. B	11. C	21. E
2. D	12. B	22. A
3. A	13. A	23. B
4. D	14. B	24. D
5. C	15. C	25. A
6. D	16. C	
7. B	17. E	
8. E	18. A	
9. B	19. A	
10. D	20. D	

SECTION 1—Critical Reading

Sentence Completion (Questions 1–7)

1. **The best answer is B.** The word "despite" at the beginning of the sentence suggests a contrast between the information preceding and following the comma. The context of the sentence implies that Melissa's "best efforts" were not good enough for her employer, who still managed to find something wrong with her work. Therefore, her employer was "critical" of her work. Answer choices A, C, D, and E do not accurately describe Melissa's boss based on the context of the sentence.

2. **The best answer is D.** The context of the sentence indicates that Jordan issues instructions in a forceful way, such that anyone receiving those instructions would simply follow them without asking any questions. Only "peremptory" is a synonym of "forceful." Answer choices A and B should be eliminated because they are opposite in meaning to "forceful." Answer choices C and E do not fit the context of the sentence.

3. **The best answer is C.** Because the actress had been rejected numerous times, it is safe to assume that she was feeling badly. "Despondent" means "to feel hopeless," which best fits the context of the sentence. Answer choices A, B, D, and E do not accurately describe the way the actress was feeling based on the context of the sentence.

4. **The best answer is B.** The context of the sentence indicates that the waitress normally behaves one way, but tonight she was behaving differently. Look for a word to insert into the first blank that describes someone who engages in "tiresome chatter." Only "garrulous," which means "talkative," works in the first blank. Answer choices A, C, D, and E do not fit the context of the sentence.

5. **The best answer is A.** The information following the semicolon is the definition of the word that should go in the blank. The word that best fits the definition of "numerous twists and turns" is "convoluted," which means "intricate and complicated." Answer choices B, C, D, and E are words that could be used to describe a storyline, but they do not fit the context of the sentence.

6. **The best answer is D.** The context of the sentence indicates that computers and motion detection equipment are doing something to the midnight security guard position. Look at each answer choice and fill in the blanks in the sentence. It does not make sense that the demand for trained guards would "escalate," or "go up" if computers and motion detection equipment "undermined" or "weakened" those positions. Eliminate answer choice A. Answer choices B, C, and E should be eliminated for similar reasons. Only answer choice D effectively completes the sentence.

7. **The best answer is A.** Look for a word to insert into the blank that means "to allow in natural sunlight." Only "translucent" fits this definition. Answer choices B and C are not words that would typically be used to describe a window curtain. Answer choices D and E have meanings that are opposite to "translucent."

Reading Comprehension (Questions 8–23)

8. **The best answer is D.** This passage primarily discusses the experiences of the author and his or her companions, specifically while exploring Buck's Pond. The passage focuses on several encounters with wildlife and nature. The passage mentions several aquatic species, but it does not include a comparison of the habitats of these animals. Although the canoe trip is a new experience, the passage does not include any analysis of the psychological effects involved. There is nothing in the passage to suggest that it is a defense of man's right to explore nature; rather, the passage explains that, at times, the group felt intrusive. The passage does not include any discussion of the different interests of people.

9. **The best answer is B.** The passage states that the author and his or her companions had been "anticipating this maiden voyage" and "could wait no longer; Buck's Pond was begging to be explored." A "maiden voyage" means the first voyage; therefore, answer choice B is correct because the "maiden voyage" refers to the first exploration of the pond. The author does not mention that the canoe (or watercraft) was new, nor does the passage suggest that the author has never been on a canoe trip. The passage does point out the "pristine wilderness," but does not refer to it as the "maiden voyage." The passage explains that the voyage had been anticipated "since" the purchase; therefore, "maiden voyage" cannot refer to the purchase of the land.

10. **The best answer is C.** The author uses words like "incredible," "beautiful," and "magnificent" to describe the "view into the private world" of "wild creatures." Clearly, the author enjoys seeing wildlife in its natural habitat; therefore, the author would most likely appreciate a visit to a nature preserve. The author mentions that there is one member of the group who enjoys bass-fishing, but does not express a personal interest in the sport. Because the author enjoys wildlife in its natural habitat, it is unlikely that he or she would appreciate a trip to the zoo. The author explains that the group tried to "cause as little interruption as possible," which is contradictory to the interruption that would be caused from a large motorboat. The passage describes the swans as "aviators," but does not mention actual pilots.

11. **The best answer is A.** "Marveled" means "to become filled with awe and wonder," and is used in the passage to describe how a bass fisherman might feel towards "the prospect of summer bass fishing." Answer choices B, C, D, and E do not fit with the context of the passage.

12. **The best answer is B.** Throughout most of the passage, the author focuses on the experiences of the group in different natural settings, which is best supported by answer choice B. The author describes "effortless paddling" and does not mention any navigation difficulties because of the size of the lake. Although the helmsman is mentioned once, the author does not focus on his ability to guide the canoe. The author does not specifically describe the location of the pond, nor does the author mention a lack of modern conveniences. Only at the beginning of the passage, the author briefly mentions clouds, a chilly temperature, and wind, but then states that the group was excited regardless of the weather. The weather and traveling conditions are not emphasized.

13. **The best answer is E.** In the third paragraph, the passage states that the group "imagined dozens of bullfrogs." The group did not actually *see* any bullfrogs, so answer choice E is correct. The passage states that the group actually saw ducks, swans, turtles, and loons.

14. **The best answer is E.** The quotation at the end of the passage reflects the main theme of the passage—that is, the appreciation of nature and the joy of observing wildlife in its natural environment. The quotation does not directly refer to visiting Buck's Pond, nor does it indicate the author's vast knowledge of natural history. It emphasizes, rather than disputes, the ideas presented in the final paragraph. The quotation does not offer a visual description, nor does it include language to enhance the reader's visual perception of nature.

15. **The best answer is B.** The passage states that polio was "a particularly devastating disease because of its effect on children." The passage further states that children who contracted the disease either died at an early age or were confined to a wheelchair. This information best supports answer choice B. The passage states that the government initiated a vaccine program, but does not state that the programs were significantly affected by the polio epidemic. Although the passage states that the polio epidemic increased when the troops returned home, the passage does not focus on the effect of polio on the troops. Neither the medical community nor the promotion of the polio vaccine experienced the most significant effects of the polio epidemic.

16. **The best answer is C.** Something that is "microscopic" is too small to be seen without a microscope. The prefix "sub" has several related but different meanings: inferior or less than, secondary or subordinate, and below or underneath. The passage indicates that it took many years for two physicians to "identify the submicroscopic virus," which implies that the virus might have been difficult to identify because of its size. Therefore, answer choice C, which mentions the "minute" or "very small" size of the virus is best. "Underneath" is a meaning for the prefix "sub," but "microscopic" does not mean "the skin." "Submicroscopic" could mean incapable of being "seen," but not incapable of being "isolated." "Sub" is a common abbreviation for a "submarine," which operates underwater," but does not apply to this situation. Answer choice E is the opposite of "submicroscopic."

17. **The best answer is A.** Paragraph 4 states that there was no "cure" for polio, so doctors focused on "managing debilitating effects" and "preventing fatalities." The "iron lung" was a primary form of treatment, and the passage indicates that the iron lung was a "common device used to assist polio patients in breathing." Answer choice A is best supported by this information because the condition of some patients with breathing problems would most likely have worsened without the "iron lung" treatment. Answer choices B, C, D, and E are not supported by information in the passage.

18. **The best answer is B.** The passage states that because there was no known cure for polio, "...doctors focused on managing the disease's debilitating effects." This information best supports answer choice B. Answer choices A, C, D, and E are not supported by information in the passage.

19. **The best answer is A.** The phrase "became typical protocol" refers
    to the polio treatment that became the standard procedure or practice.
    The passage indicates that, even though there was some debate
    regarding the proper treatment, eventually the practice of wrapping
    the affected limbs in hot compresses and exercising became the
    standard approach, "…because it seemed to relieve some pain and dis-
    comfort." Answer choices B, C, D, and E are not supported by infor-
    mation in the passage.

20. **The best answer is C.** This passage emphasizes the debilitating
    effects of polio and the efforts to combat the disease. The discussion
    of the polio virus serves to emphasize the complexity of the disease
    and the difficulty in discovering a cure. Statements such as "After
    nearly 20 years of research and trials, serum therapy was finally aban-
    doned and deemed unsuccessful" and "Even though polio was not a
    new disease, medical experts around the turn of the century were still
    uncertain about how to prevent it" support this theory. Answer choic-
    es A, B, D, and E are not supported by information in the passage.

21. **The best answer is D.** According to information in the passage,
    Jonas Salk developed an effective vaccine for polio in the early 1950s,
    based on building antibodies against the virus. Albert Sabin expanded
    on this idea by adapting the vaccine so that it could be administered
    by mouth instead of by injection. While many people did not like
    receiving injections, they were willing to take the Salk vaccine, making
    it a successful treatment until it was replaced by the Sabin oral vac-
    cine. Nothing in the passage indicates that Salk and Sabin had strong
    disagreements over a polio cure.

22. **The best answer is B.** The discussion of the polio epidemic in the
    passage focuses primarily on the devastating effects of the disease and
    the many years spent researching and developing a cure. This relates
    most directly to the current research being conducted to identify
    treatments and, eventually, a cure for cancer, a disease that affects
    large numbers of people worldwide. Answer choices A, C, D, and E
    are not supported by information in the passage.

23. **The best answer is E.** The final paragraph states that "…the scourge
    of polio is well under control in the United States…," but that
    "…approximately 500,000 Americans continue to live with the effects
    of childhood polio…" Answer choices A, B, C, and D are not support-
    ed by information in the passage.

SECTION 2—Math

1. **The correct answer is D.** To solve this problem, you must be aware that there are 2 packages that contain 8 hamburger buns each and 5 packages that contain 12 hamburger buns each.

   ➤ Answer choice A is incorrect because this is just the sum of 8 and 12; 8 + 12 = 20.

   ➤ Answer choice B is incorrect because this would be the result if all 7 packages contained 8 hamburger buns each; 7×8 = 56.

   ➤ Answer choice C is incorrect because this would be the result if there were 5 packages with 12 hamburger buns each and only 1 package with 8 hamburger buns; 5×12 + 1×8 = 60 + 8 = 68.

   ➤ Answer choice D is correct because this is the sum of 2 packages with 8 hamburger buns each and 5 packages with 12 hamburger buns each; 2×8 + 5×12 = 16 + 60 = 76.

   ➤ Answer choice E is incorrect because this would be the result if all 7 packages contained 12 hamburger buns each; 7×12 = 84.

2. **The correct answer is C.** To solve this problem, first calculate the length of BC. You are given that $AB = 12$, and BC is 13 more than AB. $BC = 12 + 13$, or 25. Now add the length of AB to the length of BC.

   ➤ Answer choice A is incorrect because this is the length of AB only.

   ➤ Answer choice B is incorrect because this is the length of BC. The question states that $BC = 13$ *more* than AC, NOT that $BC = 13$.

   ➤ Answer choice C is correct because this is the sum of the length of AB and the length of BC. The length of AB is 12 (given in the problem). The length of BC is 13 more than AB, so BC is 12 + 13 = 25. The length of AC is 12 + 25 = 37.

   ➤ Answer choice D is incorrect because this is the length of BC doubled.

   ➤ Answer choice E is incorrect because this is the product of AB times BC.

3. **The correct answer is C.** One way to solve this problem is to solve for x in the first equation, then substitute that result for x in the second equation.

➤ $x + 7 = 12a$

➤ $x = 12a - 7$

➤ $3(12a - 7) + 21$

➤ $36a - 21 + 21 = 36a$

Another way to solve this problem is to recognize that $3x + 21 = 3(x + 7)$. This means that the result of the second equation must be $3(12a)$, or $36a$.

4. **The correct answer is E.** To solve this problem, compare the Test I scores to the Test II scores for each student.

   ➤ Answer choice A is incorrect because student A scored a 50 on Test I and an 85 on Test II; Test II score is higher than Test I score.

   ➤ Answer choice B is incorrect because student B scored a 65 on Test I and an 80 on Test II; Test II score is higher than Test I score.

   ➤ Answer choice C is incorrect because student C scored a 75 on Test I and a 90 on Test II; Test II score is higher than Test I score.

   ➤ Answer choice D is incorrect because student D scored a 65 on Test I and an 85 on Test II; Test II score is higher than Test I score.

   ➤ Answer choice E is correct because student E scored an 85 on Test I and a 75 on Test II; Test II score is lower than Test I score.

5. **The correct answer is A.** To solve this problem, you need to know that the average is the sum of the test scores divided by the number of test scores. In this case, there are 5 test scores because, according to the graph, each of the 5 students took Test 1.

   ➤ Answer choice A is correct because $(50 + 65 + 65 + 75 + 85) \div 5 = 68$.

   ➤ Answer choice B is incorrect because it does not accurately represent the data given.

   ➤ Answer choice C is incorrect because it is the average of the Test II scores.

   ➤ Answer choice D is incorrect because it is the score of student E on Test I.

   ➤ Answer choice E is incorrect because it is the score of student C on Test II.

6. **The correct answer is B.** To solve this problem, you need to know how to calculate absolute value. Absolute value corresponds to a positive distance on the number line. Based on the number line shown, it appears to be at approximately $-\frac{1}{2}$, and v appears to be at approximately $-\frac{1}{4}$. Plug these values into the problem:

➤ $| -\frac{1}{2} + -\frac{1}{4} |$; find the Lowest Common Denominator

➤ $| -\frac{2}{4} + -\frac{3}{4} | = | -\frac{3}{4} |$

Since absolute value is always positive, $| u + v | = \frac{3}{4}$. Now, determine the location of the points given in the answer choice to see which one is at approximately $\frac{3}{4}$ on the number line.

➤ Answer choice A is incorrect because t is at approximately $-1\frac{3}{4}$ on the number line.

➤ Answer choice B is correct because w is at approximately $\frac{3}{4}$ on the number line.

➤ Answer choice C is incorrect because x is at approximately $1\frac{1}{4}$ on the number line.

➤ Answer choice D is incorrect because y is at approximately $1\frac{3}{4}$ on the number line.

➤ Answer choice E is incorrect because t is at approximately $2\frac{1}{2}$ on the number line.

7. **The correct answer is D.** To solve this problem, plug $\frac{1}{4}$ in for x and simplify.

➤ $\dfrac{4}{(\frac{1}{4})} + \dfrac{3}{(\frac{1}{4} - 1)} =$

➤ $\dfrac{4}{(\frac{1}{4})} + \dfrac{3}{(-\frac{3}{4})} =$

➤ $4(\frac{4}{1}) + 3(-\frac{4}{3}) =$

➤ $16 + (-\frac{12}{3}) =$

➤ $16 - 4 = 12$

8. **The correct answer is A.** To solve this problem, you need to know how to graph xy-coordinates. Since point k is in the upper left quadrant, it must be negative. Eliminate answer choices C, D, and E. In this problem, you are given another point on the line: (2,0). Since this figure is drawn to scale, you can assume that the distance along the x–axis from the origin (point O) to this point is 2 units. By the same token, if you moved 2 units to the left of the origin, you would be approximately half the distance along the x-axis to point S. Therefore, point S must be at coordinates (-4,4) in the x, y coordinate plane, putting the value of K at -4.

9. **The correct answer is C.** To answer this question, first recognize that the sum of a and b is mathematically expressed as $a + b$. Since this value is divided by the product of a and b, the correct answer choice will have $a + b$ in the numerator. Eliminate answer choices A, B, and D. The product of a and b is expressed mathematically as ab; therefore, the correct answer will have ab in the denominator. Eliminate answer choice E.

10. **The correct answer is C.** You are given that $3x$ years ago, the person was $2y$ years old. This means that at the present time, the person is $(3x + 2y)$ years old. If the person is $(3x + 2y)$ years old now, then 5 years ago, the person would have been $(3x + 2y - 5)$ years old, answer choice C.

11. **The correct answer is C.** Since the question asks you to put the letters in order from left to right, the end result must be ABCDE. Applying the given rules, the least number of changes to the original order is four, as follows: DEACB to BCAED (1) to BCADE (2) to BACDE (3) to ABCDE (4).

12. **The correct answer is D.** To answer this question, create both Set G and Set H, based on the information given.

    ➤ Set G = {24, 28, 32}, which is {(4×6), (4×7), (4×8)}

    ➤ Set H = {24, 30}, which is {(6×4), (6×5)}

    The number 30 is in Set H, but not in Set G. Because the sets include numbers between 20 and 35, they will not include 20 and 35.

13. **The correct answer is D.** Since n is a positive fraction (less than 1 but greater than 0), you should be able to conclude two things: (1) $4n$ is greater than n, and (2) n^2 is less than n. Given this information, only answer choices D and E are possible solutions. Now you must determine if n is greater than or less than $\sqrt{n}$. Since n can be any positive

fraction less than 1, choose $\frac{1}{4}$ for the value of n. You know that $\sqrt{\frac{1}{4}}$ is equivalent to $\frac{1}{2}$ because $\left(\frac{1}{2}\right)^2 = \frac{1}{4}$. Therefore, $\frac{1}{2} > \frac{1}{4}$, so the $\sqrt{n} > n$, and answer choice D is correct.

14. **The correct answer is C.** To find the median, put the slopes in order from smallest to largest. The median is the middle value. To calculate the slope of each line, first recognize that one point on each line is the origin, (0,0). The slope is equivalent to $\frac{y_1 - y_2}{x_1 - x_2}$. Plug in the values given for each line.

➤ The slope of $OA = -\frac{4}{1} = 4$

➤ The slope of $OB = -\frac{4}{2} = 2$

➤ The slope of $OC = -\frac{3}{3} = 1$

➤ The slope of $OD = -\frac{3}{6} = \frac{1}{2}$

➤ The slope of $OC = \frac{-2}{-5} = \frac{2}{5}$

The five slopes, in order, are $\frac{2}{5}, \frac{1}{2}, 1, 2, 4$. The middle value, or median, is 1, answer choice C.

15. **The correct answer is C.** First, calculate the flight time of the first plane. Its departure time was 2:00 p.m. EST, which is the same as 11:00 a.m. PST. Therefore, the time difference between the two cities is 3 hours. Since the plane arrives in Los Angeles at 4:00 p.m. PST, the flight time is 5 hours. Since the second plane leaves Los Angeles at 2:00 p.m. PST, it will arrive in Atlanta 5 hours later, 7:00 p.m. PST. Converting this time to EST, the second plane will arrive in Atlanta at 10:00 p.m. EST, answer choice C.

16. **The correct answer is D.** You are given that the radius of each of the quarter circles is 2. The area of a circle is πr^2 which means the area of a quarter circle is $\frac{1}{4} \pi r^2$. Calculate the area of the two quarter circles, as follows:

➤ $\frac{1}{4}\pi(2^2) + \frac{1}{4}\pi(2^2) =$

➤ $\frac{1}{4}\pi 4 + \frac{1}{4}\pi 4 =$

➤ $\pi + \pi = 2\pi$

Using the radius of the quarter circles, you know that the length of the rectangle is 2 and the width is 4. Therefore, the area of the rectangle is 4×2, or 8. The area of the non-shaded region is the difference between the area of the rectangle and the area of the quarter circles; $8 - 2\pi$.

17. **The correct answer is A.** To solve this problem, you must recall the rules governing exponents. First, simplify the equation, as shown below.

   ➤ $5^x + 5^x + 5^x + 5^x + 5^x = 5(5^x)$

   ➤ 5 is equivalent to 5^1, and when you multiply like-coefficients with exponents, remember that you must add the exponents.

   ➤ Therefore, $5^1(5^x) = 5^{x+1}$

18. **The correct answer is D.** You are given that $AB = BC$, which means that those sides of the large triangle are congruent. The angles opposite to congruent sides are equal in measure; therefore, angle A must equal angle C. The sum of the three angles in a triangle is 180°. Since you are given that angle $B = 40°$, the sum of angles A and C must be $180° - 40°$, or 140°. Since angle A = angle C, each must be equal to 70°. You are also given that angle CFA is equal to 120°. Since the number of degrees in a straight line is also 180°, angle AFD must be $180° - 120°$, or 60°. You now have the measure of two of the angles in the upper triangle in the figure shown. Calculate the measure of the third angle, ADF.

   ➤ $70° + 60° + ADF = 180°$

   ➤ $130° + ADF = 180°$

   ➤ $ADF = 180° - 130° = 50°$

19. **The correct answer is E.** To solve this problem, you should recognize that the first step will be to cross-multiply the proportions. Work through each answer choice; the one that is NOT equivalent to the others will be the correct choice.

   ➤ Answer choice A: $\frac{a}{b} = \frac{c}{d}$; $ad = bc$.

   ➤ Answer choice B: $\frac{a}{c} = \frac{b}{d}$; $ad = cb$. This proportion is equivalent to the proportion in answer choice A, so eliminate answer choices A and B.

➤ Answer choice C: $\frac{c}{a} = \frac{d}{b}$; $ad = cb$. This proportion is equivalent to the proportions in answer choices A and B, so eliminate answer choice C.

➤ Answer choice D: $\frac{bc}{ad} = 1$; $bc = ad$. This proportion is equivalent to the proportions in answer choices A, B, and C, so eliminate answer choice D.

➤ Answer choice E: $\frac{b}{c} = \frac{a}{d}$; $bd = ac$. This proportion is NOT equivalent to any of the proportions in the other answer choices.

Therefore, it is the correct answer.

20. **The correct answer is E.** To solve this problem, substitute the values a and b for x and y in each Roman Numeral. Set the equations equal to zero, since you are asked to determine which of the Roman Numerals can be equal to zero.

➤ Substitute a for x and b for y and set it equal to zero: $3ab - 3a = 0$. Factor out $3a$: $3a(b - 1) = 0$. Since a cannot equal zero (it must be positive based on the information given in the problem), then $(b - 1) = 0$. Solving for b gives you $b = 1$. Since b is a positive integer, Roman Numeral I can equal 0. Eliminate answer choices B and C because they do not include Roman Numeral I.

➤ Substitute $(a - b)$ for x and b for y and set it equal to zero: $3(a - b)b - 3(a - b) = 0$. Factor out $3(a - b)$: $3(a - b)(b - 1) = 0$. This is true if $a = b$ or if $b = 1$. Since either a or b can be a positive integer, Roman Numeral II can equal 0. Eliminate answer choice A because it does not include Roman Numeral II.

➤ Substitute b for x and $(a - b)$ for y and set it equal to zero: $3b(a - b) - 3b = 0$. Factor out $3b$: $3b[(a - b) - 1] = 0$. Since b cannot equal zero (it must be positive based on the information given in the problem), then $(a - b - 1) = 0$. Solving for a gives you $a = b + 1$, which can be a positive integer. Solving for b gives you $b = 1 - a$, which can also be a positive integer. So, Roman Numeral III can equal 0. Eliminate answer choice D because it does not include Roman Numeral III.

By process of elimination, you are left with answer choice E.

SECTION 3—Writing Skills

Identifying Sentence Errors (Questions 1–14)

1. **The best answer is D.** In this sentence, "important" should be replaced with "importance" because to be grammatically correct, the sentence requires a noun, not an adjective. "Stutter" agrees with the singular noun "presenter," and the adverb "uncomfortably" effectively modifies the past tense verb "stuttered." "For" is an appropriate preposition to use after "search." "Place in his" properly refers to the singular noun, "presenter," and successfully expresses a reference of location in the sentence.

2. **The best answer is B.** In this sentence, "either" requires the coordinating conjunction "or" instead of "and." The verb "arrived" is in the correct tense, and "at" is the correct preposition to use after "arrived" because it correctly refers to a location. "Contractors" correctly refers to more than one contractor. "Further" correctly refers to his degree of frustration, and "increased" is in the correct verb tense.

3. **The best answer is E.** There are no errors in this sentence. The sentence requires two different verb tenses: The first portion of the sentence describes an event that is occurring now and will occur in the future, and the second portion of the sentence describes an event that will occur in the future. The present progressive verb "is" agrees with the singular noun "preparation" and is in the correct verb tense. "Very necessary" is an appropriate phrase, and "for" is the correct preposition to use after this phrase. The phrase "who expects" correctly refers to the singular noun, "runner," and the verb "expects" correctly refers to an event that will occur in the future.

4. **The best answer is A.** The underlined phrase "animals which" is followed by information that is essential to the sentence. Therefore, "which" should be replaced with "that" to introduce the essential clause "need help." "As a result" correctly expresses the cause (never turning away animals) and the effect (receiving an award) within the sentence. The verb phrase "has received" correctly refers to the singular noun, "staff," and appropriately refers to an event that has occurred in the past and continues to the present. "Past" is the appropriate adjective.

5. **The best answer is D.** The superlative "more" must be followed by the verb "strict." It would also be correct to simply say "stricter." The past progressive verb "grew" correctly refers to an event that occurred in the past along with another event. "Increasingly" correctly modifies "grew." "To be" correctly refers to the verb tense of the sentence and the singular proper noun "Miss Murray."

6. **The best answer is E.** There are no errors in this sentence. "Applicant" correctly refers to the singular noun "director." The future verb "choose" correctly refers to an event that will occur in the future. The phrase "will probably" is appropriate and within the context of the sentence. "As much for" is an acceptable phrase for this sentence and is parallel to the phrase "as for her" that follows.

7. **The best answer is C.** In this sentence, the verb "provides" refers to the plural noun "details"; therefore, the singular verb "provides" should be replaced with the plural form "provide." "From" is the correct preposition to use after "extracted." "Contradictory to" maintains parallelism with "in agreement with," and "to" is an appropriate preposition to use after "contradictory." The phrase "information necessary" is appropriate and within the context of the sentence.

8. **The best answer is C.** To maintain parallelism within the sentence, the phrase "must drive" should be replaced with "had to drive," which agrees with the phrase "had a longer commute." "Of" is an appropriate preposition to use with "construction." The adverb "because" effectively introduces the reason for the "longer commute," and the phrase "to and from" effectively expresses a reference to distance.

9. **The best answer is E.** There are no errors in this sentence. The present perfect verb "have" correctly refers to an event that began in the past and continues into the present and agrees with the plural subject of the sentence, "actors." "Their" also agrees with the plural subject, "actors." "But" is an appropriate conjunction to express the contrast within the sentence, and the plural noun "many others" agrees with the plural noun "actors." The conjunction "or" is properly used with "either" to indicate the second of two alternatives.

10. **The best answer is A.** The adjective "patient" should modify the verb "wait" and express the manner in which the "wait" is performed; therefore, "patient" would be best expressed as "patiently." The phrase "wait as others" correctly refers to the pronoun "I," and the phrase "their views" correctly refers to the plural "others" at the meeting. "Always" is an appropriate adverb to express the frequency of an event, and "interrupts" agrees with the singular noun "someone."

11. **The best answer is B.** In this sentence, "has been" should be "have been" because the plural subject of the sentence, "the dangers," requires a plural verb. "Of" is an appropriate preposition to follow "dangers," and "to" is an appropriate preposition to follow "exposure." The adverb "strongly" effectively modifies the verb "urged," and the preposition "of" is appropriate after "use."

12. **The best answer is C.** In this sentence, the plural verb "are" should be replaced with the singular verb "is" because the phrase "which of the teams" refers to a single team and, therefore, requires a singular verb. "Rarely watch" effectively expresses the frequency in which the event occurs. The plural verb "make" correctly refers to the plural noun "predictions," and "most likely" appropriately modifies the verb "to win."

13. **The best answer is E.** There are no errors in this sentence. The phrase "highly effective teaching style" is appropriate for the context of the sentence. The phrase "who has" correctly refers to an event that began in the past and continues to the present and agrees with the singular proper noun "Dr. Adams." The verb "ensuring" appropriately refers to an event that began in the past, continues to the present, and may continue into the future. The singular verb "falls" correctly refers to the singular noun "student."

14. **The best answer is C.** To maintain parallel construction, the phrase "attempts to enter" should be replaced with "attempting to enter" to correctly parallel the phrase "attending graduate school." The verb phrase "has forced" correctly refers to the singular noun "market" and parallels the verb tense of the sentence. "To make a decision" is an appropriate phrase. The conjunction "and" is used appropriately with "between."

Improving Sentences (Questions 15–34)

15. **The best answer is A.** This sentence is best as it is written. The underlined portion clearly refers to the black hole. Answer choices B, C, D, and E are awkward and unclear.

16. **The best answer is B.** The underlined portion as it is written indicates that the "price of gold," not the price of gold is more rare than silver. The intended meaning of the sentence is that "gold" is more rare than silver. Therefore, the noun "gold" should directly follow the clause that modifies it. Eliminate answer choices A and C because they indicate that the "price of gold" not "gold" itself is more rare than

silver. In order to maintain parallel construction, the underlined portion should follow the same form as the phrase "is in greater demand worldwide." The sentence is best written when it indicates that gold "has a higher price" and gold "is in greater demand."

17. **The best answer is B.** The sentence as it is written includes a comma splice. A comma splice occurs when you use a comma to separate two independent clauses within a sentence. The phrase "*The Detroit Jewish News*" is considered a parenthetical expression because it is additional information. Therefore, it should be set off with commas. Only answer choice B clearly indicates when and where *The Detroit Jewish News* was published. Answer choices A, C, D, and E are awkward and unclear.

18. **The best answer is B.** The sentence as it is written is redundant; it uses the word "since" twice. Answer choice B completes the sentence in the most clear and effective manner and uses the common phrase "ever since" to refer to a period of time. "Whereas" is used to show contrast, which is unnecessary in this sentence. Answer choice D properly eliminates "he," but is awkward. Answer choice E includes unnecessary punctuation and is awkward and unclear.

19. **The best answer is A.** This sentence is best as it is written. The singular subject "each" requires the singular pronoun "its." Answer choices B, D, and E use the plural pronoun "their" to refer to the singular subject "each." The subordinating conjunction "when" is not appropriate for the context of the sentence; therefore, answer choice C is incorrect.

20. **The best answer is D.** To maintain parallel construction in this sentence, both phrases modifying the noun clause "diet soda products" must agree. The underlined portion should parallel the phrase "not so much for their flavor or nutritional benefits"; therefore, the underlined portion should be "but for their low sugar content." Answer choices A, B, C, and E are either awkward or contain faulty parallelism.

21. **The best answer is E.** This sentence makes a comparison between the "responsibilities" of a nurse and of a doctor. To be correct, the plural pronoun "those" should be used to refer to the plural noun "responsibilities," and the phrase "of a doctor" should be used because it agrees with the phrase "of a nurse." Answer choices A, B, and C do not agree with the rest of the sentence. Answer choice D incorrectly uses the singular pronoun "that" to refer to the plural noun "responsibilities." It also includes the possessive noun "doctor's," which is incorrect.

22. The best answer is D. To maintain parallel structure, the underlined portion of the sentence after "and" should agree with "to hear from"; therefore, "and gaining knowledge" should be replaced with "and to gain knowledge." As it is written and in answer choices B and C, the underlined portions do not maintain parallel structure. Answer choice E requires additional punctuation to be grammatically correct.

23. The best answer is C. The sentence as it is written is an incomplete sentence; the subject, "thoroughbred," is not performing an action. Answer choice E is incorrect for the same reason. Answer choices B and D are awkward; they both include the pronoun "it," which is unnecessary. Only answer choice C clearly and simply expresses the intent of the sentence. It correctly sets off the parenthetical phrase "one of the world's best-known horse breeds" with commas and places the phrase directly after the noun that it modifies.

24. The best answer is D. As it is written, the sentence suggests that "the Southwest" is "the most unique regional cuisine in the United States," which does not make sense. To make this sentence more clear and concise, the underlined portion should refer to something more specific than "the Southwest." Because the sentence focuses on cuisine, answer choice D best addresses this problem by replacing "the Southwest" with "southwest cooking." Answer choices A, B, and C refer to "the Southwest." Answer choice E uses the more specific "southwest cooking," but also uses the phrase "is including," which is not appropriate for this sentence.

25. The best answer is A. This sentence includes two related, independent clauses that need to be separated by either a semicolon or a comma followed by a coordinating conjunction. The sentence is correct as it is written because it separates the clauses with a semicolon. The subordinating conjunction "so" is not appropriate for the context of this sentence; eliminate answer choice B. Answer choice C is incorrect because it is a run-on sentence. Answer choice D is incorrect because, although it includes a comma, it does not include the necessary coordinating conjunction. The subordinating conjunction "therefore" is not appropriate for the context of this sentence; eliminate answer choice E.

26. The best answer is C. This sentence includes two related, independent clauses that need to be separated by either a semicolon or a comma followed by a coordinating conjunction. Answer choice C is correct because it is the only answer choice that properly uses a semicolon. Answer choice A uses a comma followed by "this," which is not a coordinating conjunction. Answer choice B uses a colon. Answer choice D uses a semicolon followed by the conjunctive adverb "therefore," which needs to be followed by a comma in order to be correct. Answer choice E uses a comma followed by "that," which is not a coordinating conjunction.

27. **The best answer is B.** The sentence should clearly express that there are opportunities for college graduates and even more opportunities for graduates with advanced degrees. Answer choice B makes it clear that the number of opportunities increases with an advanced degree, and properly uses a semicolon to separate two independent clauses. In answer choice A, it is unclear to whom the pronoun "they" is referring. The pronoun "who" should refer to a person(s), not "opportunities," so answer choice C is incorrect. In answer choices D and E, it is unclear what will "increase..."

28. **The best answer is C.** The singular noun "person" requires the uses of singular verbs and pronouns; therefore, the plural pronoun "they" should be replaced with the singular pronoun phrase "he or she." Answer choice A uses the plural pronoun "they." The appropriate preposition to use after "audio tapes" is "to," so answer choices B, D, and E are incorrect.

29. **The best answer is A.** This sentence is best as it is written. The underlined portion clearly and concisely completes the sentence. Without additional punctuation, "developed" is the only verb that can logically follow "team," so answer choices B, C, and E are incorrect. Although answer choice D correctly uses "developed" directly after "team," the parenthetical phrase beginning with "which" creates an awkward sentence.

30. **The best answer is E.** The underlined portion of the sentence should clearly express whose actions are being defended. Answer choice E indicates that the actions belong to the students and completes the sentence in the most clear and concise manner. Answer choices A and B use the ambiguous possessive pronoun "their," which does not clearly identify whose actions are being defended. Answer choice C is awkward and uses the present tense verb "are" instead of the past tense verb "were." Answer choice D is unclear about whose actions are being defended.

31. **The best answer is D.** This sentence refers to the singular noun "*one of the…actors*"; therefore, the plural verb "were" should be replaced with the singular verb "was." Answer choice D correctly uses "was" and "badly," which is an appropriate adverb to describe how the actor was performing. Answer choices A and B use the plural verb "were." Answer choice C correctly uses the singular verb "was" but uses the adjective "bad" instead of the adverb "badly." Answer choice E creates an awkward sentence.

32. **The best answer is A.** This sentence is best as it is written. It effectively expresses the idea and is free from ambiguity. Answer choices B, C, D, and E are awkward and unclear.

33. **The best answer is A.** This sentence is best as it is written. The adjective "unlike" properly introduces the contrast between the information before and after the comma. Answer choice B is redundant because it unnecessarily uses both "unlike" and "was different" to suggest the contrast. Answer choice C creates an awkward sentence. In answer choice D, using both "his" and "him" is unnecessary. Answer choice E is awkward and redundant.

34. **The best answer is B.** This sentence should clearly express the conditional relationship between the events. Answer choice B expresses this in the most clear and concise manner. The present tense verb "can find" and the past tense verb "would find" do not agree with the rest of the sentence. In answer choice D, "that was" is unnecessary; it makes more sense to use "highly-skilled tennis coach." Answer choice E creates an illogical sentence.

Improving Paragraphs (Questions 35–39)

35. **The best answer is C.** Sentence 7 is the last sentence that discusses Jim's era. Sentence 8 begins a description of Virgil. There is a clear shift in focus here. Therefore, this would be an ideal place to begin a new paragraph.

36. **The best answer is C.** The sentence as it is written is confusing and awkward. It is unclear to whom the pronoun "he" refers. Answer choices B and E are incorrect because they create incomplete sentences. Answer choice D is awkward and unnecessarily includes the pronoun "he." Only answer choice C clearly conveys the intended meaning and stays within the context of the paragraph.

37. **The best answer is E.** This sentence is redundant and should be deleted. The previous sentence states the same idea, so it is not necessary to mention again that the children were racist and lacked respect for people of different races.

38. **The best answer is D.** "Was" is used for one subject or item, and "were" is used for two or more subjects or items. The sentence mentions prejudice <u>and</u> racism (two items). The introductory phrase "After all" is not appropriate based on the context, so answer choice B is incorrect. Answer choice C is incorrect because inserting a semicolon would create two incomplete sentences. The apostrophe in "society's" correctly shows possession, so deleting it would be inappropriate.

39. **The best answer is A.** The author compares and contrasts the experiences and settings of Virgil and Jim. The author does not offer imaginative descriptions, ask rhetorical questions, provide personal narration, or include any direct quotations.

SECTION 4—Math

Multiple Choice (Questions 1–8)

1. **The correct answer is C.** You are given that $z = 1$, which means that you can plug 1 in for z in the second equation and solve for y.

   ➤ $y = 4(1) - 2 = 2$.

   Since $y = 2$, you can plug 2 in for y in the first equation and solve for x.

   ➤ $3x + 6(2) = 24$

   ➤ $3x + 12 = 24$

   ➤ $3x = 12$; $x = 4$, answer choice C.

2. **The correct answer is B.** You are given that Greg, g, is younger than Daniel, d. Therefore, $g < d$. Eliminate answer choices A, C, and E because they show $d < g$. You are also given that Greg, g, is older than Henry, h, so $g > h$. Only answer choice B satisfies the statement that g is less than d, but greater than h.

3. **The correct answer is A.** The average is equal to the sum of the regions divided by the number of regions. The sum of the regions is 25 and the number of regions is 4. Therefore the average is $\frac{25}{4}$, answer choice A.

4. **The correct answer is A.** The best way to solve this problem is to pick numbers for n, beginning with an easy number, and plug the numbers into the expression given in the problem. Since only one of the answer choices will be correct, you can stop when you arrive at one of the answer choices.

   ➤ When $n = 1$, $3n^2 - 4n = 3(1) - 4 = -1$. Try another number.

   ➤ When $n = 2$, $3n^2 - 4n = 3(4) - 8 = 4$, answer choice A.

5. **The correct answer is D.** The two line segments that make up angle x are equal because they are both radii of the same circle. Since they are equal, the angles opposite both line segments are also equal. Thus, angle y and the unmarked angle are equal. Since the total measure of the angles in a triangle is 180°, you can set up an equation to determine the measure of angle y.

   ➤ $2y + 30° = 180°$; $y = 75°$, answer choice D.

6. **The correct answer is E.** Since a simple square only has factors of itself, its square root, and 1, then its square root must be a prime number. Only 289 has a square root that is prime; the square root of 289 is 17. The square roots of 64, 81, 144, and 196 are 8, 9, 12, and 14, respectively. None of these numbers is a prime number.

7. **The correct answer is B.** You are given that $XZ = \frac{5}{6}h$. XZ is also the base of the triangle. The formula to calculate the area of a triangle is $\frac{1}{2}bh$. Therefore, the area of this triangle is $\frac{1}{2}(\frac{5}{6}h)h$, or $\frac{5}{12}h^2$, answer choice B.

8. **The correct answer is E.** To solve this problem, you must first recognize that 35 has four factors (1, 5, 7, 35). Based on the information given in this problem, c could be 1 and d could be 35; likewise, c could be 35 and d could be 1. Since you don't know the exact relationship between c and d, you do not have enough information to determine the ratio of c to d.

Student Produced Response (Questions 9–18)

9. **Answer: 992.** First, you know that the number must be less than 1,000 since the question asks for a three-digit integer. You also know that the number must be divisible by 8 and by 4 because 8 and 4 are factors of 16. Since 1,000 is divisible by both 8 and 4, your first try should be 8 less than 1,000 (the next lowest number divisible by both 8 and 4), or 992. As it turns out, 992 is divisible by 16, which makes 992 the greatest three-digit integer that has a factor of 16.

10. **Answer: 165.** To solve this problem, set up a proportion:

   ➤ 18 pounds for 30 people = 99 pounds for x people

   ➤ $\frac{18}{30} = \frac{99}{x} =$

   Cross multiply and solve for x:

   ➤ $18x = 2,970$

   ➤ $x = 165$

11. **Answer: 6 or 8**. The first step in solving this problem is to recognize that n increased by 5 is expressed mathematically as $n + 5$. When you double that expression, you get $2(n + 5)$. Since this value is between 20 and 30, set up an inequality and solve for n.

➤ $20 < 2(n + 5) < 30$

➤ $20 < 2n + 10 < 30$

➤ Divide each element of the inequality by 2: $10 < n + 5 < 15$

➤ Subtract 5 from each element of the inequality: $5 < n < 10$

➤ Since the question says that n is a positive even integer, n could be equal to either 6 or 8.

12. **Answer: 1,575**. The perimeter of a rectangle is calculated using the formula $P = 2(l) + 2(w)$. You are given that the perimeter is 160 and that one side is 35. Plug these values into the formula to find the length of the other side. You can set either the length (l) or the width (w) equal to 35.

➤ $160 = 2(l) + 2(35)$

➤ $160 = 2(l) + 70$

➤ $160 - 70 = 2(l)$

➤ $90 = 2(l); 45 = l$

The area of a rectangle is calculated using the formula $A = (l)(w)$. Therefore, the area is equivalent to $(45)(35)$, or 1,575.

13. **Answer: 48**. To answer this question, first recognize that the question asks you to compare a part (the number of pounds of gravel) to the whole (the number of pounds of the mixture.) The ratio of gravel to the mixture is 2:5; you are given that the mixture contains 2 parts gravel to 3 parts sand. You are also given that the mixture weighs 100 pounds. Now, set up a proportion, as follows:

➤ 2 is to 5 as x (pounds of gravel) is to 120

➤ $\dfrac{2}{5} - \dfrac{x}{120}$; cross-multiply and solve for x.

➤ $5x = 240$

➤ $x = 48$

There will be 48 pounds of gravel in a mixture of gravel and sand that weighs a total of 120 pounds.

14. Answer: $\frac{9}{2}$ **or 4.5**. The quickest way to solve this problem is to recognize that both equations have $(x - 2y)$ in common. Since $(x - 2y) = 6$, substitute 6 for $(x - 2y)$ in the first equation.

➤ $(6)(6)(2x + 3) = 324$

➤ $36(2x + 3) = 324$

➤ $72x + 108 = 324$

➤ $72x = 216$; $x = 3$

Plug 3 in for x in the second equation and solve for y.

➤ $3 - 2y = 6$

➤ $-2y = 3$

➤ $y = -\frac{3}{2}$, or -1.5

So, $x = 3$ and $y = -1.5$. Therefore, $2x + y$ equals $2(3) + (-1.5)$ or $6 - 1.5$, which is 4.5.

15. Answer: 3. If the center of the circle is at $(3,9)$ and the circle only touches the y-axis at one point, then it must touch at the point $(0,9)$. Draw a picture to help visualize the problem.

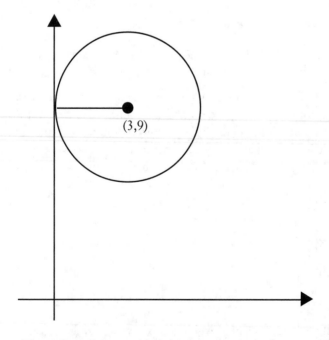

(3,9)

The radius of the circle is the distance along the x-axis, which is 3.

16. **Answer: 73.3%.** You are given that the number of people who actually voted is 60% of the voting-age population. So, $(3500 + 4200) \times .60 = 4,620$ people who actually voted. The number of registered voters is $2,700 + 3,600 = 6,300$ people. Since, according to information given in the problem, turnover is the number of people who actually voted divided by the number of registered voters, the turnover is $\frac{4,620}{6,300}$, or .733. This is equivalent to 73.3%.

17. **Answer: $\frac{13}{4}$ or 3.25.** Since the coefficient is always 3, you can deal with the exponents directly. According to the question, there are four x's, so 13 must be equal to $4x$. Solve for x.

   ➤ $13 = 4x$

   ➤ $\frac{13}{4} = x$

18. **Answer: 10,000.** A ratio can be expressed as a fraction. Count the number of places to the right of the decimal to determine the value of 0.0007. In 0.0007, the 7 is in the ten-thousandths place (four spaces to the right of the decimal). Therefore, 0.0007 is equivalent to $\frac{7}{10,000}$, or 7:10,000.

SECTION 5—Critical Reading

Sentence Completion (Questions 1–6)

1. **The best answer is B.** The context of this sentence indicates that the flowers in the garden were very colorful. Based on the context, the word that best describes the flowers is "vibrant." Answer choice A is incorrect because "homogeneous" means "uniform in composition;" the sentence states that the petunias ranged in color from yellow to blue. Answer choices C and D have meanings opposite to "vibrant." Answer choice E does not fit the context of the sentence.

2. **The best answer is D.** The definition of a "conglomerate" is a "group of consolidated corporations." "Merge" means to "consolidate." Answer choices A and C have meanings opposite to "merge." Answer choices B and E do not fit the context of the sentence.

3. **The best answer is A.** The context of the sentence indicates that Alan had to perform some specific actions. Look at each answer choice and fill in the blanks in the sentence. "Salvage" means to "rescue or save," and "concede" means to "acknowledge." These words complete the sentence effectively and make sense based on the context. Answer choices B, C, D, and E do not make sense when inserted into the sentence.

4. **The best answer is D.** Look at the answer choices and select a word to insert into the first blank that describes someone who might "bellow" and "provoke." "Passionate" in answer choice A works, and "fervent" in answer choice D also works; it means "showing great emotion." Answer choice E is still an option because "eloquent" means "persuasive or moving." The first words in answer choices B and C have meanings opposite to "fervent." Now look at the second blank. Neither "placating" in answer choice A nor "nurturing" in answer choice E fit the context of the sentence.

5. **The best answer is C.** The word "although" at the beginning of the sentence suggests a contrast between the information preceding and following the comma. Also, the context indicates that Sofia was afraid to fly, so the first blank should be filled with a word that is synonymous with "fear." Answer choices A, B, and D do not include words in the first position that are synonymous with "fear." It makes sense that Sofia would have to "overcome" her fear, based on the context of the sentence.

6. The best answer is D. The word that will best complete this sentence should relate to the idea that the suspect was able to "escape." "Abscond" means to "leave quickly and hide," which fits the context of the sentence. Answer choices A, B, C, and E do not fit the context of the sentence.

Reading Comprehension (Questions 7–25)

7. The best answer is B. Passage 1 describes Juan's upcoming attempt to escape his life of poverty in Cuba for a future of employment and freedom in America. Passage 2 describes the journey of Peter and James, "running from their war-torn country of Sudan" in hopes of better a life, first in Ethiopia, then Kenya, and, ultimately, America. Both passages discuss "traveling to America" and "providing assistance," but these details are not the theme of either passage. Answer choices D and E are not supported by the passage.

8. The best answer is E. In Passage 2, statements such as "Peter and James managed to make the best of their internment…despite the bleakness of their situation" and "Though Peter and James were unsure of what the future would hold, they remained optimistic…" suggest that the boys were both "determined" to survive and "hopeful" of their future together in America. Answer choices A, B, C, and D are not supported by information in the passage.

9. The best answer is B. The events described in Passage 1 indicate that any attempts to flee Cuba must be made in secrecy. The passage states that "Anyone attempting to flee the country would be dealt with harshly by the authorities." Therefore, the phrase "hushed voices" further describes the importance of secrecy. Answer choices A, C, D, and E are not supported by the passage.

10. The best answer is D. The passage states that "Upon hearing the plan, Juan swallowed his fear, looked his father in the eye, and nodded." This best supports the idea that Juan knew how to control his fear and self-doubt. Despite the hardships of the journey, Juan appeared determined to be strong. Answer choices A, B, C, and E are not supported by details in the passage.

11. The best answer is C. The main idea of the passage is that Juan and his family want to escape their current living conditions. It is indicated throughout the passage that, by fleeing to America, Juan and his family would be able to make a better life for themselves and "escape poverty." The description of Juan's home—"a two-room shack"—

reflects the poor living conditions that he and his seven siblings, and, presumably, other people in his country, had to endure. The passage makes clear that others had attempted the same journey that Juan and his father were about to undertake. Answer choices A, B, D, and E are not supported by the passage.

12. **The best answer is B.** The word "crude" in Passage 2 is used to describe the camp in Ethiopia where James and Peter lived for several years. Statements such as "…conditions were far from ideal…," and "…despite the bleakness of their situation…" suggest that the camps were "rough and primitive." Although "crude" can be used to mean "ignorant and rude," this definition is not supported by the context of the passage. Answer choices C, D, and E are not definitions of the word "crude."

13. **The best answer is A.** Passage 1 includes statements such as "They would never return to their homeland…" and "Anyone attempting to flee the country would be dealt with harshly by the authorities." This passage also indicates that, even if Juan and his father made it to Florida, they would still be pursued by government authorities and would have to continue to be cautious. Passage 2, on the other hand, includes more positive statements, such as "Peter and James managed to make the best of their internment in the camps…," and "…several thousand boys would have the opportunity to go to America where they would be assisted by many generous people in pursuing their education and finding a job." The overall tone of Passage 2 is more hopeful than that of Passage 1. Answer choices B, C, D, and E are not accurate descriptions of the differences between the two passages.

14. **The best answer is B.** The passage focuses on the hardships endured by many people during World War II. The discussion throughout the passage of rationing, as well as the mention of the loneliness of the American troops overseas, serve to support answer choice B. The author herself did not make any contributions to the war effort, so answer choice A is incorrect. Answer choices C, D, and E are not supported by information in the passage.

15. **The best answer is C.** The author's use of the words "crudely" and "gruesome" imply that her baking efforts were less than perfect. Answer choice A is not correct because there is nothing in the passage to suggest that the author's brother and sister even know about the little pies that the author baked. Answer choices B and E are not supported by the passage, and answer choice D is contradicted by information in the passage.

16. The best answer is C. The overall tone of the passage is positive toward the author's family. It makes sense that the author includes an example of her grandmother's good deeds because the author is proud of her grandmother. Answer choices A and D have a negative connotation, which is not supported by the context of the phrase in the question. Likewise, answer choices B and E are not supported by information in the passage.

17. The best answer is E. The sentence in the question clearly indicates that the soldiers missed their loved ones; therefore, they were most likely "lonesome." The soldiers might have been "despondent" and "terrified," but neither the context of the passage as a whole, nor the sentence mentioned in the question, support the use of those words. The passage indicates that soldiers received baked goods from home; the passage does not suggest that the soldiers were "ravenous." Likewise, answer choice D is not supported by the context of the passage.

18. The best answer is A. The passage states that "Attempts to purchase...items were curbed because the products were needed for the troops overseas." This suggests that any attempts to purchase some particular items were "restricted" because those items were needed by the troops. Answer choices B, D, and E are not supported by the context of the passage. Answer choice C directly contradicts the context of the passage.

19. The best answer is A. The passage states that "Gasoline and fuel oil were also rationed during World War II. The government allowed those registered for fuel only a limited quantity to purchase each month." According to these statements, people had to register in order to receive certain rations, which suggests that there was a process or procedure in place to allow people to buy gasoline. Answer choices B, C, D, and E are not supported by information in the passage.

20. The best answer is D. The term "war speeds," as it is used in the passage, refers to special speed limits imposed by the government, in order to "conserve fuel consumption." Answer choice E is incorrect because, although there were government restrictions on gasoline sales, this was a part of the rationing process, and did not have anything to do with the speed at which people were allowed to drive. Likewise, answer choices A, B, and C are not supported by the passage.

21. The best answer is E. The passage recalls memories of the author's mother, who grew up during World War II. The author states that "...I can imagine that he had access to gasoline and rubber tires when others did not" based on a discussion about how the author's grandfather worked for an automobile company. The author was not recalling her own memory, but was making an inference based on what her mother had told her. This best supports answer choice E. "Conjecturing" means "making a conclusion based on incomplete evidence." Answer choices A, B, C, and D are not supported by the passage.

22. **The best answer is A.** The passage states that "It was considered a romantic notion that American ladies would give up their precious nylon stockings so their brothers, husbands, and boyfriends could return home safely." It can be inferred from this statement that the author believed that most American women were happy to sacrifice their nylon stockings so that the soldiers overseas could have parachutes. Although the statement in answer choice E might be true based on the passage, it is not emphasized by the phrase "romantic notion." Answer choices B, C, and D are not supported by the passage.

23. **The best answer is B.** The quotation in the passage specifically mentions the importance of taking part in the "drive" to collect aluminum for the war effort. The radio announcer is quoted as saying, "This drive is a mighty important one. It's the first time that all of the people have had an opportunity to take part in the defense program." This best supports answer choice B. Answer choice D is not correct because no consequences are mentioned. Likewise, answer choices A, C, and E are not supported by information in the passage.

24. **The best answer is D.** Information in the passage clearly indicates that the author's mother told her stories about growing up during the war. The author herself did not experience the war, so answer choice A is incorrect. The passage does not indicate that the author's grandparents told her stories, only that her mother told her stories; therefore, answer choice B is incorrect. Likewise, answer choices C and E are not supported by information in the passage.

25. **The best answer is A.** The last sentence states that "Almost everyone on the home front was willing to do his or her part to help in the war effort as they waited anxiously for the troops to come home and life to return to normal." It can be implied that people made sacrifices during the war because they hoped that the rationing would end once the war was over and the troops came home. The passage indicates that the Great Depression occurred before World War II, so answer choice B is incorrect. Likewise, answer choices C, D, and E are not supported by the passage.

Practice Exam 2

This practice PSAT consists of 125 questions, divided into five sections. To achieve the best results, time yourself strictly on each section. Use the Answer Sheet at the end of the chapter to mark your answers. Read the directions carefully, and remember not to guess at random. A scoring guide is included in Appendix D that should be used to calculate an approximate test score. Your score on the actual PSAT will be dependant on many factors, including your level of preparedness and your fatigue level on test day.

We suggest that you make this practice test as much like the real test as possible. Find a quiet location, free from distractions, and make sure that you have pencils, a calculator, and a timepiece. You should read the chapters for each specific section of the PSAT prior to taking this practice test.

SECTION 1

Time—25 Minutes

23 Questions

Directions: For each question, select the best answer from among the choices listed. Fill in the corresponding circle on your answer sheet.

Each sentence below has either one or two blanks. Each blank indicates that a word has been omitted from the sentence. Beneath each sentence are five words or sets of words. Select the word or set of words that, when inserted into the sentence in place of the blank(s), best fits the context of the sentence as a whole.

1. Some students complained that the teachers were _____, focusing on short-term goals while ignoring the long-term benefits of classroom reorganization.
    - (A) ambiguous
    - (B) myopic
    - (C) perceptive
    - (D) discerning
    - (E) mindful

2. Although he appeared to be very _____ at the meeting with his investors, Frank was actually _____ of participating in such a daunting venture.
    - (A) acute . . culpable
    - (B) complacent . . hesitant
    - (C) collected . . assured
    - (D) confident . . terrified
    - (E) deferential . . bereft

3. The residents of my dormitory lived _____ lives, often indulging in wild and _____ behavior.
    - (A) chaotic . . impulsive
    - (B) temperate . . frenzied
    - (C) moderate . . destructive
    - (D) arbitrary . . leisurely
    - (E) boisterous . . unpretentious

4. Given the inclement weather and hazardous road conditions, it was rather _____ of Jonathan, who has never driven a car, to ignore the warning reports and attempt to drive into town.
   (A) shrewd
   (B) brash
   (C) comical
   (D) noble
   (E) valiant

5. Quickly ascending to high altitudes may have a _____ effect on the body; those who hike should climb very slowly to allow the body to _____, or get used to the conditions at various altitudes.
   (A) damaging . . transgress
   (B) noxious . . transform
   (C) deleterious . . acclimate
   (D) regrettable . . modify
   (E) moderating . . normalize

6. The attorney argued that his client was a secretive man by nature, and that his _____ was not an indication of guilt.
   (A) sincerity
   (B) forthrightness
   (C) furtiveness
   (D) integrity
   (E) candor

7. Though it is considered the _____ Italian dish and is a primary staple of the Italian diet, pasta is rumored to have actually originated in China.
   (A) thorough
   (B) quintessential
   (C) regular
   (D) innovative
   (E) punctilious

Each passage below is followed by several questions based on the content of the passage. Answer the questions based on what is either stated or implied in each passage. Be sure to read any introductory material that is provided.

Questions 8–15 are based on the following passage.

Recently, my curiosity was aroused while watching a movie. In the film, an offhand remark was made regarding the tradition of the Mexican piñata. The film stated that originally, piñatas were cast in the likeness of a particular person in order to pay homage to that
5 individual. I questioned the authenticity of this statement because I had never heard this claim before. I discovered that designing piñatas to resemble specific people is not actually a common practice. My research also revealed that contrary to popular belief, piñatas are not of Mexican origin.

10 While the history of the piñata is somewhat murky, most scholars believe that the piñata originated in China and later became popular in Europe. Some historians believe that the modern version of the piñata was created centuries ago in China where most piñatas were made to resemble animals. These animal figures were covered with
15 colorful paper and filled with seeds, rather than candy or toys as is customary today. Once the seeds were spilled, they were gathered and burned as a ritualistic practice. The ashes of the seeds were kept until the end of the year and were thought to bring good luck to their owners.

20 The Italian explorer, Marco Polo, is probably responsible for bringing the Chinese piñata to Europe. The piñata quickly became associated with religious ceremonies and was also used in many celebratory events. Often, the piñata was made into the shape of a star, which represented the Star of Bethlehem. During this time in Italy,
25 the piñata was often made of fragile clay. In fact, the Italian word "pignatta" translates to "fragile pot." The clay pots would be hung from a tree or a pole, and a stick would be used to strike the pot until it broke. The broken pots dispensed tiny treasures that would fall to the ground, where eager children and adults would quickly gather
30 them up. These clay pots could be unadorned or decorated with colorful ribbons and paper. In some areas of Mexico today, clay pots are still favored over papier-mâché creations. Whether made of clay or papier-mâché, piñatas are used in Mexico for many different events. One of these events is a ceremony called *posados*. During *posados*, a
35 piñata game is played for nine consecutive nights.

In the United States, piñatas are generally made either of papier mâché or a cardboard-type material. American piñatas come in almost

every shape and design imaginable. Every holiday has its own host of
possible choices and themes. In America, baseball bats, instead of tra-
40 ditional sticks, are the preferred tool used to break open the piñata.
In general, using a baseball bat should make it simple to break open
the piñata, laden with pounds of candy and toys; however, each person attempting the feat is first blindfolded and then spun around several times. This routine is similar to "Pin the Tail on the Donkey,"
45 which is another popular party game. Both games require the blindfolded participant to locate his or her target before either swinging
the bat or pinning on the tail. Onlookers will generally try to help the
participant by offering suggestions, but the audience most enjoys
watching the blindfolded person swing mightily at nothing but thin
50 air. In the piñata game, everyone wins when the broken piñata spills
its contents and onlookers scramble to collect the fun surprises.

8. According to the passage, modern day piñatas are typically used
  (A) as part of a celebratory activity
  (B) to honor a particular person of Mexican origin
  (C) as an expression of artistic talent or regional artistry
  (D) only during religious holidays
  (E) as a symbol of fertility or good fortune

9. As used in line 10, "murky" most nearly means
  (A) contrary or adverse
  (B) clear or straightforward
  (C) secretive or obvious
  (D) explicit or certain
  (E) vague or indefinite

10. According to the passage, what did the Chinese do with the seeds
from their piñatas?
  (A) They shared them with the rest of their community during harvest
    time.
  (B) They saved the seeds in a jar for good luck.
  (C) They used them again the following year during religious ceremonies.
  (D) They burned them and kept the ashes.
  (E) They planted them and grew crops.

11. It can be inferred from lines 21–22 ("The piñata quickly ... celebrato-
ry events.") that
  (A) the piñata was only popular in China
  (B) the piñata's popularity spread swiftly
  (C) Marco Polo had never heard of the piñata
  (D) Europeans were not very religious
  (E) the piñata was not celebrated in Italy

12. The tone of lines 47-50 ("Onlookers will … thin air.") is best described as

(A) serious
(B) trivial
(C) contemplative
(D) lighthearted
(E) somber

13. The author's discussion of how a piñata is used during a celebration (lines 39–51) emphasizes the

(A) importance of the contents of the piñata
(B) fun created by special rules in modern American piñata games
(C) decorative and artistic value of piñatas
(D) details in constructing a modern papier mâché piñata
(E) comparison with several other popular American party games

14. The information in the passage suggests that a museum's exhibition of traditional piñatas would

(A) consist primarily of Chinese clay pots
(B) be nonexistent as the piñata is strictly a modern day object
(C) be highly diverse and colorful
(D) not include Mexican piñatas
(E) show mostly Italian "pignattas"

15. Which statement best summarizes the author's perspective on the use of piñatas?

(A) Piñatas can be a festive addition to almost any celebration.
(B) Piñatas should be characterized as a serious religious icon rather than as a game.
(C) The piñata game will soon be replaced by other, more popular games.
(D) Piñatas should be more appreciated for their role in celebrations.
(E) Mexico should be attributed with the invention of the piñata game.

Questions 16–23 are based on the following passage.

A new recreational activity has been introduced that is bound to capture the attention of anyone fascinated with technology or utilizing a global positioning system (GPS). The only equipment necessary for this activity is a GPS receiver and some sort of trivial prize posi-
5   tioned in another location. The common name for this new technology sport is "geocaching." "Geo" refers to geography, and "caching" signifies the hidden stash at the end of this alleged treasure hunt.

In order to play this game, one must understand the principles behind a GPS device. The GPS is operated by the U. S. government.
10 This complex system allows anyone using a GPS device to determine his or her exact location anywhere on Earth. This is achieved by

using satellites that were first launched into orbit by the Department of Defense. In simple terms, the GPS determines location by calculating the difference between the transmission and receiving of a par-
15 ticular signal. As numerous satellites are involved in the broadcasting of these signals, information is constantly and instantly being computed by the GPS receiver.

While the primary purpose of these satellites is to aid in target location and detection of nuclear detonation, the GPS is not used
20 solely for defense. In fact, GPS is used in numerous areas and is now routinely installed in airplanes, personal watercrafts, ships, and automobiles. As GPS has become more affordable, many serious hikers, campers, and other outdoor enthusiasts refuse to travel without a GPS device. A simple handheld receiver can be had for as little as one
25 hundred dollars. More expensive devices cost up to one thousand dollars.

Besides their more serious and functional uses, many other more entertaining applications, such as "geocaching," have evolved. In "geocaching," a "geocacher" can go to several different websites and
30 find a cache in a specific area. Each cache listing will include the geographical coordinates (latitude and longitude) of the cache, along with other clues such as a general description of the topography or the level of difficulty in finding the cache. In "geocaching," a cache seeker technically already knows *where* the treasure is. However, he or she
35 does not know exactly what the process of finding it will entail. There can be, and often are, numerous obstacles to face while making one's way from point A to point B. The success a player has in overcoming these impediments will determine whether he or she will find the hidden cache.

40   There are many rules of etiquette guiding the "geocaching" process. First and foremost, both the person hiding the cache and those looking for it must be vigilant regarding the land or property they are traversing. A cache should never be hidden on private property without the owner's permission. By the same token, authorization should be
45 obtained for the use of public property. There have been many recorded cases of fear and panic when a hidden cache, often a metal canister or an old army ammunition case, is found by a "non-cacher" in a usually quiet public park. "Geocachers" should also be mindful of the techniques they use to surmount difficulties along the way. For example,
50 "bushwhacking," the act of cutting away bushes and branches, should not be used when moving through thick trees or brambles. In fact, it is a good idea to obtain a topographical map of the area before heading out. By using a topographical map, some of the potential obstacles can be anticipated ahead of time. With any luck, proper planning will help
55 reduce frustration and save valuable time.

"Geocachers" should always dress appropriately. A topographical map might help reveal any boggy areas where proper footwear is essential and mosquito repellant will be a desired commodity. "Geocachers" should always have plenty of drinking water and food as well. Like

60 any hiker in unfamiliar territory, "geocachers" should be prepared for anything. Getting lost is a real possibility because the GPS is only a receiver, and cannot transmit the "cacher's" location to anyone.

What might the "geocacher" find if the treasure is actually located? Usually, the treasure is unimpressive and the real reward is having

65 successfully located it. Often, the cache container will harbor only a log book and a disposable camera. The successful hunter is asked to record information about the adventure and to take a photo of him or herself. However, there will sometimes be inexpensive items hidden within the container. It is customary to take an item out and replace it

70 with something else. Therefore, "cachers" should always be prepared and have an alternate trinket on hand.

Many variations of the basic "geocaching" game are developing. For instance, one game requires moving the cache to another location once it is discovered. Multi-caching, which involves finding several

75 different caches in a series of searches, is also popular. A cache can also be something that is a permanent fixture, like a marker or a statue. "Geochaching" is becoming a popular pastime and is just one more reason to purchase a personal GPS.

16. The primary purpose of the passage is to

(A) explain the principles behind the global positioning system (GPS)
(B) compare "geocaching" with more serious uses of the GPS
(C) defend the fees associated with personal use of the GPS
(D) describe an activity referred to as "geocaching"
(E) examine how satellites are used to assist the Department of Defense

17. In line 7, "alleged" primarily signifies that

(A) geocaching is a fleeting trend
(B) geocaching is a technological version of a treasure hunt
(C) GPS systems are highly regarded and respected
(D) there is no actual treasure at the end of a GPS hunt
(E) a personal GPS system is overpriced

18. The author suggests in lines 9–17 that the GPS

(A) is a sophisticated and elaborate tracking system
(B) is not available to non-military personnel
(C) relies on satellites located in the United States
(D) can only be utilized by "geocachers" in the United States
(E) is unreliable and overly complicated

19. In line 28, "applications" most nearly means

    (A) petitions

    (B) appeals

    (C) treatments

    (D) purposes

    (E) proposals

20. The purpose of lines 41-43 ("First and foremost... traversing.") is to

    (A) emphasize the importance of a particular rule

    (B) create a sense of foreboding regarding a specific act

    (C) discredit the views of a certain group of people

    (D) introduce a topic of interest to most landowners

    (E) present a difference in opinion regarding etiquette

21. The author's conclusion in lines 77–78 would be most directly supported by information that

    (A) revealed the exact locations of caches placed in the United States

    (B) detailed the number of currently active "geocaches"

    (C) told the reader how to obtain a GPS receiver

    (D) described other specific uses of a GPS personal device

    (E) provided testimonials from treasure hunters

22. The author suggests that people who enjoy "geocaching" are most likely

    (A) government employees

    (B) resistant to new experiences

    (C) adventure seekers

    (D) ill-prepared

    (E) hoping for great monetary rewards

23. The author suggests that topographical maps can be used to

    (A) supplement the GPS in coordinating defense efforts

    (B) show various physical properties of the land

    (C) promote knowledge about dealing with insect bites

    (D) advertise the need for GPS to outdoor enthusiasts

    (E) decrease the risk of alarming "non-cachers" in public parks

---

STOP

If you finish before your time is up, check your work on this section only. You may not turn to any other section in the test.

SECTION 2

Time—25 Minutes

20 Questions

Directions: Solve each problem and determine which is the best of the answer choices given. Fill in the corresponding circle on your answer sheet. Use any available space to solve the problems.

Notes

1. The use of a calculator is permitted.
2. All numbers are real numbers.
3. Figures that accompany problems in this test are intended to provide information useful in solving the problems. They are drawn as accurately as possible EXCEPT when it is stated in a specific problem that the figure is not drawn to scale. All figures lie in a plane unless otherwise indicated.
4. Unless otherwise specified, the domain of any function f is assumed to be the set of all real numbers x for which $f(x)$ is real number.

Reference Information

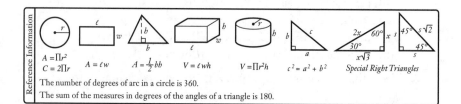

$A = \Pi r^2$
$C = 2\Pi r$

$A = \ell w$

$A = \frac{1}{2}bh$

$V = \ell wh$

$V = \Pi r^2 h$

$c^2 = a^2 + b^2$

Special Right Triangles

The number of degrees of arc in a circle is 360.

The sum of the measures in degrees of the angles of a triangle is 180.

1. If $5x + 7 = 27$, what is the value of $3x - 9$?

(A) 3
(B) 4
(C) 12
(D) 21
(E) 30

2. There are 6 sections in the school gymnasium. Each section contains at least 100 seats but not more than 175 seats. Which of the following could be the number of seats in this gymnasium?

(A) 550
(B) 850
(C) 1,150
(D) 1,250
(E) 1,350

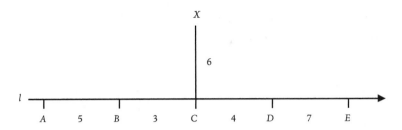

Note: Figure not drawn to scale.

3. In the figure above, *XC* is perpendicular to *l*. Which of the following line segments (not shown) has the greatest length?

(A) *AX*
(B) *BX*
(C) *CX*
(D) *DX*
(E) *EX*

JASON'S TROPHY COLLECTION

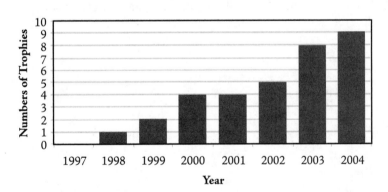

4. The graph above shows how Jason's trophy collection has grown between 1997 and 2004 by indicating the total number of trophies he has at the end of each year. In which year did Jason win three separate trophies?

(A) 1999
(B) 2000
(C) 2002
(D) 2003
(E) 2004

5. The average of x and y is 16, and the average of x, y, and z is 22. What is the value of z?

(A) 16
(B) 22
(C) 34
(D) 45
(E) 66

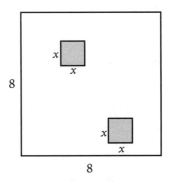

6. In the figure above, 2 small squares are inside a larger square. What is the area, in terms of x, of the non-shaded region?

(A) $16 - 2x^2$
(B) $16 - 4x$
(C) $64 - 2x^2$
(D) $64 - x^2$
(E) $2x^2 - 64$

7. If $pqrs = 24$ and $prst = 0$, which of the following must be true?

(A) $p > 0$
(B) $q > 0$
(C) $t = 0$
(D) $p = 0$
(E) $r = 0$

8. During its most recent basketball game, the red team scored one-eighth of its points in the first quarter, one-third of its points in the second quarter, 23 points in the third quarter, and the remaining points in the fourth quarter. If the red team scored a total of 72 points, how many points did the red team score in the fourth quarter?

(A) 9
(B) 16
(C) 23
(D) 24
(E) 56

9. If $3^{6x} = 27^{4x-2}$, what is the value of x?

    (A) -1

    (B) 0

    (C) 1

    (D) 2

    (E) 3

10. If 9 more than 5 times a certain number is 3 less than twice the number, what is the number?

    (A) -4

    (B) -2

    (C) 0

    (D) 2

    (E) 4

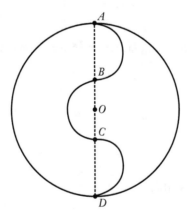

11. The circle above has center O and diameter AD. The three semicircles have diameters AB, BC, and CD. If the circumference of the circle is 90π and the three semicircles are all of equal size, what is the length of the curved path from A to D through B and C?

    (A) 15π

    (B) 30π

    (C) 45π

    (D) 60π

    (E) 90π

x	$f(x)$
0	a
2	27
4	b

12. The table above shows some values for the function f. If f is a linear function, what is the value of $a + b$?

(A) 3

(B) 9

(C) 27

(D) 54

(E) It cannot be determined from the information given.

$$\frac{4(3+\oplus)}{3} = 5\frac{2}{3}$$

13. What number, used in place of $\oplus$ above, makes the statement true?

(A) $\dfrac{2}{3}$

(B) $\dfrac{5}{4}$

(C) 3

(D) 12

(E) 17

14. If $x - 13 = 13 - x$, then $x =$

(A) -26

(B) -13

(C) 0

(D) 13

(E) 26

ANTIQUE VALUE

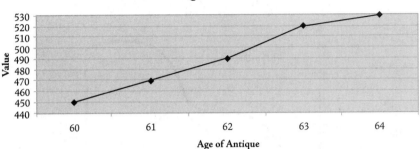

15. The graph above shows the value of Martin's antique chair in dollars from the age of 60 to the age of 64. The value of Martin's antique chair at the age of 64 was what percent (to the nearest percent) greater than the value of the antique chair at the age of 60?

    (A) 15%
    (B) 18%
    (C) 25%
    (D) 50%
    (E) 80%

16. It takes 8 buckets of dirt to fill 6 empty holes. At this rate, how many buckets of dirt will it take to fill 9 empty holes of the same size?

    (A) 6
    (B) 9
    (C) 12
    (D) 15
    (E) 18

17. If $7a + 4(x - 2) = s$, what is $x - 2$, in terms of s and a?

    (A) $\dfrac{s}{7a}$

    (B) $\dfrac{(s + 7a)}{4}$

    (C) $\dfrac{(s - 7a)}{4}$

    (D) $\dfrac{4s}{7a}$

    (E) $7a + 4 + s$

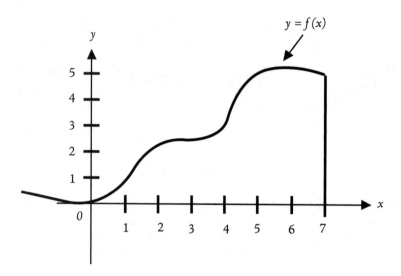

18. The enclosed region in the figure above is bounded by the x-axis, the line x = 7, and the graph of f(x). If the point (c,d) lies in the enclosed region, which of the following must be true?

   I. $c \leq 7$

   II. $d \leq f(c)$

   III. $c = d$

   (A) I only
   (B) II only
   (C) III only
   (D) I and II only
   (E) I, II, and III

19. The length of a rectangular kitchen floor is 3 feet more than its width. If the length of the floor is 12 feet, what is the area of the floor in square feet?

   (A) 9
   (B) 15
   (C) 42
   (D) 108
   (E) 144

The sum of $7a$ and the square of $4b$ is equal to the sum of $3a$ and $5b$.

20. Which of the following is an expression for the statement above?

    (A) $7a + (4b)^2 = 3a + 5b$

    (B) $7a + 4b^2 = 3a + 5b$

    (C) $7a + 4b^2 = 3a + 5b$

    (D) $7a + (4b)^2 = (3a)(5b)$

    (E) $7a + \sqrt{4b} = (3a)(5b)$

STOP

If you finish before your time is up, check your work on this section only. You may not turn to any other section in the test.

SECTION 3

Time—30 Minutes

39 Questions

> **Directions:** For each question, select the best answer from among the choices listed. Fill in the corresponding circle on your answer sheet.

> The following questions test your ability to recognize grammar and usage errors in standard written English. Each sentence contains either a single error or no error at all. Refer to the underlined, lettered portions of each sentence. If the sentence contains no error, select answer choice E. If the sentence contains an error, select the one underlined and lettered portion (A, B, C, or D) that is incorrect.

1. The laboratory <u>requires</u> <u>technicians to wear</u> safety goggles at all times
            A   B

   <u>of the day</u> <u>to protect against</u> injury. <u>No error</u>
      C   D   E

2. For many young people in the 1920s, <u>attending</u> high school <u>was</u> a
                            A   B

   way <u>to prolong</u> youth, not a way to further <u>your</u> education. <u>No error</u>
        C   D   E

3. Although the restaurant <u>boasted</u> a <u>pleasurable</u> atmosphere, neither
                    A   B

   the food <u>or</u> the service <u>was worthy</u> of a four-star rating. <u>No error</u>
         C   D   E

4. Mr. Reed, unlike the other neighbors who live <u>at our street</u>, <u>failed</u> to
                                       A   B

   maintain the landscaping on his property, <u>which fueled</u> the neighbor-
                                       C

   hood committee <u>to report his</u> negligence to the city. <u>No error</u>
               D   E

5. Because the <u>increase in</u> gas prices <u>has made</u> the cost of driving to
                A   B

   Florida <u>too high</u>, we <u>booked</u> a flight to Orlando to save hundreds of
        C   D

   dollars. <u>No error</u>
        E

6. The highest of the charity board's priorities, contradictory to the

mission of the group, <u>are</u> to install a state-of-the-art exercise facility
                       A
<u>in the office</u> for use <u>by</u> members of the board <u>only</u>. <u>No error</u>
   B   C   D   E

7. In 1580, the crew of the *Golden Hind*, <u>guided by</u> European explorer
                                                    A
Sir Francis Drake, <u>triumphantly</u> <u>arrived in</u> England after an arduous
                        B   C
three-year journey across <u>both the</u> Pacific and Atlantic Oceans.
                              D
<u>No error</u>
   E

8. <u>Just as those</u> <u>who were working</u> on the project prepared to throw in
        A   B
the towel, the supervisors, <u>determined</u> to see the group finish,
                               C
<u>become</u> the most encouraging. <u>No error</u>
   D   E

9. The company <u>introduced</u> a new line of health beverages in addition
                     A
to <u>its</u> standard soft drinks, because <u>consumers responded</u> very well to
   B   C
<u>these</u> in focus groups. <u>No error</u>
   D   E

10. The risk <u>of</u> cross-contamination between foods, surfaces, and
                 A
equipment, for example, <u>prove that</u> proper training <u>is</u> necessary for all
                           B   C
foodservice <u>workers</u>. <u>No error</u>
               D   E

11. <u>Whereas</u> <u>most novice</u> gardeners <u>attempting to revive</u> an ailing plant
         A   B   C
by placing it in direct sunlight, many experts know that the plant is

<u>more likely to</u> survive in the shade. <u>No error</u>
   D   E

12. The casting announcement, <u>previously scheduled</u> for 1:00 p.m. today,

                                          A

   <u>would</u> be postponed because the director cannot choose <u>between</u> the

    B   C

   two actors <u>vying for</u> the lead role. <u>No error</u>

                D   E

13. <u>Most experts</u> in the medical field <u>find it difficult</u> to determine

      A   B

   <u>what factor </u>contributes more to obesity: lifestyle choices <u>or</u> heredity.

     C   D

   <u>No error</u>

    E

14. The university programs committee <u>maintain</u> that the dynamic

                                      A

   curriculum is in <u>accordance with</u> the <u>frequently</u> changing demands

                       B   C

   <u>of both</u> <u>the students </u>and the job market. <u>No error</u>

      D   E

The following questions test the correct and effective use of standard written English in expressing an idea. Part of each sentence (or the entire sentence) is underlined. Beneath each sentence are five different ways of phrasing the underlined portion. Answer choice A repeats the original phrasing. If you think that the original phrasing is best, select answer choice A. Otherwise, select from the remaining four choices. Your selection should result in the most effective, clear sentence, free from awkwardness or ambiguity.

15. To ensure that all of the navy beans will have the same suppleness after cooking, <u>it is the chef who must use beans that are approximately the same size</u>.

    (A) it is the chef who must use beans that are approximately the same size

    (B) the chef must use beans that are approximately the same size

    (C) beans used must be approximately the same size, by the chef

    (D) the beans, approximately the same size, used by the chef

    (E) the chef is the one using beans approximately the same size

16. Clear-cutting is cheaper, more profitable, and easier than other logging methods, but <u>the greater is its toll on the local ecology</u>.

    (A) the greater is its toll on the local ecology

    (B) in its local ecology toll it is greater

    (C) it has a greater local ecology toll

    (D) its toll on local ecology is greater

    (E) there is the greater local ecology toll

17. Marcia had overwhelming support from her party during the election, <u>this</u> partisan assistance enabled her to win handily.

    (A) this

    (B) of which

    (C) therefore

    (D) and this

    (E) so that

18. <u>Revered for their impeccable breeding, dog enthusiasts will spend a small fortune on purebred dogs rather than settle for a common mutt</u>.

    (A) Revered for their impeccable breeding, dog enthusiasts will spend a small fortune on purebred dogs rather than settle for a common mutt

    (B) Revered as impeccable, dog enthusiasts will spend a small fortune on purebred dogs as opposed to settling for a common mutt

    (C) Revered for their impeccable breeding, purebred dogs command a small fortune among dog enthusiasts unwilling to settle for a common mutt

    (D) As opposed to common mutts, dog enthusiasts will spend a small fortune to obtain a purebred dog with impeccable breeding

    (E) Dog enthusiasts unwilling to settle for a common mutt will spend a small fortune on obtaining a purebred dog revered for their impeccable breeding

19. Evidence from surveys and interviews <u>show that babies fed breast milk tend to be healthier</u> than those fed formula.

    (A) show that babies fed breast milk tend to be healthier
    (B) shows that babies fed breast milk tend to be healthier
    (C) are showing that babies fed breast milk tend to be healthier
    (D) show, that babies fed breast milk tend to be healthier
    (E) tend to show that healthier babies are fed breast milk

20. <u>Before reading a new magazine, my mother studies the table of contents, my father flips through the advertisements.</u>

    (A) Before reading a new magazine, my mother studies the table of contents, my father flips through the advertisements
    (B) My mother studies the table of contents, my father flips through the advertisements before reading a new magazine
    (C) Before reading a new magazine, my mother studies the table of contents; my father flips through the advertisements
    (D) Before reading a new magazine, my mother studies the table of contents; my father flipping through the advertisements
    (E) My father flips through the advertisements with my mother studying the table of contents before reading a new magazine

21. <u>Claude Monet is best known for his representations of landscapes and natural beauty, and</u> his most beautiful painting, *Houses of Parliament* (London 1908), presents a breathtaking view of the historic building.

    (A) Claude Monet is best known for his representations of landscapes and natural beauty, and
    (B) Claude Monet is best known for his representations of landscapes and natural beauty,
    (C) Claude Monet is best known for his representations of landscapes and natural beauty
    (D) Although Claude Monet is best known for his representations of landscapes and natural beauty,
    (E) Because Claude Monet is best known for his representations of landscapes and natural beauty;

22. After attending a well-known music school in New York City, Jennifer, Kate, and Kahla shared a determination <u>to become singing trio sensations</u> known worldwide.

    (A) to become singing trio sensations
    (B) to becoming a singing trios sensation
    (C) to become a singing trio sensation
    (D) to become sensational singing trios
    (E) to become a singing trios sensations

23. One of the most fascinating regions in North America, <u>the New England coast is noted for its natural attractions</u>.

    (A) the New England coast is noted for its natural attractions

    (B) the New England coast is notable for attractions that are natural

    (C) the New England coast is naturally noted for attractions

    (D) the New England coast has among its natural attractions

    (E) the New England coast, is noted for natural attractions

24. <u>Michael's honesty and integrity is what will help him</u> tackle the hardships of this government position.

    (A) Michael's honesty and integrity is what will help him

    (B) Michael's honesty and integrity will help him

    (C) Honesty and integrity is going to help Michael

    (D) Michael will be helped by: honest and integrity to

    (E) This honesty and integrity is what will help Michael

25. Babe Ruth had a record-setting career in major league baseball: <u>in 1916 when he pitched 13 scoreless innings in his first World Series it began</u>.

    (A) in 1916 when he pitched 13 scoreless innings in his first World Series it began

    (B) when he pitched 13 scoreless innings in his first World Series it began in 1916

    (C) in 1916 it began when he pitched 13 scoreless innings in his first World Series

    (D) it began in 1916 when he pitched 13 scoreless innings in his first World Series

    (E) it began in 1916 when in his first World Series he pitched 13 scoreless innings

26. Although Frank is very interested in the German culture, he does not speak the language, <u>he</u> has never visited Germany.

    (A) he

    (B) Frank

    (C) somehow

    (D) as a result

    (E) and he

27. <u>National standards are difficult to agree on even for educators</u>.

    (A) National standards are difficult to agree on even for educators

    (B) National standards are difficult even for educators to agree on

    (C) Even educators find it difficult to agree on national standards

    (D) Even educators, find that reaching an agreement on national standards is difficult

    (E) Educators find that national standards is difficult to agree on

28. <u>Colin Powell has had other occupations other than Secretary of State such as; he has been a general, and an army officer, along with a government official</u>.

    (A) Colin Powell has had other occupations other than Secretary of State such as; he has been a general, and an army officer, along with a government official

    (B) Colin Powell has had other occupations rather than Secretary of State including: general, army officer, along with a government official

    (C) In addition to being the Secretary of State, Colin Powell has been a general, an army officer, and a government official

    (D) In addition to being the Secretary of State, Colin Powell has been: a general, army officer, and a government official

    (E) In addition, to being Secretary of State, Colin Powell has been a general, and army officer, along with a government official

29. <u>Buying a dog is not necessarily costly, but paying for food, toys, and trips to the veterinarian can become increasingly expensive</u>.

    (A) Buying a dog is not necessarily costly, but paying for food, toys, and trips to the veterinarian can become increasingly expensive

    (B) A dog is not necessarily costly, increasingly expensive are paying for food, toys, and trips to the veterinarian

    (C) Buying a dog is not necessarily costly but paying for food, toys and trips to the veterinarian becomes expensive increasingly

    (D) Even though buying a dog is not necessarily costly, increasingly expensive are: paying for food, toys, and trips to the veterinarian

    (E) Buying a dog, paying for food, toys, and trips to the veterinarian, is not necessarily costly but can become increasingly expensive

30. In an endeavor to increase parent participation, <u>teachers have planned too many field trips hence they hinder student achievement</u>.

    (A) teachers have planned too many field trips hence they hinder student achievement

    (B) teachers have planned too many field trips and so have hence hindered student achievement

    (C) teachers have planned too many field trips and hinders student achievement as a result

    (D) teachers have planned too many field trips and hence hinder student achievement

    (E) teachers have planned too many field trips that have hindered student achievement

31. In grocery stores across town, shoppers can discover dozens of brands of bread <u>with its own unique nutritional claims</u>.

    (A) with its own unique nutritional claims

    (B) that have its own unique nutritional claims

    (C) with their own unique nutritional claims

    (D) which have their own uniquely nutritional claims

    (E) have uniquely nutritional claims of its own

32. Processed food is less nutritious <u>then restaurant food but homemade food is usually more nutritious than restaurant food</u>.

  (A) then restaurant food but homemade food is usually more nutritious than restaurant food

  (B) then restaurant food, but homemade food is usually more nutritious then restaurant food

  (C) than restaurant food; but homemade food is usually more nutritious than restaurant food

  (D) than restaurant food, and homemade food, is usually more nutritious than restaurant food

  (E) than restaurant food, and homemade food is usually more nutritious than restaurant food

33. <u>The court released their opinion</u> on the controversial case and answered questions to reporters after the trial.

  (A) The court released their opinion

  (B) The court released there opinion

  (C) The court released its opinion

  (D) The court's opinion was released

  (E) The court did release its opinion

34. Because San Francisco is located on the ocean and receives an almost constant <u>breeze, this keeps temperatures fairly mild</u>.

  (A) breeze, this keeps temperatures fairly mild

  (B) breeze: this is the reason temperatures are fairly mild

  (C) breeze is the reason why temperatures are fairly mild

  (D) breeze, keeps temperatures fairly mild

  (E) breeze, temperatures stay fairly mild

Directions: The following passage is a rough draft of a student essay. Some parts of the passage need to be rewritten in order to improve the essay.

Read the passage and select the best answer for each question that follows. Some questions ask you to improve the structure or word choice of specific sentences or parts of sentences, while others ask you to consider the organization and development of the essay. Follow the requirements of standard written English.

(1) In the book *The House On Mango Street*, there are many different characters introduced throughout the short stories. (2) Each one of them plays an important role in the story, and each explains a bit about Esperanza and her crazy life. (3) Esperanza Cordero does not like a lot of things about herself, and does not like the house she lives in. (4) Her whole family wishes for the "All-American" home, but never seems to achieve that dream. (5) In the beginning, Esperanza does not have many friends and is quite lonely however, by the end of the book, Esperanza meets many different people who surround her in their little neighborhood. (6) She soon becomes very good friends with Rachel, Lucy, Sally, and many other people in the neighborhood. (7) Each person in her neighborhood is a little different and has troubles and problems of his or her own.

(8) The Cordero family "American Dream" is to have that white house with the blue shutters and the walk way to the door, more than one bathroom, and where each kid can have their own room. (9) But sadly, by the end of the story, the family is not able to achieve this goal.

(10) I think that, even though Esperanza and her family never achieved the "American Dream," their determination will get them what they want in the end. (11) Esperanza started out to be a shy, lonely girl with no confidence, but through the time she spent living on Mango Street, she learned that there are people with lives more difficult than her own, and that she has many friends surrounding her; she just has to open her mind to new experiences, and she will see it. (12) With the proper attitude, Esperanza will find her "dream home," and never forget all of the people who made her life more interesting.

35. In the first paragraph, (sentences 1–7), the author is primarily

(A) informing the reader about Esperanza Cordero's acquaintances

(B) proving that the All-American home does not exist

(C) providing background information about the novel *The House on Mango Street* and its main character

(D) explaining the loneliness that adolescent girls feel after a move

(E) describing the problems of the families who live on Mango Street, placing emphasis on Rachel, Lucy, and Sally

36. Which of the following should be done with sentence 5 (reproduced below)?

In the beginning, Esperanza does not have many friends and is quite lonely however, by the end of the book, Esperanza meets many different people who surround her in their little neighborhood.

(A) Delete it; the point has already been made

(B) Delete " In the beginning"

(C) Move it to the end of paragraph 1 (after sentence 7)

(D) Form two sentences by placing a period after "lonely" and capitalizing "however"

(E) Insert a comma after "friends"

37. In context, which of the following is the best version of sentence 8 (reproduced below)?

The Cordero family American dream is to have that white house with the blue shutters and the walk way to the door, more than one bathroom, and where each kid can have their own room.

(A) (As it is now.)

(B) The Cordero family's American Dream includes having a white house with blue shutters, a walkway to the door, more than one bathroom, and a bedroom for each kid.

(C) A white house with blue shutters and a walkway to the door with more than one bathroom, and a bedroom for each kid is the Cordero family's American Dream.

(D) The Cordero family's, American Dream, is to have that white house with blue shutters with the walkway to the door, more than one bathroom, and where each kid can have their own room.

(E) The Cordero family American Dream is: to have a white house with blue shutters, a walkway to the door, more than one bathroom and a room for each child.

38. The primary effect of the final paragraph (sentences 10–12) is to

(A) continue the essay's tone of lighthearted humor

(B) summarize the importance of achieving the American Dream

(C) give an example of a family who succeeds in achieving the American Dream, no matter the cost

(D) use persuasion to change the reader's opinion of the Cordero family

(E) offer the author's predictions and opinions about the ending of *The House on Mango Street* and Esperanza's future

39. In context, which is the best way to revise the underlined portion of sentence 12 (reproduced below)?

With the proper attitude, Esperanza will find her "dream home," and never forget all of the people who made her life more interesting.

(A) Leave it as it is.
(B) Delete "With" at the beginning of the sentence and replace with "This is"
(C) Add the word "never" before the phrase "will find her 'dream home'"
(D) Add a semicolon after "dream home"
(E) Delete "will find" and replace with "did find"

STOP

If you finish before your time is up, check your work on this section only. You may not turn to any other section in the test.

SECTION 4

Time—25 Minutes

18 Questions

Directions: This section includes two types of questions. For questions 1–8, solve each problem and determine which is the best of the answer choices given. Fill in the corresponding circle on your answer sheet. Use any available space to solve the problems. For questions 9–18, solve each problem and fill in your answer on the answer sheet.

Notes

1. The use of a calculator is permitted.
2. All numbers are real numbers.
3. Figures that accompany problems in this test are intended to provide information useful in solving the problems. They are drawn as accurately as possible EXCEPT when it is stated in a specific problem that the figure is not drawn to scale. All figures lie in a plane unless otherwise indicated.
4. Unless otherwise specified, the domain of any function f is assumed to be the set of all real numbers x for which $f(x)$ is real number.

Reference Information

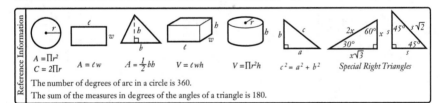

$A = \Pi r^2$
$C = 2\Pi r$ $A = \ell w$ $A = \frac{1}{2}bh$ $V = \ell wh$ $V = \Pi r^2 h$ $c^2 = a^2 + b^2$ *Special Right Triangles*

The number of degrees of arc in a circle is 360.

The sum of the measures in degrees of the angles of a triangle is 180.

---

1. If $\dfrac{2x + 3 = 8 + 3}{2x = 8}$, then x can equal which of the following?

(A) $\dfrac{1}{8}$

(B) $\dfrac{1}{4}$

(C) $\dfrac{1}{2}$

(D) 4

(E) 8

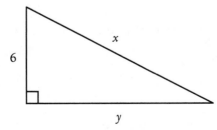

Note: Figure not drawn to scale.

2. In the right triangle above, if $x = 9$, what is the value of y?

   (A) 3
   (B) $\sqrt{45}$
   (C) $\sqrt{55}$
   (D) $\sqrt{65}$
   (E) 15

All numbers that are divisible by both 3 and 12 are also divisible by 9.

---

3. Which of the following numbers can be used to show that the statement above is FALSE?

   (A) 15
   (B) 24
   (C) 36
   (D) 72
   (E) 81

4. If $6x = 108$ and $xy = 8$, what is the value of y?

   (A) $\dfrac{2}{9}$

   (B) $\dfrac{1}{3}$

   (C) 4
   (D) 18
   (E) 32

5. A colored marble is to be chosen at random from a bag of marbles. The probability that the marble chosen will be green is $\dfrac{4}{9}$. Which of the following could NOT be the total number of marbles in the bag?

   (A) 36
   (B) 64
   (C) 72
   (D) 81
   (E) 108

6. A square has a perimeter of 32. What is the area of the square?

   (A) 8
   (B) 16
   (C) 32
   (D) 40
   (E) 64

7. Dave's daily newspaper route consists of three neighborhoods A, B, and C in that order. He delivers to Neighborhood C faster than he delivers to Neighborhood A. He delivers to Neighborhood B faster than he delivers to Neighborhood C, even though he delivers the same number of newspapers to each neighborhood. If he does not rest between neighborhoods, which of the following could be the graph of the number of newspapers he delivers during the entire time of his route?

(A)

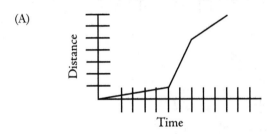

(B)

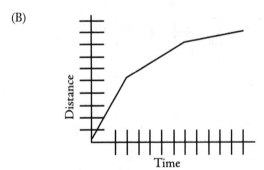

(C)

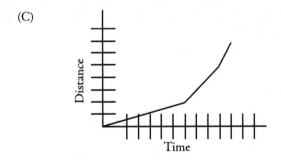

(D)

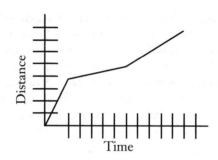

(E)

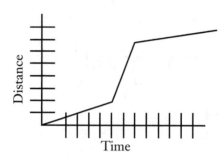

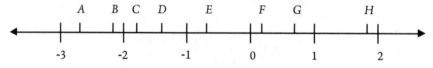

8. Which of the lettered points on the number line above could represent the result when the coordinate of point *D* is multiplied by the coordinate of point *H*?

    (A) *A*

    (B) *B*

    (C) *E*

    (D) *F*

    (E) *G*

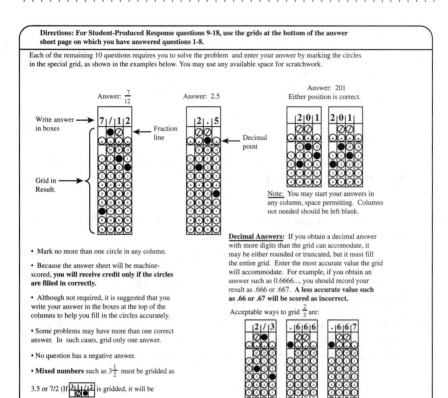

Directions: For Student-Produced Response questions 9-18, use the grids at the bottom of the answer sheet page on which you have answered questions 1-8.

Each of the remaining 10 questions requires you to solve the problem and enter your answer by marking the circles in the special grid, as shown in the examples below. You may use any available space for scratchwork.

Write answer in boxes

Fraction line

Grid in Result.

Answer: $\frac{7}{12}$

Answer: 2.5

Decimal point

Answer: 201
Either position is correct.

Note: You may start your answers in any column, space permitting. Columns not needed should be left blank.

• Mark no more than one circle in any column.

• Because the answer sheet will be machine-scored, **you will receive credit only if the circles are filled in correctly.**

• Although not required, it is suggested that you write your answer in the boxes at the top of the columns to help you fill in the circles accurately.

• Some problems may have more than one correct answer. In such cases, grid only one answer.

• No question has a negative answer.

• **Mixed numbers** such as $3\frac{1}{2}$ must be gridded as

3.5 or 7/2 (If $3|1|/|2$ is gridded, it will be

interpreted as $\frac{31}{2}$, not $3\frac{1}{2}$.)

Decimal Answers: If you obtain a decimal answer with more digits than the grid can accomodate, it may be either rounded or truncated, but it must fill the entire grid. Enter the most accurate value the grid will accommodate. For example, if you obtain an answer such as 0.6666..., you should record your result as .666 or .667. **A less accurate value such as .66 or .67 will be scored as incorrect.**

Acceptable ways to grid $\frac{2}{3}$ are:

9. If $7y - 3x = 18$ and $x = y - 8$, what is the value of y?

10. A company sold 200 bookcases in the first month of the year. After some cost-saving strategies, the company reduced its prices and the number of bookcases sold increased 30 percent from the first month to the second month. How many bookcases did the company sell the second month?

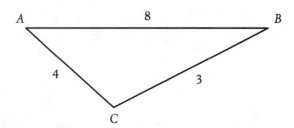

11. Each angle of $\triangle ABC$ above has the same measure as an angle in $\triangle XYZ$ (not shown). If the length of one side of $\triangle XYZ$ is 48, what is one possible perimeter of $\triangle XYZ$?

12. If r and s are integers greater than 1 and if s is a factor of both $r + 5$ and $r + 18$, what is the value of s?

13. The length of a model airplane is $\frac{4}{7}$ of the length of the actual airplane. If the length of the actual airplane is 140 feet, what is the length, in feet, of the model airplane?

14. If the number of students enrolled at a university doubles every 20 years, the number of students enrolled in the year $Y + 100$ will be how many times the number of students enrolled in the year Y?

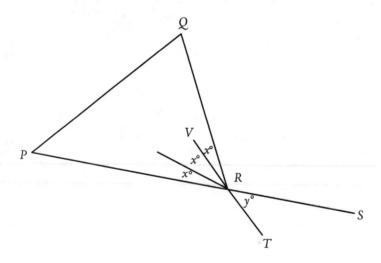

15. In the figure above, $\triangle PQR$ is equilateral and SP and TV intersect at point R. What is the value of $2x + y$?

16. Let the operations $\boxtimes$ and $\varnothing$ be defined for all real numbers a and b as follows.

$a \boxtimes b = 4ab + 3b$

$a \varnothing b = 10a + 4b$

If $2 \boxtimes (3y) = 3 \varnothing (2y)$, what is the value of y?

17. If $\frac{a}{2} = b$ and $3b = b$, what is the value of a?

18. Amanda drives to work in the morning using the highway, but returns home from work using back roads because of heavy traffic on the highway. Both routes are equal in distance. She averages 50 miles per hour going to work and 25 miles per hour returning home from work. Her total commute time to and from work is 45 minutes. How many miles does Amanda drive to work in the morning?

STOP

If you finish before your time is up, check your work on this section only. You may not turn to any other section in the test.

SECTION 5

Time—25 Minutes

25 Questions

Directions: For each question, select the best answer from among the choices listed. Fill in the corresponding circle on your answer sheet.

Each sentence below has either one or two blanks. Each blank indicates that a word has been omitted from the sentence. Beneath each sentence are five words or sets of words. Select the word or set of words that, when inserted into the sentence in place of the blank(s), best fits the context of the sentence as a whole.

---

1. Her disheveled clothing and _____ hair surprised me; Jane's appearance is normally very polished and smart.
   - (A) orderly
   - (B) capacious
   - (C) unkempt
   - (D) formal
   - (E) striking

2. Although he desperately wanted to believe that the story was a _____, Dan could not discount the mounting evidence that showed the facts were undeniably _____.
   - (A) delusion . . welcome
   - (B) reality . . compelling
   - (C) fabrication . . untrue
   - (D) deception . . false
   - (E) rumor . . valid

3. Frank believes that the _____ of a necktie, which serves no functional purpose, is reason enough to avoid wearing a suit and tie for his job.
   - (A) futility
   - (B) importance
   - (C) humility
   - (D) efficacy
   - (E) integrity

4. My inability to follow the film, even though I have already read the novel, explains why I do not like to watch films based on novels: the storyline in the film almost always _____ that of the novel.

(A) adheres to
(B) deviates from
(C) mimics
(D) endangers
(E) protracts

5. Some of the more _____ designs painted on the Indonesian artifacts at the museum must have required an exceptionally _____ artist, one capable of the painstaking creation of very elaborate details.

(A) delicate . . amateur
(B) intricate . . adroit
(C) unpretentious . . agile
(D) winsome . . spurious
(E) austere . . experienced

6. The editors of the newspaper are often criticized for the _____ of their opinion column, which frequently _____ from one side of an issue to the other.

(A) monotony . . continues
(B) ingenuity . . settles
(C) unpredictability . . scuttles
(D) inconsistency . . vacillates
(E) rigidity . . dithers

Each passage below is followed by several questions based on the content of the passage. Answer the questions based on what is either stated or implied in each passage. Be sure to read any introductory material that is provided.

Questions 7–13 are based on the following passages.

Passage 1

American literature encompasses many different and unique styles and genres. One of the most interesting of these is the Southern Gothic subgenre. As its name implies, Southern Gothic literature is reflective of life in the American South. Southern Gothic maintains
5 some of the characteristics of Gothic writing, such as plot development of the supernatural or the ironic. However, Southern Gothic does not focus on creating tension and suspense like other Gothic genres. Instead, Southern Gothic story lines examine Southern society and its underlying and often implicit social structure.

10   Southern Gothic writers generally spurn the stereotype of the
gentleman on the plantation and the glamorous Southern belle.
Instead, the authors develop characters who are sinister or reclusive
and not particularly pleasant on the surface. However, these characters usually have redeeming qualities that allow and encourage the
15   reader to empathize with their situations or dilemmas. It is through
these immoral and unhappy personalities that the Southern Gothic
writer is able to present and explore moral issues of the American
South, such as slavery and bigotry, without blatant accusations.

Many American authors are known for their Southern Gothic
20   style. Playwright Tennessee Williams (1911–1983) is among the most
celebrated of these writers. Williams's long list of plays and novels
include Pulitzer Prize winning dramas *A Streetcar Named Desire*
(1948) and *Cat on a Hot Tin Roof* (1955). It is said that many of
Williams's characters were based on his own family. For instance, it is
25   speculated that the pitiable character Laura in *The Glass Menagerie* is
modeled after Williams's mentally incapacitated sister, Rose. In the
same play, Amanda Wingfield is said to mirror Williams's own mother, a Southern belle who later turned to prostitution. Williams even
portrays himself in *Suddenly, Last Summer* and *The Glass Menagerie*.
30   His own adult life battling depression and alcoholism seemed to
mimic much of the strife and agony of his characters. Certainly,
Williams's work reflected the deep emotion and questions about
morality that Williams experienced firsthand. Williams's experiences
living in New Orleans and his family connections to the South gave
35   him plenty of inspiration. Williams used this influence to create mas-
terpieces that continue to leave lasting impressions on his audiences.

Passage 2

William Shakespeare (1564–1616) is considered the greatest
English playwright and poet of all time. Although he passed away at
age 52, Shakespeare managed to write dozens of plays that continue to
be performed worldwide. Shakespeare also wrote 154 sonnets and
40   other poems and songs. Shakespeare's various works included famous
lines such as "pomp and circumstance" and "foregone conclusion,"
which have become common everyday phrases. Many individual words
have also been attributed to Shakespeare's works. These include such
colloquialisms as "cheap," "fashionable," and "addiction."

45   Shakespeare was raised in a fairly prosperous household. His
father was a glove maker and town official. Very few detailed records
exist regarding Shakespeare's life. However, court records indicate
that Shakespeare's father was prosecuted for participating in illegal
wool trade.

50   At the age of 18, Shakespeare married Anne Hathaway, a lady
eight years his senior. Soon after their marriage, Hathaway gave birth

to two daughters and a son. Unfortunately, Shakespeare's only son
died at the tender age of twelve. Shakespeare continued working, and
by his mid-thirties, was a top actor. During this time, he also gained
55 recognition as a playwright. Shakespeare even formed his own acting
company called "the Lord Chamberlain's Men." Later, this renowned
group became known as "the King's Men."

Some controversy exists regarding the true authorship of
Shakespeare's works. It is believed by some that Shakespeare, as
60 owner of the acting company, signed his own name to all works done
by those under his employ. Despite this controversy, Shakespeare is
best known for his ability to understand and portray the vast array of
human emotions. He was a master of both tragedy and comedy and
perfected these two important dramatic genres. Shakespeare's talent
65 was as unique as it was highly regarded.

Shakespeare's works continue to entertain and inspire audiences.
Troupes all over the world, both amateur and professional, regularly
perform classic tragedies such as *Romeo and Juliet* and *Macbeth*, as well
70 as comedies such as *Much Ado About Nothing*.

7. Both passages are primarily concerned with the theme of

(A) English playwrights and writers of the American South

(B) contrasting the works of popular playwrights

(C) comparing writing poetry with writing plays

(D) examining the life of an important playwright and briefly discussing
his work

(E) American writing styles and specific American genres during the fif-
teenth century

8. Passage 1 is developed primarily through

(A) stating facts about the development of American literature

(B) presentation of an idea with a supporting example

(C) narration of an explicit literary occurrence

(D) dialogue between two main characters

(E) quotations from specific biographies

9. According to the passages, plays written by Tennessee Williams were
probably most like

(A) Shakespearean comedies

(B) accounts of historical events in the American South

(C) Shakespeare's tragedies

(D) modern day situation comedies

(E) sonnets written by William Shakespeare

10. The phrase "...Pulitzer Prize winning..." in line 22 emphasizes the

(A) recognition Williams earned with his writing

(B) politics involved in writing plays

(C) multifarious themes tackled by Tennessee Williams

(D) acceptance of the Southern Gothic sub genre

(E) popularity of the Gothic style of writing

11. The statement in lines 40–43 ("Shakespeare's various works included famous lines...") suggests that

(A) few scholars regard Shakespeare's plays as original or innovative

(B) Shakespeare's language and plays were easy for the common person to understand

(C) Shakespeare used complicated language that has only now begun to be accepted

(D) Shakespeare probably did not write many of the works attributed to him

(E) some elements of Shakespeare's works have influenced modern society

12. In Passage 2, the word "master" (line 63) refers to Shakespeare's

(A) attitude

(B) professionalism

(C) accomplishments

(D) experiences

(E) perceptiveness

13. The tone of the author of Passage 2 in lines 64–65 ("Shakespeare's talent ... regarded.") is best described as

(A) insipid

(B) satirical

(C) disrespectful

(D) impudent

(E) deferential

Questions 14–25 are based on the following passage.

Sometimes an object in nature is so rare that it escapes mention in nature books. Such is the case with the delightful Kirtland's warbler. The Kirtland's warbler is a plump, yellow-breasted bird that can be found nesting almost exclusively in the upper half of Michigan's
5 Lower Peninsula. Although this bird does migrate to the Bahamas during the winter months, Michigan is its natural habitat. Unfortunately, the Kirtland's warbler is considered an endangered species because so few of them exist. The remaining Kirtland's warblers now enjoy living among the jack pine trees located in protected
10 Michigan forests.

Ironically, the Kirtland's warbler nests on the ground and not in the jack pine trees themselves. The male warblers generally arrive back in Michigan for the summer before the female birds. Often, the male warblers return in May. When they arrive, the male warblers
15 stake out their territories and choose a nesting area. At the completion of the long journey from the Bahamas to Michigan, the female warblers begin to collect leaves and grass to build their nests. During this process, the female warbler's chosen mate provides food. The female Kirtland's warbler will lay four to five speckled eggs. The eggs
20 hatch in two to three weeks, and both the male and female warblers tend to their chicks. Five weeks after the eggs hatch, the fledglings will be able to survive on their own.

Kirtland's warblers are extremely fastidious about their habitat. This is most likely why these birds have become endangered.
25 Kirtland's warblers will generally only be found in stands of jack pine trees that are 80 acres or larger. Kirtland's warblers also prefer to be in areas containing "Grayling sand." Grayling sand is fine and powdery, and prevents the flooding of nests because water seeps through the sand very quickly. This is important because the warblers' nests are
30 built on or near the ground. Grayling sand also supports the type of plant material that the warblers prefer for their diets and nest building.

If not for ongoing human conservation efforts, these special habitats and this rare bird would probably not exist today. As logging subsided in Michigan and natural fires increased, the jack pine popula-
35 tion increased dramatically. The heat created by the fires allowed the cones of the jack pine to release their seeds. However, in the early 1900s, natural fires were suppressed by new forest management policies, and the jack pine forests quickly diminished. This greatly reduced the number of nesting areas available for the Kirtland's war-
40 bler.

To correct this problem, jack pine areas are currently managed on a rotational basis. This ensures an appropriate number of nesting sites. These nesting sites encourage the warblers to return and reproduce annually. The protected jack pine forests are also home to
45 white-tailed deer, black bear, the Eastern bluebird, the upland sandpiper, and the snowshoe hare. Unfortunately for the Kirtland's warbler, the brown-headed cowbird is also prevalent in these woods. Cowbirds are well known for their tendency to steal the nests of other birds by taking out the other bird's eggs and secretly laying
50 cowbird eggs in their place. When the chicks are hatched, the warblers will raise the young cowbirds as their own. This, of course, negatively impacts the population of the Kirtland's warbler. Studies have shown that when a cowbird lays one egg in a warbler's nest, generally only one to three warbler chicks will survive. If two or more cowbird
55 chicks survive in a single warbler nest, none of the warblers will

survive. To combat this dilemma, government programs have been established to trap and eradicate cowbirds that attempt to nest in the warblers' habitat. These efforts have greatly improved the survival and proliferation of the Kirtland's warbler over the past few decades.

60   The male Kirtland's warbler sings a loud, persistent, and melodic song that can be heard up to a quarter mile away. Counting these songs becomes important during mating season, because scientists trying to save the warbler from extinction use this as a census to determine the annual population and to ensure that efforts to save the

65 bird are successful.

Debates periodically surface over whether to replace the robin with the Kirtland's warbler as Michigan's state bird. Admirers of the Kirtland's warbler argue that it is strictly a Michigan bird. Supporters of the robin point out that the Kirtland's warbler is only present in

70 Michigan for, at most, half of the year. Perhaps this debate will continue until more Michigan residents have a chance to see the beautiful and somewhat exotic bird known as the Kirtland's warbler that calls Michigan home.

14. The first paragraph of the passage implies that the author is

    (A) disinterested in the fate of Kirtland's warbler

    (B) a proponent of Kirtland's warbler

    (C) a native of Michigan

    (D) reluctant to discuss the migratory patterns of Kirtland's warbler

    (E) annoyed that Kirtland's warbler is not mentioned in nature books

15. Lines 21-22 indicate that the word "fledgling" most likely refers to

    (A) Kirtland's warbler eggs

    (B) Kirtland's warbler nests

    (C) Kirtland's warbler chicks

    (D) Kirtland's warbler habitat

    (E) Kirtland's warbler food

16. The underlying sentiment in lines 23–24 ("Kirtland's warblers...endangered.") reflect the author's

    (A) familiarity with the Kirtland's warbler's characteristics

    (B) distress about the programs assisting the Kirtland's warbler

    (C) disapproval for attempts to save the Kirtland's warbler from extinction

    (D) regard for the jack pine tree stands of Michigan

    (E) reverence for bird enthusiasts and wildlife experts

17. In lines 27–31, the author suggests that Grayling sand is

    (A) non-porous

    (B) ideal for Kirtland's warblers

    (C) deficient in important nutrients

    (D) a hostile environment for songbirds

    (E) imported

18. The author's attitude toward human conservation efforts is primarily one of

(A) disappointment at their failure

(B) disapproval of their tactics

(C) satisfaction because of their success

(D) regret for their many setbacks

(E) frustration at their inconsistency

19. In the sentence beginning in line 36 ("However, in the early...for the Kirtland's warbler"), the author suggests that

(A) the forest service wanted to destroy the Kirtland's warbler

(B) forest fires destroyed the jack pine trees

(C) new forest fire controls were harmful to the Kirtland's warbler

(D) Kirtland's warblers chose other habitats once the jack pine trees started disappearing

(E) the jack pine tree reproduces unlike any other tree

20. In line 47, "prevalent" most nearly means

(A) unheard of

(B) predatory

(C) obscure

(D) well protected

(E) commonly occurring

21. The cowbird is accused of stealing (line 48) because it

(A) uses Kirtland's warbler nests for its own eggs

(B) removes the Kirtland's warbler nests from the trees

(C) takes over the jack pine forests

(D) destroys the Kirtland's warbler nests

(E) raises Kirtland's warbler chicks as its own

22. The sentence "Studies have shown that when a cowbird lays one egg in a warbler's nest, generally only one to three warbler chicks will survive." (lines 52–54) emphasizes the idea that

(A) Kirtland's warblers are unable to survive in areas that contain cowbirds

(B) Kirtland's warbler enthusiasts dislike cowbirds

(C) cowbirds should be destroyed in order to promote the propagation of Kirtland's warblers

(D) cowbirds have the ability to affect the Kirtland's warbler population

(E) Kirtland's warbler chicks will always survive if no cowbird eggs are present in their nest

23. The statement in line 51 ("This, of course,...") primarily serves as a warning about

    (A) the impact that human intervention can have on a species' survival

    (B) government controls over natural occurrences

    (C) the lack of information about the interaction between the warblers and cowbirds

    (D) the real dangers that the cowbird poses to the warbler's survival

    (E) protecting natural habitats for birds in general

24. The "loud, persistent, and melodic song" (lines 60–61) is used primarily to indicate

    (A) an important characteristic of the male Kirtland's warbler

    (B) an unnecessary detail about Kirtland's warbler

    (C) the reason for the possible extinction of Kirtland's warbler

    (D) consequences resulting from the extinction of Kirtland's warbler

    (E) the means by which the male Kirtland's warbler attracts a mate

25. It can be inferred from the final paragraph that

    (A) Kirtland's warbler is more popular than the robin

    (B) Kirtland's warbler will soon replace the robin as Michigan's state bird

    (C) fewer residents of Michigan have seen the Kirtland's warbler than have seen a robin

    (D) admirers of Kirtland's warbler do not particularly like robins

    (E) many supporters of the robin have also seen the Kirtland's warbler in its native habitat

---

STOP

If you finish before your time is up, check your work on this section only. You may not turn to any other section in the test.

PSAT PRACTICE TEST 2
ANSWER SHEET

For each new section, begin with number 1. Some sections have fewer than 40 questions-
leave the rest of the answer spaces blank. Completely erase any unnecessary marks.

SECTION 1

1 Ⓐ Ⓑ Ⓒ Ⓓ Ⓔ 11 Ⓐ Ⓑ Ⓒ Ⓓ Ⓔ 21 Ⓐ Ⓑ Ⓒ Ⓓ Ⓔ 31 Ⓐ Ⓑ Ⓒ Ⓓ Ⓔ
2 Ⓐ Ⓑ Ⓒ Ⓓ Ⓔ 12 Ⓐ Ⓑ Ⓒ Ⓓ Ⓔ 22 Ⓐ Ⓑ Ⓒ Ⓓ Ⓔ 32 Ⓐ Ⓑ Ⓒ Ⓓ Ⓔ
3 Ⓐ Ⓑ Ⓒ Ⓓ Ⓔ 13 Ⓐ Ⓑ Ⓒ Ⓓ Ⓔ 23 Ⓐ Ⓑ Ⓒ Ⓓ Ⓔ 33 Ⓐ Ⓑ Ⓒ Ⓓ Ⓔ
4 Ⓐ Ⓑ Ⓒ Ⓓ Ⓔ 14 Ⓐ Ⓑ Ⓒ Ⓓ Ⓔ 24 Ⓐ Ⓑ Ⓒ Ⓓ Ⓔ 34 Ⓐ Ⓑ Ⓒ Ⓓ Ⓔ
5 Ⓐ Ⓑ Ⓒ Ⓓ Ⓔ 15 Ⓐ Ⓑ Ⓒ Ⓓ Ⓔ 25 Ⓐ Ⓑ Ⓒ Ⓓ Ⓔ 35 Ⓐ Ⓑ Ⓒ Ⓓ Ⓔ
6 Ⓐ Ⓑ Ⓒ Ⓓ Ⓔ 16 Ⓐ Ⓑ Ⓒ Ⓓ Ⓔ 26 Ⓐ Ⓑ Ⓒ Ⓓ Ⓔ 36 Ⓐ Ⓑ Ⓒ Ⓓ Ⓔ
7 Ⓐ Ⓑ Ⓒ Ⓓ Ⓔ 17 Ⓐ Ⓑ Ⓒ Ⓓ Ⓔ 27 Ⓐ Ⓑ Ⓒ Ⓓ Ⓔ 37 Ⓐ Ⓑ Ⓒ Ⓓ Ⓔ
8 Ⓐ Ⓑ Ⓒ Ⓓ Ⓔ 18 Ⓐ Ⓑ Ⓒ Ⓓ Ⓔ 28 Ⓐ Ⓑ Ⓒ Ⓓ Ⓔ 38 Ⓐ Ⓑ Ⓒ Ⓓ Ⓔ
9 Ⓐ Ⓑ Ⓒ Ⓓ Ⓔ 19 Ⓐ Ⓑ Ⓒ Ⓓ Ⓔ 29 Ⓐ Ⓑ Ⓒ Ⓓ Ⓔ 39 Ⓐ Ⓑ Ⓒ Ⓓ Ⓔ
10 Ⓐ Ⓑ Ⓒ Ⓓ Ⓔ 20 Ⓐ Ⓑ Ⓒ Ⓓ Ⓔ 30 Ⓐ Ⓑ Ⓒ Ⓓ Ⓔ 40 Ⓐ Ⓑ Ⓒ Ⓓ Ⓔ

SECTION 2

1 Ⓐ Ⓑ Ⓒ Ⓓ Ⓔ 11 Ⓐ Ⓑ Ⓒ Ⓓ Ⓔ 21 Ⓐ Ⓑ Ⓒ Ⓓ Ⓔ 31 Ⓐ Ⓑ Ⓒ Ⓓ Ⓔ
2 Ⓐ Ⓑ Ⓒ Ⓓ Ⓔ 12 Ⓐ Ⓑ Ⓒ Ⓓ Ⓔ 22 Ⓐ Ⓑ Ⓒ Ⓓ Ⓔ 32 Ⓐ Ⓑ Ⓒ Ⓓ Ⓔ
3 Ⓐ Ⓑ Ⓒ Ⓓ Ⓔ 13 Ⓐ Ⓑ Ⓒ Ⓓ Ⓔ 23 Ⓐ Ⓑ Ⓒ Ⓓ Ⓔ 33 Ⓐ Ⓑ Ⓒ Ⓓ Ⓔ
4 Ⓐ Ⓑ Ⓒ Ⓓ Ⓔ 14 Ⓐ Ⓑ Ⓒ Ⓓ Ⓔ 24 Ⓐ Ⓑ Ⓒ Ⓓ Ⓔ 34 Ⓐ Ⓑ Ⓒ Ⓓ Ⓔ
5 Ⓐ Ⓑ Ⓒ Ⓓ Ⓔ 15 Ⓐ Ⓑ Ⓒ Ⓓ Ⓔ 25 Ⓐ Ⓑ Ⓒ Ⓓ Ⓔ 35 Ⓐ Ⓑ Ⓒ Ⓓ Ⓔ
6 Ⓐ Ⓑ Ⓒ Ⓓ Ⓔ 16 Ⓐ Ⓑ Ⓒ Ⓓ Ⓔ 26 Ⓐ Ⓑ Ⓒ Ⓓ Ⓔ 36 Ⓐ Ⓑ Ⓒ Ⓓ Ⓔ
7 Ⓐ Ⓑ Ⓒ Ⓓ Ⓔ 17 Ⓐ Ⓑ Ⓒ Ⓓ Ⓔ 27 Ⓐ Ⓑ Ⓒ Ⓓ Ⓔ 37 Ⓐ Ⓑ Ⓒ Ⓓ Ⓔ
8 Ⓐ Ⓑ Ⓒ Ⓓ Ⓔ 18 Ⓐ Ⓑ Ⓒ Ⓓ Ⓔ 28 Ⓐ Ⓑ Ⓒ Ⓓ Ⓔ 38 Ⓐ Ⓑ Ⓒ Ⓓ Ⓔ
9 Ⓐ Ⓑ Ⓒ Ⓓ Ⓔ 19 Ⓐ Ⓑ Ⓒ Ⓓ Ⓔ 29 Ⓐ Ⓑ Ⓒ Ⓓ Ⓔ 39 Ⓐ Ⓑ Ⓒ Ⓓ Ⓔ
10 Ⓐ Ⓑ Ⓒ Ⓓ Ⓔ 20 Ⓐ Ⓑ Ⓒ Ⓓ Ⓔ 30 Ⓐ Ⓑ Ⓒ Ⓓ Ⓔ 40 Ⓐ Ⓑ Ⓒ Ⓓ Ⓔ

SECTION 3

1 Ⓐ Ⓑ Ⓒ Ⓓ Ⓔ 11 Ⓐ Ⓑ Ⓒ Ⓓ Ⓔ 21 Ⓐ Ⓑ Ⓒ Ⓓ Ⓔ 31 Ⓐ Ⓑ Ⓒ Ⓓ Ⓔ
2 Ⓐ Ⓑ Ⓒ Ⓓ Ⓔ 12 Ⓐ Ⓑ Ⓒ Ⓓ Ⓔ 22 Ⓐ Ⓑ Ⓒ Ⓓ Ⓔ 32 Ⓐ Ⓑ Ⓒ Ⓓ Ⓔ
3 Ⓐ Ⓑ Ⓒ Ⓓ Ⓔ 13 Ⓐ Ⓑ Ⓒ Ⓓ Ⓔ 23 Ⓐ Ⓑ Ⓒ Ⓓ Ⓔ 33 Ⓐ Ⓑ Ⓒ Ⓓ Ⓔ
4 Ⓐ Ⓑ Ⓒ Ⓓ Ⓔ 14 Ⓐ Ⓑ Ⓒ Ⓓ Ⓔ 24 Ⓐ Ⓑ Ⓒ Ⓓ Ⓔ 34 Ⓐ Ⓑ Ⓒ Ⓓ Ⓔ
5 Ⓐ Ⓑ Ⓒ Ⓓ Ⓔ 15 Ⓐ Ⓑ Ⓒ Ⓓ Ⓔ 25 Ⓐ Ⓑ Ⓒ Ⓓ Ⓔ 35 Ⓐ Ⓑ Ⓒ Ⓓ Ⓔ
6 Ⓐ Ⓑ Ⓒ Ⓓ Ⓔ 16 Ⓐ Ⓑ Ⓒ Ⓓ Ⓔ 26 Ⓐ Ⓑ Ⓒ Ⓓ Ⓔ 36 Ⓐ Ⓑ Ⓒ Ⓓ Ⓔ
7 Ⓐ Ⓑ Ⓒ Ⓓ Ⓔ 17 Ⓐ Ⓑ Ⓒ Ⓓ Ⓔ 27 Ⓐ Ⓑ Ⓒ Ⓓ Ⓔ 37 Ⓐ Ⓑ Ⓒ Ⓓ Ⓔ
8 Ⓐ Ⓑ Ⓒ Ⓓ Ⓔ 18 Ⓐ Ⓑ Ⓒ Ⓓ Ⓔ 28 Ⓐ Ⓑ Ⓒ Ⓓ Ⓔ 38 Ⓐ Ⓑ Ⓒ Ⓓ Ⓔ
9 Ⓐ Ⓑ Ⓒ Ⓓ Ⓔ 19 Ⓐ Ⓑ Ⓒ Ⓓ Ⓔ 29 Ⓐ Ⓑ Ⓒ Ⓓ Ⓔ 39 Ⓐ Ⓑ Ⓒ Ⓓ Ⓔ
10 Ⓐ Ⓑ Ⓒ Ⓓ Ⓔ 20 Ⓐ Ⓑ Ⓒ Ⓓ Ⓔ 30 Ⓐ Ⓑ Ⓒ Ⓓ Ⓔ 40 Ⓐ Ⓑ Ⓒ Ⓓ Ⓔ

For each new section, begin with number 1. Some sections have fewer than 40 questions-leave the rest of the answer spaces blank. Completely erase any unnecessary marks.

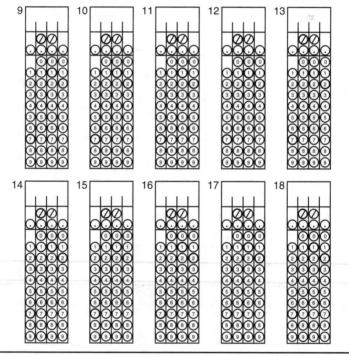

CAUTION Only use the answer grids below for Section 4 if you are instructed to do so in the corresponding test.

Student-Produced Responses

ANY ANSWERS WRITTEN IN THE BOXES ABOVE THE CIRCLES WILL NOT COUNT TOWARDS YOUR SCORE. ONLY ANSWERS FILLED IN ON THE GRID WILL BE SCORED.

For each new section, begin with number 1. Some sections have fewer than 40 questions-leave the rest of the answer spaces blank. Completely erase any unnecessary marks.

SECTION 5

1 ⒶⒷⒸⒹⒺ	11 ⒶⒷⒸⒹⒺ	21 ⒶⒷⒸⒹⒺ	31 ⒶⒷⒸⒹⒺ
2 ⒶⒷⒸⒹⒺ	12 ⒶⒷⒸⒹⒺ	22 ⒶⒷⒸⒹⒺ	32 ⒶⒷⒸⒹⒺ
3 ⒶⒷⒸⒹⒺ	13 ⒶⒷⒸⒹⒺ	23 ⒶⒷⒸⒹⒺ	33 ⒶⒷⒸⒹⒺ
4 ⒶⒷⒸⒹⒺ	14 ⒶⒷⒸⒹⒺ	24 ⒶⒷⒸⒹⒺ	34 ⒶⒷⒸⒹⒺ
5 ⒶⒷⒸⒹⒺ	15 ⒶⒷⒸⒹⒺ	25 ⒶⒷⒸⒹⒺ	35 ⒶⒷⒸⒹⒺ
6 ⒶⒷⒸⒹⒺ	16 ⒶⒷⒸⒹⒺ	26 ⒶⒷⒸⒹⒺ	36 ⒶⒷⒸⒹⒺ
7 ⒶⒷⒸⒹⒺ	17 ⒶⒷⒸⒹⒺ	27 ⒶⒷⒸⒹⒺ	37 ⒶⒷⒸⒹⒺ
8 ⒶⒷⒸⒹⒺ	18 ⒶⒷⒸⒹⒺ	28 ⒶⒷⒸⒹⒺ	38 ⒶⒷⒸⒹⒺ
9 ⒶⒷⒸⒹⒺ	19 ⒶⒷⒸⒹⒺ	29 ⒶⒷⒸⒹⒺ	39 ⒶⒷⒸⒹⒺ
10 ⒶⒷⒸⒹⒺ	20 ⒶⒷⒸⒹⒺ	30 ⒶⒷⒸⒹⒺ	40 ⒶⒷⒸⒹⒺ

Answer Key 2

The Scoring Guide included in Appendix D should only be used to approximate your test score. Your focus should be on reading the explanations for each of the questions that you missed, and working toward strengthening your weak areas.

PRACTICE TEST 2 ANSWER KEY

<table>
<tr><td colspan="2" align="center">SECTION 1
Critical Reading</td><td colspan="2" align="center">SECTION 2
Math</td></tr>
<tr><td>1. B</td><td>13. B</td><td>1. A</td><td>11. C</td></tr>
<tr><td>2. D</td><td>14. C</td><td>2. B</td><td>12. D</td></tr>
<tr><td>3. A</td><td>15. A</td><td>3. E</td><td>13. B</td></tr>
<tr><td>4. B</td><td>16. D</td><td>4. D</td><td>14. C</td></tr>
<tr><td>5. C</td><td>17. D</td><td>5. C</td><td>15. B</td></tr>
<tr><td>6. C</td><td>18. A</td><td>6. C</td><td>16. C</td></tr>
<tr><td>7. B</td><td>19. D</td><td>7. C</td><td>17. C</td></tr>
<tr><td>8. A</td><td>20. A</td><td>8. B</td><td>18. D</td></tr>
<tr><td>9. E</td><td>21. B</td><td>9. C</td><td>19. D</td></tr>
<tr><td>10. D</td><td>22. C</td><td>10. A</td><td>20. A</td></tr>
<tr><td>11. B</td><td>23. B</td><td></td><td></td></tr>
<tr><td>12. D</td><td></td><td></td><td></td></tr>
</table>

SECTION 3
Writing Skills

1. E	21. D
2. D	22. C
3. C	23. A
4. A	24. B
5. E	25. D
6. A	26. E
7. E	27. C
8. D	28. C
9. D	29. A
10. B	30. E
11. C	31. C
12. B	32. E
13. C	33. C
14. A	34. E
15. B	35. C
16. D	36. D
17. D	37. B
18. C	38. E
19. B	39. A
20. C	

SECTION 4
Math

1. D
2. B
3. B
4. A
5. B
6. E
7. A
8. A
9. $-\frac{3}{2}$ or -1.5
10. 260
11. 90, 180, or 240
12. 13
13. 80
14. 32
15. 100
16. $\frac{6}{5}$ or 1.2
17. 0
18. 12.5

SECTION 5
Critical Reading

1. C	11. E	21. A
2. E	12. C	22. D
3. A	13. E	23. D
4. B	14. B	24. A
5. B	15. C	25. C
6. D	16. A	
7. D	17. B	
8. B	18. C	
9. C	19. C	
10. A	20. E	

SECTION 1—Critical Reading

Sentence Completion (Questions 1–7)

1. **The best answer is B.** The information following the blank helps to define the word that should go in the blank. The word "myopic" means "short-sighted or near-sighted." Both "perceptive" and "discerning" have meanings that are opposite to "myopic," so answer choices C and D should be eliminated. Answer choice A, "ambiguous," and answer choice E, "mindful," do not fit the context of the sentence.

2. **The best answer is D.** The word "although" at the beginning of the sentence suggests that Frank appeared to be one way, but actually felt another way. To determine the correct answer, look at the second blank, which is followed by descriptive information. A "daunting venture" would most likely make someone "terrified," and "confident" appropriately contrasts "terrified." Answer choice A does not fit the context of the sentence. Answer choice B could work in this sentence, but "complacent" and "hesitant" are not as effective. Answer choices C and E do not fit the context of the sentence.

3. **The best answer is A.** The information following the first blank helps to define the word that should go in the blank. People who indulge in "wild behavior" could lead either "chaotic" or "boisterous" lives. "Temperate" and "moderate" do not describe such people, so eliminate answer choices B and C. Now look at the second blank, which should be filled with a word that has a meaning similar to "wild." Neither "leisurely" nor "unpretentious" will work in the second blank, so eliminate answer choices D and E.

4. **The best answer is B.** Because of the bad weather and Jonathan's inexperience, you can conclude that Jonathan's actions were "bold," but also "reckless." Only "brash" means both "bold" and "reckless." Answer choice A suggests intelligent and practical behavior, and answer choice C does not fit the context of the sentence. Answer choices D and E are related favorably to "bravery," but are not associated with "recklessness."

5. **The best answer is C.** The phrase "get used to," which is the same as "to adapt" or "to adjust," helps to define the word that should go in the second blank. To determine the word that should go in the first blank, notice that the sentence states that hikers should "climb slowly"

so that the body can "get used to the conditions." Because the sentence suggests climbing "very slowly" to be safe, you can assume that "quickly ascending" is not safe and has an opposite, or harmful, effect on the body. "Damaging," "noxious," and "deleterious" all mean "harmful," but only "acclimate" means to "get used to."

6. **The best answer is C.** The word that fills in the blank must be similar to the adjective "secretive" and must be a noun. "Furtiveness" relates to a tendency to be "secretive or stealthy" and best fits the context of the sentence. Answer choices A, B, D, and E are all opposite in meaning to "secretive."

7. **The best answer is B.** The word "though" at the beginning of the sentence introduces the contradiction in the sentence: Pasta is considered to be Italian, but actually might have come from China. The word that fills the blank must indicate that pasta is a "representative" dish of Italy. "Quintessential" means "most typical" or describes the "perfect example or representation" of a certain quality or category. "Regular," which means "expected" or "usual," almost works in this sentence, but does not effectively convey the intended contrast. The remaining answer choices do not fit the context of the sentence.

Reading Comprehension (Questions 8–21)

8. **The best answer is A.** The passage states that, in "Mexico today," piñatas are used "for many different events," including a ceremony in which a "piñata game is played." The passage continues to describe the modern-day use of piñatas in the United States. Therefore, answer choice A is best. The passage mentions the use of piñatas to "honor a particular person," "during religious holidays," and "to bring good luck," but only in the description of the history of piñatas, not in the use of modern day piñatas. Likewise, answer choice E is not supported by the passage.

9. **The best answer is E.** The word "murky" is generally used to describe something that is "unclear" or "vague." Here, it is used to suggest that the history of the piñata is not very well known. Answer choices B, C, and D include words that are opposite in meaning to "murky." Answer choice A is not supported by the context of the passage.

10. **The best answer is D.** Paragraph 2 clearly indicates that Chinese piñatas were "filled with seeds" that, once "spilled," were "burned," and "the ashes of the seeds were kept." Answer choices A, C, and E

are not mentioned in the passage. The Chinese saved the ashes, not the seeds, for good luck, so answer choice B is incorrect.

11. **The best answer is B.** The context of the sentence indicates that after the piñata was introduced in Europe, it quickly became associated with religious ceremonies and other celebratory events. "Swiftly" is a synonym of "quickly." Answer choices A, C, D, and E are not supported by the passage.

12. **The best answer is D.** The passage states that onlookers generally offer suggestions regarding the location of the piñata, but that they actually most enjoy watching people swing the bat and miss the piñata. The tone of this sentence is best described as "lighthearted" because the onlookers are playing a sort of joke. Answer choices A, B, C, and E are not supported by the context of the passage.

13. **The best answer is B.** The author's discussion of American piñatas focuses on how the use of a "baseball bat" and a routine similar to "Pin the Tail on the Donkey" adds a humorous element to the game because the "audience most enjoys watching the blindfolded person swing mightily at nothing but thin air." Therefore, answer choice B is best. Although the passage mentions the remaining answer choices in the paragraph, none of them are the focus of the author's discussion.

14. **The best answer is C.** This passage emphasizes that many different types of piñatas were used throughout history, including "animal figures...with colorful paper" in China, piñatas in the "shape of a star" in Europe, "clay pots...unadorned or decorated with colorful ribbons and paper" in Italy, "clay or papier-mâché" in Mexico. The passage also states that "American piñatas come in almost every shape and design imaginable." Therefore, a museum's exhibition of piñatas would be "highly diverse and colorful" because so many different varieties of piñatas exist. Answer choices A, B, D, and E are not supported by the passage.

15. **The best answer is A.** The main theme of the passage is the use of piñatas in religious ceremonies and various other celebrations. Therefore, it makes sense that the author's view would include the use of piñatas at almost any type of celebration. Answer choices B, C, D, and E are not supported by information in the passage.

16. **The best answer is D.** Almost all the information given in this passage directly pertains to or is related to the activity of "geocaching." Therefore, the main purpose of the passage is to describe this activity. The passage states that the principles of GPS must be understood for effective "geocaching," but does not actually explain the principles

behind GPS. The passage also mentions other uses of GPS and the cost of a GPS device, but neither is the primary purpose of the passage. Although the Department of Defense is credited for launching the satellites, the passage does not focus on this fact or "how satellites...assist the Department of Defense." Therefore, you should eliminate answer choices A, B, C, and E.

17. **The best answer is D.** The passage indicates that the geocacher will receive a "trivial prize," which suggests that the prize will be small or unimportant. The word "alleged" used before the word "treasure" indicates that the treasure is not a real treasure in the true sense of the meaning of the word treasure. This best supports answer choice D.

18. **The best answer is A.** The passage states that GPS is a "...complex system...," and that "...numerous satellites are involved in broadcasting..." the signals. This suggests that GPS is sophisticated and elaborate. Answer choices B, C, D, and E are not supported by the passage.

19. **The best answer is D.** As it is used in the context of the passage, the word "applications" refers to the different "purposes" or "uses" of the GPS. Answer choices A, B, C, and E could be used as synonyms of "applications," but they do not fit the context of the passage.

20. **The best answer is A.** The phrase "first and foremost..." emphasizes the importance of the rule that follows. "Foreboding" signifies some kind of warning, which does not describe the purpose of the lines mentioned in the question, so eliminate answer choice B. Likewise, answer choices C, D, and E are not supported by the passage.

21. **The best answer is B.** The author states that "geocaching" is "becoming a popular pastime." To support this statement, the author should include information about the number of people actually playing the game or the number of currently active "geocaches." "Geocaching" can be done anywhere in the world, and the location of caches most likely changes, so the exact location of caches in the United States is not relevant, nor does location have anything to do with the author's conclusion that geocaching is becoming a popular pastime. Eliminate answer choice A. Likewise, answer choices C, D, and E do not support the author's conclusion.

22. **The best answer is C.** The passage indicates that geocachers will likely have to travel extensively and will encounter "numerous obstacles" along the way. This best supports the idea that geocachers are adventure seekers. Answer choices A, B, D, and E are not supported by information in the passage.

23. **The best answer is B.** The passage states that a "topographical map might help reveal any boggy areas where proper footwear is essential…" In other words, the author suggests that topographical maps show various physical properties of the land. Answer choices A, C, D, and E are not mentioned in relation to topographical maps.

SECTION 2—Math

1. The correct answer is A. The first step is to solve for x in the first expression.

➤ $5x + 7 = 27$

➤ $5x = 20$

➤ $x = 4$

Now, substitute 4 for x in the expression $3x - 9$.

➤ $3(4) - 9 = 3$.

2. The correct answer is B. Based on information given in the problem, the minimum number of seats that could be in the gymnasium is 6×100, or 600 seats. The maximum number of seats that could be in the gymnasium is $6 \times 175 = 1,050$ seats. The correct answer must be a number between 600 and 1,050. Answer choice A is too small, and answer choices C, D, and E are too large.

3. The correct answer is E. To calculate the length of each of the line segments, use the Pythagorean theorem, $a^2 + b^2 = c^2$.

➤ Answer choice A: given $AC = 8$, $AX = \sqrt{(6^2 + 8^2)}$

➤ $\sqrt{(36 + 64)} = \sqrt{100} = 10$. Line segment $AX = 10$.

➤ Answer choice B: given $BC = 3$, $BX = \sqrt{(6^2 + 3^2)}$

➤ $\sqrt{(36 + 9)} = \sqrt{45} = 3\sqrt{5}$. Line segment $BX = 3\sqrt{5}$, which is approximately equal to 6.7.

➤ Answer choice C: $CX = 6$

➤ Answer choice D: given $CD = 4$, $DX = \sqrt{(6^2 + 4^2)}$

➤ $\sqrt{(36 + 16)} = \sqrt{52} = 2\sqrt{13}$. Line segment $DX = 2\sqrt{13}$, which is approximately equal to 7.2.

➤ Answer choice E: given $CE = 11$, $EX = \sqrt{(6^2 + 11^2)}$

➤ $\sqrt{(36 + 121)} = \sqrt{147} = 7\sqrt{3}$. Line segment $EX = 7\sqrt{3}$, which is approximately equal to 12.12.

Line segment EX has the greatest length.

4. The correct answer is D. To answer this question, look closely at the graph. At the end of 2002, Jason had 5 trophies, and at the end of 2003, he had 8 trophies. Thus, he must have won three trophies during 2003.

5. The correct answer is C. You are given that the average of x and y is 16. Therefore, $(x + y) \div 2 = 16$, which means that $x + y = 32$. It is not important to know what x and y equal individually, only to know that their sum is 32. Given that the average of x, y, and z is 22, then $(x + y + z) \div 3 = 22$, and $x + y + z = 66$. Since $x + y = 32$, then $32 + z = 66$, and $z = 34$.

6. The correct answer is C. To solve this problem, first find the area of the larger square. The formula for the area of a square is $A = s^2$. The length of each side is given as 8, so the area is $A = 8 \times 8$, or 64. The area of each of the smaller squares is $A = (x)(x)$, or x^2. Since you are asked for the area of the non-shaded region, subtract the area of the two smaller squares $(2x^2)$ from the area of the larger square (64). Thus, the area of the non-shaded region is $64 - 2x^2$, answer choice C.

7. The correct answer is C. Since $pqrs = 24$, none of these variables can equal 0. If one of them did equal 0, the product would be 0, not 24. Thus, eliminate answer choices D and E. It is possible for both p and q to be greater than 0, but neither must be greater than 0, so eliminate answer choices A and B. Because you are given that $prst = 0$ and you have determined that p, q, r, and s cannot equal 0, t must equal 0.

8. The correct answer is B. Given that the total number of points scored is 72, you can determine how many points were scored in each of the quarters, as follows.

> ➤ In the first quarter, one-eighth of the points were scored;
> $\left(\dfrac{1}{8}\right)72 = 9$

> ➤ In the second quarter, one-third of the points were scored;
> $\left(\dfrac{1}{3}\right)72 = 24$

> ➤ In the third quarter, 23 points were scored.

> ➤ Therefore, in the fourth quarter, $72 - 9 - 23 - 24$, or 16 points were scored.

9. **The correct answer is C.** The first step in solving this problem is to recognize that 27 can be rewritten as 3^3. Therefore, you can rewrite the equation as $3^{6x} = 3^{3(4x - 2)}$. Now, because the base is the same (3), you can set the exponents equal to each other and solve for x, as follows:

> ➤ $6x = 3(4x - 2)$

> ➤ $6x = 12x - 6$

> ➤ $-6x = -6$

> ➤ $x = 1$

10. **The correct answer is A.** Set up the equation based on the statement given. "9 more than 5 times a certain number" translates to $9 + 5x$; "3 less than twice the number" translates to $2x - 3$.

> ➤ $9 + 5x = 2x - 3$

> ➤ $9 + 3x = -3$

> ➤ $3x = -12$

> ➤ $x = -4$

11. **The correct answer is C.** The formula for the circumference of a circle is $C = 2\pi r$, where r is the radius, or $C = \pi d$, where d is the diameter. You are given that the circumference of the circle is 90π; therefore, $90\pi = \pi d$, and $d = 90$. If the diameter of the circle is 90, the diameter of each of the three small semicircles is $90 \div 3$, or 30. The diameter is twice as long as the radius, so the radius of each of the three small semicircles is $30 \div 2$, or 15. Because the circumference of each of the semicircles is equal to half the circumference of a full circle, the formula for the circumference of a semicircle is $\frac{1}{2}(2\pi r)$. Thus, each of the semicircles has a circumference of $\frac{1}{2}[2\pi(15)]$, or $\frac{1}{2}(30\pi)$, which equals 15π. The length of the curve is the sum of the circumferences of the three small semicircles: $15\pi + 15\pi + 15\pi$, or 45π, answer choice C.

12. **The correct answer is D.** Because the function is linear, the difference between each term and its succeeding term is equal. Thus, $b - 27 = 27 - a$. Solve for $a + b$.

> ➤ $b - 27 = 27 - a$; add a to both sides

> ➤ $a + b - 27 = 27$; add 27 to both sides

> ➤ $a + b = 54$

13. **The correct answer is B**. To solve this problem, work through the answer choices, replacing the $\oplus$ symbol with the quantity in each answer choice. The answer choice that satisfies the equation will be the correct answer.

➤ Answer choice A: First, convert $5\frac{2}{3}$ into the improper fraction $\frac{17}{3}$.

➤ $\dfrac{4\left(3+\frac{2}{3}\right)}{3}=\dfrac{17}{3}$; multiply both sides by 3 to get rid of 3 in the denominator.

➤ $4\left(3+\frac{2}{3}\right)=17$; convert $3\frac{2}{3}$ into the improper fraction $\frac{11}{3}$.

➤ $4\left(\frac{11}{3}\right)$ does not equal 17, so eliminate answer choice A.

➤ Answer choice B: First, convert $5\frac{2}{3}$ into the improper fraction $\frac{17}{3}$.

➤ $\dfrac{4\left(3+\frac{5}{4}\right)}{3}=\dfrac{17}{3}$; multiply both sides by 3 to get rid of 3 in the denominator.

➤ $4\left(3+\frac{5}{4}\right)=17$; convert $3\frac{5}{4}$ into the improper fraction $\frac{17}{4}$.

➤ $4\left(\frac{17}{4}\right)=17$, so answer choice B is correct.

➤ Answer choice C: First, convert $5\frac{2}{3}$ into the improper fraction $\frac{17}{3}$.

➤ $\dfrac{4\left(3+\frac{5}{4}\right)}{3}=\dfrac{17}{3}$; multiply both sides by 3 to get rid of 3 in th denominator.

➤ $4(3+3)=17$

➤ $4(6)$ does not equal 17, so eliminate answer choice C.

➤ Answer choice D: First, convert $5\frac{2}{3}$ into the improper fraction $\frac{17}{3}$.

➤ $\dfrac{4(3+12)}{3} = \dfrac{17}{3}$; multiply both sides by 3 to get rid of 3 in the denominator.

➤ $4(3 + 12) = 17$

➤ $4(15)$ does not equal 17, so eliminate answer choice D.

➤ Answer choice E: First, convert $5\dfrac{2}{3}$ into the improper fraction $\dfrac{17}{3}$.

➤ $\dfrac{4(3+17)}{3} = \dfrac{17}{3}$; multiply both sides by 3 to get rid of 3 in the denominator.

➤ $4(3 + 17) = 17$

➤ $4(20)$ does not equal 17, so eliminate answer choice E.

14. **The correct answer is C.** To solve this problem, replace x in the given equation with each of the answer choices. The answer choice that satisfies the equation will be correct.

➤ Answer choice A: $(-26) - 13 = 13 - (-26)$

   ➤ -39 does not equal 39, so eliminate answer choice A.

➤ Answer choice B: $(-13) - 13 = 13 - (-13)$

   ➤ -26 does not equal 26, so eliminate answer choice B.

➤ Answer choice C: $(0) - 13 = 13 - (0)$

   ➤ -13 does not equal 13, so eliminate answer choice C.

➤ Answer choice D: $(13) - 13 = 13 - (13)$

   ➤ $0 = 0$, so answer choice D is correct.

➤ Answer choice E: $(26) - 13 = 13 - (26)$

   ➤ 13 does not equal -13, so eliminate answer choice E.

15. **The correct answer is B.** This question requires you to calculate the percent change in value from age 60 to age 64. To find the percent change, first calculate the difference of the value at age 64 (530) and the value at age 60 (450), and then divide by the value at age 60 (450).

➤ $(530 - 450) \div 450 = 17.77\%$

Because the question asks for the nearest percent, round up to 18%.

16. **The correct answer is C.** The best way to solve this problem is to set up a proportion. You are given that 8 buckets will fill 6 holes, and are asked for the number of buckets that will fill 9 holes. Set up a proportion as follows:

    8 buckets is to 6 holes as x buckets is to 9 holes; this can be expressed mathematically as $\frac{8}{6} = \frac{x}{9}$.

    ➤ $\frac{8}{6} = \frac{x}{9}$; solve for x.

    ➤ $6x = 72$

    ➤ $x = 12$

17. **The correct answer is C.** To solve this problem, isolate the $(x - 2)$ term on the left side of the equation.

    ➤ $7a + 4(x - 2) = s$; subtract $7a$ from both sides.

    ➤ $4(x - 2) = s - 7a$; divide both sides by 4.

    ➤ $(x - 2) = \frac{(s - 7a)}{4}$

18. **The correct answer is D.** To solve this problem, look closely at the information that is given. You are given that point (c,d) lies inside the enclosed region. Since c is the x-value and $x = 7$ is a boundary, c must be less than or equal to 7 to lie within the enclosed region; therefore, the statement in Roman Numeral I is true. Eliminate answer choices B and C, because they do not include Roman Numeral I. Because d is the y-value and you are given that $y = f(x)$, then d must be less than or equal to $f(c)$ to lie within the enclosed region; therefore, the statement in Roman Numeral II is true. Eliminate answer choice A because it does not include Roman Numeral II. If you look closely at the graph, you will see that c does not have to equal d; for example, one point that lies within the enclosed region is $(6,1)$. Therefore, the statement in Roman Numeral III is not true, so eliminate answer choice E.

19. **The correct answer is D.** You are given that the length of the floor is 12 feet and that the length is 3 more than the width. Set the width equal to w, and set up an equation to find the width.

    ➤ $3 + w = 12$

    ➤ $w = 9$

    To calculate the area, multiply the length by the width.

    ➤ $12 \times 9 = 108$

    The area of the kitchen floor is 108 square feet.

20. **The correct answer is A.** To answer this question, you must translate the word problem into a mathematical expression. The square of $4b$ is equivalent to $(4b)^2$. The sum is the result of addition, so add $7a$ to $(4b)^2$: $7a + (4b)^2$. You can now eliminate answer choices B and C because they include the quantity $4b^2$, which is incorrect because it shows that only the b is squared. You can also eliminate answer choice E because it includes the square root of $4b$, not the square of $4b$. The problem states that $7a + (4b)^2$ is equal to the sum of $3a$ and $5b$, which is expressed mathematically as $7a + (4b)^2 = 3a + 5b$.

SECTION 3—Writing Skills

Identifying Sentence Errors (Questions 1–14)

1. **The best answer is E.** There are no errors in this sentence. The singular, present tense verb "requires" agrees with the singular noun "laboratory." The phrase "technicians to wear" effectively completes the phrase that begins with the word "requires." "Of the day" is an appropriate phrase to follow "times" and the preposition "against" effectively follows "to protect."

2. **The best answer is D.** In this sentence, the singular pronoun "your" should be replaced with the plural pronoun "their" because the plural subject of the sentence, "young people," requires a plural pronoun. The past progressive verb "attending" correctly refers to an event that was ongoing in the past. The verb "was" correctly refers to an event that occurred in the past, and the phrase "to prolong" appropriately precedes "youth."

3. **The best answer is C.** In this sentence, "neither" requires the coordinating conjunction "nor" instead of "or." The word "boasted" correctly refers to an event that occurred in the past and fits within the context of the sentence. The adjective "pleasurable" effectively modifies the noun "atmosphere." The phrase "was worthy" correctly refers to an event that occurred in the past and fits within the context of the sentence.

4. **The best answer is A.** Although the preposition "at" does indicate place, the correct idiomatic expression is "on our street." The verb "failed" correctly refers to an event that occurred in the past. "Which" appropriately introduces the nonessential clause, and "fueled" agrees with the verb tense of the sentence. The phrase "to report his" agrees with the singular proper noun "Mr. Reed" and is within the context of the sentence.

5. **The best answer is E.** There are no errors in this sentence. "In" is an appropriate preposition to indicate where there was an "increase." The phrase "has made" correctly refers to the singular noun "increase" and an event that began in the past and continues to the present. "Too high" is an appropriate phrase for the context of the sentence. The past tense verb "booked" effectively describes an event that occurred because of the "increase in gas prices."

6. The best answer is A. In this sentence, the "highest of the charity board's priorities" refers to a single priority; therefore, the plural verb "are" should be replaced with the singular verb "is." The preposition "in" effectively indicates location when followed by "the office." "By" and "only" are appropriate for indicating who will use the "facility."

7. The best answer is E. There are no errors in this sentence. The phrase "guided by" correctly refers to an event that occurred in the past. The adverb "triumphantly" effectively modifies the past tense verb "arrived." "In" is an appropriate preposition to follow "arrived" and indicate location. "Both" is used correctly to refer to the things that follow: "the Pacific and Atlantic."

8. The best answer is D. The present tense verb "become" should be replaced with the past tense verb "became" to agree with the other past tense verbs in the sentence ("were," "prepared," "determined"). "Just as those" appropriately expresses the relationship of the events that occur in the sentence. "Who were working" correctly refers to the multiple people working on the project and the verb tense of the sentence. "Determined" agrees with the verb tense of the sentence and is within the context of the sentence.

9. The best answer is D. In this sentence, "these" is a modifying adjective that needs to either be followed by a noun or replaced with the plural pronoun "them." The verb "introduced" correctly refers to an event that occurred in the past. The adjective "its" is the correct way to show possession of the singular noun "company," and effectively modifies the noun, "standard soft drinks." "Consumers responded" is an appropriate phrase to describe the actions of the "consumers."

10. The best answer is B. The singular subject of the sentence, "risk," requires that the plural verb phrase "prove that" be replaced by the singular verb phrase "proves that." "Of" is an appropriate preposition to use after "risk." The singular verb "is" properly refers to the singular noun "training." The plural noun "workers" is effectively modified by the preceding adjective "foodservice."

11. The best answer is C. The progressive verb "attempting" suggests an ongoing action. The context of this sentence requires that all verbs be in present tense and refer to the plural noun "gardeners"; therefore, "attempting to revive" should be "attempt to revive." "Whereas" is effective in introducing the direct contrast within the sentence, and the superlative adjective "most" effectively modifies the noun "novice." The adjective "more" effectively expresses the extent to which the event is "likely to" occur.

12. **The best answer is B.** The word "because" indicates a cause and effect relationship. In this sentence, an event will occur in the future as a result of an event that occurs in the present; therefore, the past tense verb "would" should be replaced with the present tense verb "will." "Previously scheduled" begins a nonessential clause that is appropriate for this sentence. "Between" is an appropriate preposition to use after "choose." The progressive verb "vying" effectively describes an event that is ongoing, and "for" is an appropriate preposition to follow "vying."

13. **The best answer is C.** The pronoun "what" should be used when there are an unlimited number of choices, and the pronoun "which" should be used when a specific number of choices have been identified. This sentence identifies only two choices, so "what factor" should be replaced with "which factor." The superlative "most" effectively modifies the noun "experts." The verb "find" is in the correct verb tense, and the adverb "difficult" appropriately modifies the verb phrase "to determine." The conjunction "or" is effectively used between "lifestyle choices" and "heredity."

14. **The best answer is A.** The singular noun, "committee," requires that the plural verb "maintain" be replaced by the singular verb "maintains." "With" is an appropriate preposition to use after the noun "accordance." The adverb "frequently" effectively modifies the "changing demands." The preposition "of" correctly follows "demands," and "both" is used correctly to refer to two of two things that follow: "the students and the job market."

Improving Sentences (Questions 15–34)

15. **The best answer is B.** In this sentence, the phrase "it is the chef who" is unnecessary; simply using "the chef" is appropriate, so answer choice B is the best choice. The underlined portion in answer choice C creates an awkward sentence, and the underlined portion in answer choice D creates an incomplete sentence. The sentence requires that the verbs in the underlined portion refer to activities in the present tense; the verb "using" describes an event in progress, so answer choice E is incorrect.

16. **The best answer is D.** The idea being conveyed in the sentence is that clear-cutting exacts a toll on the local ecology. Answer choice D effectively uses the pronoun "its" to indicate that the "toll" belongs to

"clear-cutting." Answer choices B, C, and E indicate that the "toll" belongs to the "local ecology," not to "clear-cutting." As it is written, the sentence is awkward.

17. **The best answer is D.** Using a comma to separate two independent clauses requires a coordinating conjunction after the comma. Answer choice D correctly uses the coordinating conjunction "and." The sentence as it is written creates a "comma splice." Answer choices B, C, and E do not effectively complete the sentence.

18. **The best answer is C.** The introductory phrase "revered for their impeccable breeding" should refer to, or modify, the "purebred dogs," not the "dog enthusiasts." Answer choice C correctly rearranges the sentence so that the introductory phrase clearly modifies the "purebred dogs." As the sentence is written, is not clear whether the "dogs" or the "enthusiasts" are "revered." In answer choice B, it is not clear who is "revered as impeccable." Answer choice D incorrectly compares "common mutts" to "dog enthusiasts." Answer choice E incorrectly uses the plural pronoun "their" to refer to the singular noun, "purebred dog."

19. **The best answer is B.** The singular noun "evidence" requires that the plural verb "show" be replaced with the singular verb "shows." The rest of the underlined portion is appropriate, and no other corrections are necessary. The progressive verb "showing" could be used in this sentence, but only with the singular verb "is," not the plural verb "are." Answer choice D incorrectly uses a comma after "show." Answer choice E incorrectly uses the plural verb "tend" to refer to the "evidence."

20. **The best answer is C.** The separation of two independent clauses requires either a semicolon or a comma followed by a coordinating conjunction. Answer choice C correctly uses a semicolon to separate the independent clauses. Answer choices A and B both use a comma, but no coordinating conjunction, to separate the independent clauses. The clause following the semicolon in answer choice D is a dependent clause. Answer choice E is awkward and unclear.

21. **The best answer is D.** The information in the first portion of this sentence appears to contrast with the information in the second portion of the sentence; therefore, answer choice D is correct because it uses "although" to introduce the contrast in the sentence. Answer choices A, B, and C do not introduce the contrast, making the sentence less clear and concise. Instead of introducing a contrast, answer choice D indicates a cause and effect relationship with "because."

22. **The best answer is C.** In the underlined portion of the sentence, the adjective "singing" should modify the singular noun, "trio sensation." Answer choice A uses the plural noun "sensations," answer choice B uses the incorrect form of the verb "become" and the plural noun "trios," answer choice D uses the plural noun "trios," and answer choice E uses the plural nouns "trios" and "sensations."

23. **The best answer is A.** This sentence is best as written. It is clear that the "New England coast" is a "fascinating region." It is also clear why the "New England Coast" is a "fascinating region." Answer choice B is not as concise as answer choice A. Answer choice C incorrectly uses "naturally" to modify "noted." Answer choice D is an incomplete sentence. Answer choice E includes an extraneous comma after "coast."

24. **The best answer is B.** Because this sentence makes it clear that "honesty and integrity" are the virtues that "help" Michael do something, the phrase "is what" is unnecessary. Answer choice B correctly deletes this phrase from the sentence. Answer choice C includes the unnecessary phrase "is going to" instead of "will." When a colon is used to introduce a list, the clause in front of the colon must be independent, so answer choice D is incorrect. Answer choice E is unclear as to who or what possesses the "honesty and integrity."

25. **The best answer is D.** The phrase in answer choice D correctly uses the pronoun "it" to refer to Babe Ruth's career, and effectively conveys the intended meaning of the sentence. Answer choices A, B, C, and E are awkward and unclear.

26. **The best answer is E.** This sentence requires a coordinating conjunction after the comma that separates the two independent clauses, "he does not speak the language" and "he has never visited Germany." Answer choice E uses the correct coordinating conjunction "and." Answer choices A, B, and C do not use a coordinating conjunction after the comma. "As a result" should be used to introduce a cause and effect relationship, which is not appropriate for this sentence. Also, a semicolon would be necessary before the transitional phrase "as a result."

27. **The best answer is C.** The sentence in answer choice C is clear and concise, and quickly indicates the intended meaning of the sentence. Answer choices A, B, and D are awkward and unclear. Answer choice E incorrectly uses the singular verb "is."

28. **The best answer is C.** The first portion of this sentence would be more effective if it began with "in addition to." Furthermore, the proper coordinating conjunction for the list is "and," not "along with."

Answer choice C uses the proper introductory phrase, maintains parallel structure with the elements in the list, and uses the correct conjunction "and." As it is written, the sentence incorrectly uses a semicolon, places the coordinating conjunction "and" in the middle of a series of elements, and improperly uses "along with." Answer choice B incorrectly uses "rather than" to suggest additional occupations and uses "along with" instead of "and." Answer choice D incorrectly uses a semicolon and fails to maintain the parallelism of the list by using "a" before "general" and "government official," and not using "an" before "army officer." Answer choice E uses an unnecessary comma after "in addition," places the coordinating conjunction "and" in the middle of a series of elements, and improperly uses "along with."

29. **The best answer is A.** This sentence is best as written. The use of the coordinating conjunction "but" clearly indicates a contrast between the first and second portions of the sentence. The sentence is correctly punctuated, and the verb tense of the sentence is consistent. Answer choice B is contradictory because it suggests that a dog is both "not necessarily costly" and "increasingly expensive." Answer choice C fails to use a comma before the coordinating conjunction "but;" it is also awkward. In answer choice D, "even though" is an acceptable introduction, but the rest of the sentence is awkward. Answer choice E fails to communicate a logical contrast.

30. **The best answer is E.** In the sentence as it is written, it is unclear as to whom or to what "they" is referring. In addition, using the adverb "hence" requires the use of extra punctuation. Answer choice E correctly uses "that," which requires no comma, to introduce an essential clause of the sentence. Answer choice E also eliminates "they," making it clear that the "field trips" modify "student achievement." Answer choice B uses the phrase "and so have" and the adverb "hence," which is redundant. In answer choice C, the singular verb "hinders" is incorrect because it refers to the plural verb "field trips." Answer choice D suggests that the "teachers," not the "field trips," "hinder student achievement."

31. **The best answer is C.** The plural possessive pronoun "their" should be used in reference to the plural noun phrase "dozens of brands." Answer choices A, B, and E incorrectly use the singular possessive pronoun "its." "Which" is generally used to indicate a nonessential clause and should be preceded by a comma. In addition, answer choice D incorrectly uses "uniquely" to modify "nutritional" when it is intended to modify "claims."

32. **The best answer is E.** This sentence does not intend to contrast the first and second portions of the sentence; it is merely stating two comparisons. Therefore, the conjunction "and" is more appropriate than the conjunction "but." In addition, when making a comparison, the conjunction "than" should be used instead of "then." Answer choice E correctly places a comma before the conjunction "and" to separate the two independent clauses and properly uses "than." Answer choice B uses the conjunction "but," and "then" instead of "than." Answer choice C uses a semicolon instead of a comma and uses "then" instead of "than." Answer choice D places an unnecessary comma after "homemade food."

33. **The best answer is C.** In this sentence, the singular noun "court" requires that the plural pronoun "their" be replaced with the singular pronoun "its." Answer choice B uses "there," which is commonly confused with the plural pronoun "their." The phrase "on the controversial case" should directly follow the "opinion," so answer choice D is incorrect. It is not necessary to include the past tense verb "did," so answer choice E is incorrect.

34. **The best answer is E.** This sentence begins with "because," which sufficiently indicates the cause (located on the ocean) and the effect (mild temperatures) of the sentence. Therefore, no additional information or explanation is necessary after the comma. Answer choice E correctly states that the reason for the mild temperatures is the location. In answer choices A, B, and C, it is unnecessary to refer to the cause as "this." Answer choice D creates an incomplete, unclear sentence.

Improving Paragraphs (Questions 35–39)

35. **The best answer is C.** The first sentence of this paragraph provides information about the format of the book. The rest of the paragraph focuses on describing Esperanza and her experiences. Although the first paragraph mentions that Esperanza's family does not have an "All-American" home, the author does not state that the "All-American" home does not exist for anyone. Eliminate answer choice B Likewise, answer choices A, D, and E are not supported by the first paragraph.

36. **The best answer is D.** The original sentence is a run-on sentence. There are two separate sentences and ideas in the original sentence. Therefore, the best option is to actually form separate sentences. Answer choices A, B, C, and E do not correct or improve the sentence.

37. **The best answer is B.** The sentence as written includes numerous grammatical errors, such as using the plural pronoun "their" to refer to the singular noun phrase "each kid." Only answer choice B effectively identifies both that the Corderos have an "American dream," as well as what that dream is. Answer choice C is awkward, and answer choices D and E are not punctuated correctly.

38. **The best answer is E.** The focus of the final paragraph is on what the author thinks will happen to Esperanza and her family. This best supports answer choice E. Answer choices A, B, C, and D are not supported by information in the final paragraph.

39. **The best answer is A.** The sentence is best as it is written, and requires no revision. Answer choice B is incorrect because if you replace "with" at the beginning of the sentence with "this is," you must also change the comma after "attitude" to a semicolon. Answer choice C is incorrect because adding "never" changes the context of the sentence. Answer choice D is incorrect because the phrase that follows "dream home" is not an independent clause. Answer choice E is incorrect because "did find" does not fit the context of the paragraph.

SECTION 4—Math

Multiple Choice (Questions 1–8)

1. The correct answer is D. To solve this problem, simplify the equation and solve for x, as follows:

➤ $\dfrac{2x+3}{(2x)} = \dfrac{11}{8}$

➤ $11(2x) = 8(2x + 3)$

➤ $22x = 16x + 24$

➤ $8x = 24$

➤ $x = 4$

2. The correct answer is B. To solve, use the Pythagorean Theorem $(a^2 + b^2 = c^2)$, as follows:

➤ $6^2 + y^2 = 9^2$

➤ $36 + y^2 = 81$

➤ $y^2 = 81 - 36$

➤ $y^2 = 45$

➤ $y = \sqrt{45}$

3. The correct answer is B. To solve this problem, you must choose the answer that is divisible by 3 and 12, but is NOT divisible by 9

➤ Answer choice A is not correct because 15 is not divisible by 12.

➤ Answer choice B is correct because 24 is divisible by 3 and 12, but is not divisible by 9.

➤ Answer choice C is not correct because even though 36 is divisible by 3 and 12, it is also divisible by 9. This holds true for answer choice D as well.

➤ Answer choice E is not correct because 81 is not divisible by 12.

4. The correct answer is A. To solve this problem, solve the first equation for x, as follows:

➤ $6x = 108$

➤ $x = 18$

Now, substitute 18 for x in the second equation and solve for y.

➤ $18y = 4$

➤ $y = \dfrac{4}{18}$, or $\dfrac{2}{9}$

5. The correct answer is B. You are given that the probability of drawing a green marble is $\dfrac{4}{9}$, or 4 out of 9. This means that the total number of marbles in the bag must be a multiple of 9. The question asks for the answer choice that cannot be the number of marbles in the bag. Therefore, the answer choice that is not a multiple of 9 will be the correct answer. Only 64 is not a multiple of 9.

6. The correct answer is E. The perimeter is equal to the distance around an object. To calculate the perimeter of a square, you would add the length of the 4 sides. Because the sides have equal length, the formula for the perimeter of square is $P = 4s$. You are given that the perimeter of the square is 32. Therefore, the length of each side must be $32 \div 4$, or 8. The formula for the area of a square is $A = s^2$. Therefore, the area of the square is 8^2, or 64.

7. The correct answer is A. According to information in the problem, Dave delivers first to neighborhood A, then B, then C. You are also given that Dave completes route B the fastest, then C, and finally A. Since he does A, the slowest route, first, the graph should indicate the passage of a lot of time during the first phase. You can eliminate answer choices B and D, which indicate that very little time passed during the first phase. Since route B is completed next, and this is the fastest route, the graph should then have a very steep incline showing that a lot of distance was covered in a short period of time. Eliminate answer choice C, because A and E show a steeper incline during the second phase. Dave completes route C last, and in a shorter amount of time than he completed route A. Therefore, the final phase of the graph should be fairly steep as well. Graph A most accurately portrays the speed and duration of each route.

8. The correct answer is A. To solve this problem, first estimate the value of points D and H. Point D is at about -1.5 on the number line and Point H is located about 1.8. The product of $D \times H$ is -1.5×1.8, or -2.7. Next, estimate the value of the point in each answer choice. The point with a value closest to -2.7 will be correct.

➤ Answer choice A: Point A lies between -2 and -3, but is much closer to -3.

➤ Answer choice B: Point B lies between -2 and -3, but is much closer to -2. Eliminate answer choice B.

> Answer choice C: Point C lies between -1 and -2, which means that the value cannot be -2.7. Eliminate answer choice C. Answer choice D can be eliminated for the same reason.

> Answer choice E: Point F is a positive number; eliminate answer choice E.

Answer choice A includes the only point that could be equal to -2.7, so it is correct.

Student Produced Response (Questions 9–18)

9. **Answer: $-\frac{3}{2}$ or –1.5.** To solve this problem, first substitute $y - 8$ for x into the first equation.

> $7y - 3(y - 8) = 18$

> Expand and combine like terms to get $4y + 24 = 18$ (Remember to keep track of negatives!)

> Subtract 24 from both sides to get $4y = -6$

> Divide both sides by 4 to get $y = \frac{-3}{2}$, or -1.5.

10. **Answer: 260.** To solve this problem, simply multiply the number of bookcases sold in the first month by 130%, or 1.3, its decimal equivalent. This is the same as multiplying by 30%, or 0.3, and then adding that result to the number of bookcases sold in the first month. The number of bookcases sold in the second month is 200×1.3, or 260 bookcases.

11. **Answer: 90, 180, or 240.** Since the angles in $\triangle XYZ$ have the same measure as the angles in $\triangle ABC$, the two triangles must be similar. Given that one side of $\triangle XYZ$ is 48, you have three possible scenarios:

> #1: The side that is 48 in $\triangle XYZ$ corresponds to the side that is 8 in $\triangle ABC$.

> #2: The side that is 48 in $\triangle XYZ$ corresponds to the side that is 4 in $\triangle ABC$.

> #3: The side that is 48 in $\triangle XYZ$ corresponds to the side that is 3 in $\triangle ABC$.

In Scenario 1, the sides of $\triangle XYZ$ would be 48, 24, and 18. In Scenario 2, the sides of $\triangle XYZ$ would be 48, 96, and 36. In Scenario 3, the sides of $\triangle XYZ$ would be 48, 64, and 128. To calculate the perimeter, add the lengths of the sides. The three possible perimeters would be $48 + 24 + 18 = 90$; $48 + 96 + 36 = 180$; and $48 + 64 + 128 = 240$.

12. **Answer: 13.** To solve this problem, you must recognize that if s is a factor of both $r + 5$ and $r + 18$, then $\frac{(r+5)}{s}$ must be an integer and $\frac{(r+18)}{s}$ must be an integer. The difference of two integers is also an integer, so $\frac{[(r+18)-(r+5)]}{s}$ is also an integer.

➤ $\frac{[(r+18)-(r+5)]s}{s} =$

➤ $\frac{r-r+(18-5)}{s} = \frac{18-5}{s}$, or $\frac{13}{s}$

Thus, $\frac{13}{s}$ is an integer, which means that s must equal 13.

13. **Answer: 80.** To solve this problem, calculate $\frac{4}{7}$ of 140 as follows:

➤ $140\left(\frac{4}{7}\right) =$

➤ $\frac{560}{7} = 80$

Alternatively, divide 140 by 7 to get 20. Then, simply multiply 20 by 4 to get 80.

14. **Answer: 32.** You are given that the number of enrolled students doubles every 20 years. Let p equal the population in year Y.

➤ In 20 years, the number of enrolled students will be $2p$.

➤ In 20 more years (40 years), the number of enrolled students will be $2(2p)$. You can express $2(2p)$ as 2^2p.

➤ In 20 more years (60 years), the number of enrolled students will be $2(2^2p)$, which is equivalent to 2^3p.

➤ In 20 more years (80 years), the number of enrolled students will be $2(2^3p)$, which is equivalent to 2^4p.

➤ In 20 more years (100 years), the number of enrolled students will be $2(2^4p)$, which is equivalent to 2^5p.

So, the number of enrolled students in the year $Y + 100$ will be 2^5, or 32 times the number of enrolled students in year Y.

15. **Answer: 100.** Since $\triangle PQR$ is equilateral, each interior angle must equal 60°. Thus, $x = 20°$. Since angle y is opposite angle QRP, which measures 60°, angle y must also measure 60°. Therefore, the value of $2x + y$ is $2(20) + 60$, or 100.

16. **Answer:** $\dfrac{6}{5}$ **or 1.2.** Don't let the strange symbols scare you. To solve this problem, simply substitute the given values into the newly defined operations, as follows:

   ➤ You are given that $a \boxtimes b = 4ab + 3b$. Therefore, $2 \boxtimes (3y)$ is equivalent to $4(2)(3y) + 3(3y)$, or $24y + 9y$, which is $33y$.

   ➤ You are also given that $a \oslash b = 10a + 4b$. Therefore, $3 \oslash (2y)$ is equivalent to $10(3) + 4(2y)$, or $30 + 8y$.

   ➤ $33y = 30 + 8y$

   ➤ $25y = 30$

   ➤ $y = \dfrac{30}{25}$, or $\dfrac{6}{5}$. The decimal equivalent of $\dfrac{6}{5}$ is 1.2.

17. **Answer: 0.** To solve this problem, start with the second equation. If $3b = b$, then b must equal 0. No other value of b will satisfy the equation. Now, replace b with 0 in the first equation.

   ➤ $\dfrac{a}{2} = 0$

   ➤ $a = (2)(0)$

   ➤ $a = 0$

18. **Answer: 12.5 miles.** To solve this problem, let x be the number of miles that Amanda drives each way.

   ➤ Going to work: $\dfrac{x \text{ miles}}{50 \text{ mph}}$

   ➤ Returning from work: $\dfrac{x \text{ miles}}{25 \text{ mph}}$

   ➤ Total distance: $\dfrac{x \text{ miles}}{50 \text{ mph}} + \dfrac{x \text{ miles}}{25 \text{ mph}} = 45$

45 minutes is equal to .75 hours.

   ➤ The LCD is 50, so $\dfrac{x \text{ miles}}{50 \text{ mph}} + \dfrac{2(x)}{50 \text{ mph}} = \dfrac{3x \text{ miles}}{50 \text{ mph}} = .75$ hours

   ➤ $\dfrac{3x}{50} = .75$ hours

   ➤ $3x = 37.5$

   ➤ $x = 12.5$

SECTION 5—Critical Reading

Sentence Completion (Questions 1–6)

1. **The best answer is C.** The phrase "surprised me" indicates that the description of Jane before the semicolon contrasts with Jane's normal appearance. "Messy" or "dirty" hair logically fits with "disheveled clothing" and contrasts a "polished and smart" appearance. Only "unkempt" is a synonym for "messy" and "dirty," so answer choice C is correct. Answer choice A has a meaning opposite to "untidy." Answer choices B, D, and E do not fit with the context of the sentence.

2. **The best answer is E.** The word "although" at the beginning of the sentence indicates that the information before the comma will contrast with information after the comma. In other words, Dan wanted the rumor to be one thing, but the evidence proved that it was actually another. Look for two words that contrast each other and fit the context of the sentence. A "fallacy" would suggest that the rumor was based on a notion that is "false or erroneous," and "valid" would suggest that, despite what Dan wanted, the facts were actually based on "truth." The remaining answer choices do not contain words that contrast one another and fit the context of the sentence.

3. **The best answer is A.** The context of this sentence suggests that Frank does not like neckties. The clause that begins with "which" describes why he does not like ties, and helps to define the word that fills in the blank. Something that "serves no functional purpose" is the same as something that is "useless." "Futility" is a synonym for "useless." Frank believes that neckties are "useless," not "important" or "effective," so eliminate answer choices B and D. Answer choices C and E do not fit the context of the sentence.

4. **The best answer is B.** The word that fills in the blank should complete the phrase after the semicolon, which identifies why the person who wrote this sentence does not like these types of films. It would be hard to follow a film, based on a novel that you have already read, if the story line of the film was "different" from the story line of the novel. Therefore, if the story line of the film "deviates from" the story line of the novel, it would be more difficult to follow the film. Answer choices A and C are opposite in meaning to "deviates from." Answer choices D and E do not fit the context of the sentence.

5. **The best answer is B.** The context of this sentence indicates that the details and designs are "elaborate." The first blank should describe these "elaborate" designs. "Intricate" is a synonym for "elaborate," and "delicate" could also be used to describe the designs. Eliminate answer choices C, D, and E because the first word choice is not appropriate for the first blank. The context of this sentence also indicates that the artist must be capable of creating these "elaborate" designs. The second blank should describe this type of artist. "Amateur" is used to describe someone who lacks the skill of a professional or an expert, which does not fit the context of the sentence. "Adroit" means "skillful," so answer choice B is best.

6. **The best answer is D.** The context of this sentence indicates that something about the column is often criticized. Look at each answer choice and fill in the blanks in the sentence. The words in answer choice A do not fit the context of the sentence. "Ingenuity" is not usually criticized and does not make sense with "settles." "Unpredictability" could very well be criticized, but "scuttles" does not logically define an opinion. "Rigidity" could very well be criticized, but something that is "rigid," or inflexible, does not usually "dither," which describes something uncertain or undecided. Therefore, answer choice D is best. The column is criticized for "inconsistency" (the opinions disagree or are not predictable) because the opinions stated often "vacillate" (vary between two opposing beliefs).

Reading Comprehension (Questions 7–25)

7. **The best answer is D.** Passage 1 discusses the life and work of playwright Tennessee Williams, and Passage 2 discusses the life and work of playwright William Shakespeare. Therefore, both passages are primarily concerned with "examining the life of an important playwright and briefly discussing his work." Neither passage discusses "English playwrights and writers of the American South" together, so answer choice A is incorrect. Passage 2 does mention that Shakespeare wrote "plays," "sonnets," "poems," and "songs," but neither passage compares writing "poetry" with writing "plays." Passage 1 discusses American literature, but Passage 2 discusses English literature, so answer choice E is incorrect.

8. **The best answer is B.** Passage 1 begins with a description of the Southern Gothic style. Tennessee Williams is introduced later as an example of one of the most "celebrated" Southern Gothic writers. Therefore, the development of Passage 1 is most like answer choice B:

the presentation of an idea (Southern Gothic style) with a supporting example (the life and work of Southern Gothic writer Tennessee Williams). The remaining answer choices are not supported by the passage.

9. **The best answer is C.** Like most other Southern Gothic works, the characters in Williams's plays were "sinister," "reclusive," or had "immoral and unhappy personalities." In particular, Williams's characters included "Laura," who was "mentally incapacitated," "Amanda," a "prostitute," and other characters whose lives modeled his own life of "battling depression and alcoholism." Likewise, the characters in a tragedy often suffer from some sort of tragic flaw or moral weakness, and are often involved in unfortunate situations. Therefore, Williams's work is most like "Shakespeare's tragedies." The remaining answer choices are not supported by the passage.

10. **The best answer is A.** The Pulitzer Prize is a distinguished award given to important and influential people or literary works. Therefore, you can safely assume that mentioning a Pulitzer Prize emphasizes the "recognition Williams earned with his writings." Answer choices B, C, D, and E are not supported by the passage.

11. **The best answer is E.** This statement indicates that Shakespeare's "famous lines...have become common everyday phrases." In other words, these phrases have, over time, become part of our modern language, therefore influencing modern society. This best supports answer choice E. The passage does not support answer choices A, B, or C. The passage quickly discusses a "controversy...regarding the true authorship of Shakespeare's works," but not in relation to his "famous lines," so answer choice D is incorrect.

12. **The best answer is C.** The word "master," as it is used in this context, means that Shakespeare was "skilled" or "an expert," most likely because of his many "accomplishments." Answer choices A, B, D, and E do not convey the same meaning.

13. **The best answer is E.** The phrase "Shakespeare's talent was as unique as it was highly regarded" indicates that the author most likely respected Shakespeare's talent. The word "deferential" means "marked by deference or respect." Answer choice C, "disrespectful" is opposite in meaning to "deferential." Answer choices A, B, and D are not supported by the context of the passage.

14. **The best answer is B.** Statements in the first paragraph such as "…delightful Kirtland's warbler," and "unfortunately, the Kirtland's warbler is considered an endangered species…," indicate that the author feels positively about the Kirtland's warbler. A "proponent" is a supporter; the information contained in the first paragraph best supports the idea that the author is a "proponent" or supporter of the Kirtland's warbler. Answer choices A, C, D, and E are not supported by the first paragraph.

15. **The best answer is C.** Details in the passage indicate that "fledgling" refers to the young Kirtland's warblers. Answer choices A, B, D, and E are not supported by details in the passage.

16. **The best answer is A.** The first paragraph of the passage gives a detailed physical description of the Kirtland's warbler and also mentions the bird's habitat. Clearly, the author of this passage is very familiar with the Kirtland's warbler. The author is very informative, but does not convey sentiments of "distress" or "denigration" anywhere in the passage, so answer choices B and C are incorrect. Likewise, the author discusses jack pines and appears to enjoy nature and wildlife, but does not convey either positive or negative sentiments about either jack pines or bird enthusiasts and wildlife experts, so answer choices D and E are incorrect.

17. **The best answer is B.** The passage indicates that warblers "prefer" Grayling sand because the sand not only "prevents flooding" of nests "built on or near the ground," but also "supports…plant material that the warblers prefer." These birds have unique requirements that are satisfied by Grayling sand; therefore, the sand is "ideal for Kirtland's warblers." If Grayling sand were "non-porous," water could not pass through, so answer choice A is incorrect. The sand is not "deficient" or "hostile"; in fact, the passage mentions that the sand supports the habitat of the warblers, so answer choices C and D are incorrect. The passage does not suggest that Grayling sand is "imported," so answer choice E is incorrect.

18. **The best answer is C.** Statements in the passage such as "if not for ongoing human conservation efforts, these special habitats and this rare bird would probably not exist today" and "these efforts have greatly improved the survival and proliferation of the Kirtland's warbler over the past few decades" indicate that the author is satisfied with the success of human conservation efforts. Answer choices A, B, D, and E are not supported by the passage.

19. **The best answer is C.** The passage indicates that "fires allowed the cones of the jack pine to release their seeds." This increased the number of jack pine stands and thus the number of nesting habitats for warblers. Conversely, new forest management policies suppressed these fires, decreasing the number of jack pine stands and thus the number of nesting habitats. Therefore, the author is suggesting that "new forest fire controls were harmful to the Kirtland's warbler." The author does not suggest that the forest service had any desire to destroy the warbler, so answer choice A is incorrect. According to the passage, forest fires are beneficial to the jack pines, so answer choice B is incorrect. The passage does not support answer choices D or E.

20. **The best answer is E.** The word "prevalent" means "commonly occurring." The context of the passage indicates that the number of cowbirds has a negative effect on the number of Kirtland's warbler. This information best supports answer choice E. Answer choices A, B, C, and D are not supported by the context of the passage.

21. **The best answer is A.** The passage states that cowbirds "…steal the nests of other birds by taking out the other bird's eggs and secretly laying cowbird eggs in their place." This best supports answer choice A. Answer choices B, C, D, and E are not supported by information in the passage.

22. **The best answer is D.** According to the statement from the passage, fewer than normal Kirtland's warbler chicks will survive if a cowbird takes over the warbler's nest. This suggests that the presence of cowbirds could negatively impact the Kirtland's warbler population. There is no evidence presented in the passage to suggest that Kirtland's warblers are unable to survive in areas that contain cowbirds or that Kirtland's warbler chicks will always survive if no cowbird eggs are present in their nest, so eliminate answer choices A and E. Destroying the cowbird population might lead to an increase in the number of Kirtland's warblers, but this conclusion does not logically follow from the statement in the question. Eliminate answer choice C. Likewise, the opinions of Kirtland's warbler enthusiasts are not emphasized by the statement from the passage, so eliminate answer choice B.

23. **The best answer is D.** The statement "This, of course, negatively impacts the population of the Kirtland's warbler" serves to warn the reader about the real dangers that the cowbird poses to the warbler's survival. According to the passage, fewer than normal Kirtland's warbler chicks will survive if a cowbird takes over the warbler's nest, which could most definitely have a negative impact on the Kirtland's

warbler population. Answer choices A, B, C, and E are not supported by information in the passage.

24. **The best answer is A.** The passage states that "The male Kirtland's warbler sings a loud, persistent, and melodic song that can be heard up to a quarter mile away. Counting these songs becomes important during mating season, because scientists trying to save the warbler from extinction use this as a census to determine the annual population and to ensure that efforts to save the bird are successful." This suggests that the song of the male Kirtland's warbler is an important characteristic. Answer choices B, C, D, and E are not supported by information in the passage.

25. **The best answer is C.** The final paragraph indicates that the debate regarding whether the Kirtland's warbler will replace the robin as Michigan's state bird will "...continue until more Michigan residents have a chance to see the beautiful and somewhat exotic bird known as the Kirtland's warbler that calls Michigan home." This suggests that fewer residents of Michigan have seen the Kirtland's warbler than have seen a robin. Answer choices A, B, D, and E are not supported by information in the passage.

What's Next?

Once you have successfully tackled the PSAT exam, you will still need to deal with the SAT and, perhaps, the ACT. Those tests are the subjects of other books. We hope that you will hang on to this book and remember that many of the strategies apply to most of the exams that you will take for the rest of your life.

It's not too early to think about the rest of the college admissions process. This chapter is meant to provide some useful suggestions to help you to make decisions about what colleges and programs to apply to, as well as how to improve your chances of getting into the program of your choice.

Choosing the Best College or University for You

Many books and websites are available that include lists of the "best" schools. There might be more than one "best" school for you, and you might not be a good fit for any of the "top schools" that appear on those ranking lists. There are positive and negative features of all institutions, and the final decision is up to you and your family. You should not rely on somebody else's list to make your decision. The following are some factors to consider when making your choices. There are many areas where the factors overlap.

Size

The largest university campuses are in the 35,000–50,000 student range. They are similar to small cities with their own fire departments and police forces and their own streets and power plants. At the other end of the spectrum are small colleges with only a few hundred students.

Large campuses tend to have more interesting activities and a larger variety of resources such as libraries and museums. There will be people from all walks of life, and from many places on Earth. On the negative side, large campuses typically have horrible parking problems. One large university takes in more than $1,000,000 dollars every year in parking tickets alone. There can be more serious crime issues also. Another negative is the fact that many students at large schools find that it is ever more difficult to graduate within four years. Graduation times for a first bachelor's degree are closer to five years than four at many larger schools. This adds up to one extra year of tuition and expenses.

Location

Some students prefer to stay close to the their parents. They like weekend visits and short travel times. Others like the idea of striking out on their own and being more self-reliant. However, the expense and inconvenience of travel during holiday breaks can be a hassle. There is also the issue of residency to consider. At most state colleges, nonresidents pay a higher tuition rate. The financial differences can make an out-of-state public school just as expensive as any in-state private school.

Climate is another major factor to consider. Try to visit the schools you are considering during the worst times of the year so that you can better decide whether you are cut out for the climate extremes.

Finances

There are several money issues that you must consider. Sometimes, tuition is not the most important financial factor to consider; housing might be. Be sure that you look into the cost of housing and parking. In many places, it is simply not affordable for most students to own a car. Some campuses have such serious parking issues that they do not allow undergraduates to have cars on campus.

There is also financial aid, which is a big question for most students. Make sure that you contact the Financial Aid Office at each school you are seriously considering. Learn about loans, scholarships, and grants. Don't simply assume that your family is too affluent to qualify for aid. Many scholarships are not based on financial need and are awarded to students based only on academic performance or test scores.

Reputation

The reputation of an institution is very subjective. There are some well-known schools, and there are many that are known only to specialists in a certain field or industry or a specific geographic area. There might be some connection between the school you attend and the opportunities available to you immediately after graduation; those connections usually break down as time moves on and you build a career of your own.

The reputation of an institution can be affected by factors that are completely unrelated to anything that will impact your life as a student. For example, schools that win national athletic championships tend to be famous and some people therefore assume that they are academically superior to other schools, even though there is usually no connection at all between athletics and academics.

Resources

If you plan to study chemistry, you should look for a school that has advanced chemistry lab equipment. If you want to study business, you should seek a college that has connections to industry employers. We have seen many students disappointed by the facilities available at campuses.

Athletics

There are two different groups of students involved in athletics: players and fans. Do you want a school where you can be an athlete or a fan? Are there scholarship dollars available for your chosen sport? Is your sport a varsity sport or a club sport at the schools you are interested in? Does your sport even exist at the colleges you are considering?

Instructors

Some larger schools have many classes taught by graduate students, (called TA's "Teaching Assistants" or GA's "Graduate Assistants"). Like many college professors, they usually have had no training on how to be a teacher. They are woefully underpaid and usually sleep deprived. Some of them have a weak grasp of English. However, there are some stars. Some of these instructors will probably be among the best teachers you have ever met. However, some students find it is worth being certain that they can access their professors and that class size is manageable. Some classes have hundreds of students in a large lecture hall.

Many professors and instructors are focused on delivering quality education to their students, and some colleges go out of their way to arrange for frequent and high-quality interaction between students and instructors.

Social Environment

Everyone knows that part of your college experience will be social interaction.

Generally, smaller schools tend to be more homogeneous. Students tend to act, dress, and think more like each other. Larger colleges consist of a wider variety of subcultures. Your comfort level with the social environment at your school can have a bearing on your success.

Diversity

To most people, diversity usually means racial diversity. There are other aspects to diversity at college: opinion, socio-economic background, sex, majors, and countries of origin. All of these are factors on most college campuses. Some students think that they will learn better in an environment in which people much like themselves will surround them. Others are interested in experiencing a greater level of diversity and learning from people with different backgrounds and experience.

The best way to get the real picture is to visit campuses. Do some research on the World Wide Web, but remember that the colleges' websites are basically sales brochures. They have a financial interest in signing you up. Be a smart consumer. Try to meet some students if you do a campus visit.

Applying to College

The general rule is that you should get your applications in to your colleges no later than the holiday break of your senior year. This means that you should have all your personal statements completed, applications filled out, letters of recommendation sent in, and your test scores available by New Year's Day if you want to be ahead of the rest of the applicants.

Five is a good average number of colleges to apply to. Choose one or two fallback schools that you will attend if something goes terribly wrong with your other choices. Two or three should be schools that are realistic choices for you based on GPA, test scores, and other factors. One or two should be long shot schools where you have some small chance at getting in and you will certainly attend if you are accepted.

Applications

Don't send an application in too early. Admissions officials appreciate promptness and neatness. What they don't like is messiness, inability to follow instructions, aggressive or annoying follow up calls and letters, last minute applications, or applications that come too early.

If you call an admissions department, be focused. Write down your question ahead of time and keep your call brief and polite. Don't expect anyone on the telephone to tell you whether you will or will not be accepted. Admissions offices have procedures for making such decisions, and they cannot change the rules for you.

Recommendations

Be careful about the people you ask to write recommendations for you. Be certain that they are people who know you well and can discuss your academic strengths and your strength of character. Give them a lot of time, and don't be afraid to be certain that your letters are ready on time. Give each recommender a pre-addressed, stamped envelope if the letter is to be sent via U.S. Mail. Offer a copy of your resume, or work that you did in his or her class, or a list of points that you hope he or she will mention in your letter.

Resume

Most colleges will either ask you for a resume, or accept one, even if it is not required. Keep it simple and straightforward. Lay out the information in an easy format using common fonts so that the person who will be looking at it can quickly find what he or she needs.

Personal Statements

Many schools require you to write an essay. Some schools are vague about their requirements. They ask you to write an essay explaining why you would be a positive addition to the school. Other colleges will give you very detailed requirements. Follow the directions. Don't go over the page limits given. Do make sure that the essays you send in are your own work. There is nothing wrong with asking a family member, teacher, or admissions consulting professional for a little guidance and editing assistance. But, if you let someone else write your essays for you, it will be easy for experienced admissions officials to spot.

Start early. Brainstorm. List all the topics and points that you want to include. Make outlines. Get input from friends, family, and so on. Do first drafts of the best ideas you can come up with. Put them aside for a week or so, and then take them back out and compare them to teach other. If the idea still looks good when you review it several days later, it's worth finishing. You will probably go through many drafts. Your personal statement is often your only chance to get the admissions officials to see you as a person instead of a set of statistics.

Tell a story about yourself that illuminates a positive characteristic of yours. If you have some negative information such as a few bad grades that you need to explain, do so. However, avoid whining or asking for "sympathy points." It never works. Instead, try to frame the discussion in terms of overcoming obstacles. Everyone likes a good come-from-behind success story, and admissions officials are no different.

High School Course Work

These are the courses that you should take to help raise your PSAT score and to get ready for college.

Mathematics: Algebra, Geometry

Basic, intermediate, and a few advanced Algebra concepts will be tested on the PSAT. There won't be any geometry proofs, but there will be plenty of circles and triangles.

English: Writing/Composition Courses

The English courses that focus on writing skills will help most with the PSAT. The tougher the instructor, the better he or she will prepare you for the PSAT and college.

Languages: Latin, Spanish, Italian, French

Most English vocabulary comes from Latin. If you study Latin, or a Romance Language, (the modern versions of Latin that are still spoken today), you'll have a much better English vocabulary. Many native English speakers learn much more about English grammar by studying a foreign language than students who only take English courses.

Good luck!

If you have worked through this entire book, you should give yourself a pat on the back, and remember that you have put in a lot of effort to ensure your testing success. Thank you for allowing us help you get ready for the PSAT. Good luck with your exam and the rest of your education!

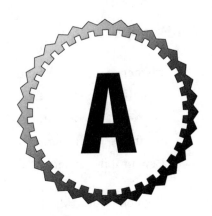

PSAT Vocabulary List

Following are words that have appeared on actual PSAT and SAT tests. They are included here because they have been selected by experienced PSAT and SAT instructors as representative of the vocabulary level that is expected on both the PSAT and the SAT.

A

absurd—extremely ridiculous or completely lacking reason

abundance—having considerably more than is necessary or adequate; more than plenty

accommodate—to adapt or adjust in a way that makes someone else comfortable; make room

acrid—harsh or bitter taste or smell

acute—sharp; quick and precise; intense

adjacent—in the nearest position; next to

aesthetic—appeals to the senses because it is beautiful

alienate—to isolate oneself from others or another person from oneself

ambiguous—unclear or capable of having more than one meaning

amiable—friendly and pleasant

annotate—to provide with extra notes or comments

anomaly—something that is different from the norm

anticipate—to look forward to or expect

apathy—a lack of any emotion, concern, or interest

aristocracy—the upper class

aristocrat—a member of the elite, ruling class

articulate—to clearly explain; the quality of being able to speak clearly

assert—to demonstrate power; to defend a statement as true

assiduous—characteristic of careful and persistent effort

assumption—something believed to be true without proof, unsupported evidence

aversion—strong dislike

B

banish—to force to leave; to exile

belittle—to cause someone to feel as if he or she is smaller or less worthy; to put down

beneficiary—recipient of benefits, such as funds or property

benign—kind; mild

bereft—being deprived of or losing something

buoyant—tending to float; lighthearted

burgeoning—thriving or growing rapidly

C

calamity—a horrible event that results in extreme loss

capacity—maximum amount that an object or area can hold; mental ability

capricious—impulsive

censure—a formal criticism or intense disproval

chaos—a state of complete disarray or confusion

chronicle—a detailed narrative

circumscribe—to enclose or define limits

coherent—the quality of being logical and clear

coincidental—occurring by chance

commendable—worthy of praise

competence—the quality of having adequate skill, knowledge, and experience

comprehensive—all-inclusive

concede—to admit or reluctantly yield; to surrender

concoct—to prepare by mixing ingredients together; devise a plan

consequence—result of an action

contemporary—current; modern

context—text or spoken words that surround a word or passage and help determine meaning; circumstances that surround an event

contradict—to assert the opposite

converge—to meet or come together at a common point

cordial—sincere; courteous

correlate—to have corresponding characteristics

corroborate—to confirm, to substantiate with evidence

criterion—requirements on which judgment can be based

crucial—extremely important; vital

D

debilitate—to weaken or impair

decipher—to interpret the meaning, usually of a code or hard to read handwriting

decry—to denounce or criticize

delve—to deeply search through

demean—to reduce in worth

demur—to express opposition

derive—infer certain knowledge; to trace the origin or development of something

descend—to come from a particular origin; to move down from a higher point

deter—to prevent from taking a particular course of action

deviant—differing from the normal path

didactic—intended for the purposes of teaching or instructing

diligent—continuously putting in great effort

discern—to differentiate or distinguish; to perceive

disconcerting —unsettling

discriminatory—showing a bias

disdainful—scornful and sneering

dispel—to rid one's mind of; to drive out

disperse—to scatter or spread out

docile—easy to train or teach

dominant—the most prominent; exuding authority

drastic—extreme

dubious—unsure, skeptical, or uncertain

E

egregious—noticeably bad or offensive

eloquent—very clear and precise; quality of being skilled in clear and precise speech

elucidate—to clarify

emit—to release or give out

empirical—based on or can be proven by observation and experiment

emulate—to follow an admirable example; imitate

endorse—to support or sign

enigmatic—unexplainable; puzzling

enumerate—to state things in a list

ephemeral—temporary; fleeting

espouse—to choose to follow or support something

ethical—in line with the principles of right and wrong

exacerbate—to intensify bitterness or violence

exceptional—having uncommonly great qualities

exhort—to urge or provoke

expatriate—(v) to banish someone; (v) to move from one's native land; (n) one who lives in a foreign country

expunge—to get rid of or erase

exquisite—characterized by great beauty and intricacy

extravagant—lavish beyond the norm

exultant—gleeful because of success

F

fabricate—to create or make something up

facilitate—to aid or make easier

fallacy—an error in reasoning

fathomable—capable of being understood

feign—to fabricate or deceive

figurative—using symbolic figures

fickle—constantly changing one's mind

flourish—to thrive; a dramatic gesture; a written embellishment

forage—to hunt around or search for food

formidable—awe-inspiring, capable of causing fear

fortuitous—happening by accident or chance

frivolous—unnecessary and silly

frugal—thrifty, not wasteful

G

galvanize—to provoke or stimulate

garrulous—very talkative

gaudy—tastelessly flashy

glib—doing something with ease and slickness, but lacking sincerity

gluttonous—overindulgent

grandiose—of great size of magnitude; pompous

gratuitous—for no reason and at no cost

gullible—easily tricked; too trusting of others

H

hackneyed—unoriginal; overused

hamper—to slow something down or get in the way

hierarchy—a way to rank or place things in order

hostile—unfriendly; adversarial

hypocritical—pretending to be something or believe in something when one actually does not

hypothetical—based on an assumption or a theory

I

ideological—relating to the fundamental ideas of an individual or group

idiosyncrasy—a peculiar characteristic

idolatrous—having an excessive adoration of someone or something

imminent—close to happening; impending

impartiality—characterized by fairness

implicit—something that is not obvious but still capable of being understood

imply—to indirectly suggest, often confused with *infer*, which means to conclude

improvise—to do or perform without preparation

incarcerate—to put in prison

incinerate—to set fire to and burn until reduced to ashes

incorporate—to bring two things or certain aspects of two things together

incorrigible—impossible to change or reform

indifference—total lack of concern or interest

indignation—anger because of unfairness

indulge—to freely partake in; to yield to the wish or desire of oneself or others

inexplicable—impossible to give the reason for; unexplainable

inevitable—bound to happen; unavoidable

infer—to deduce from evidence; to guess

infuse—for one substance to penetrate into another (for example, steak infused with garlic flavor)

ingenious—brilliant and clever

inherent—naturally occurring, permanent element or attribute

insinuate—to subtly imply

intricacy—a detail of something complex

invaluable—priceless

involuntary—an action done without one's consent or free will

irony—use of words to express a meaning that is the opposite of the real meaning; similar to and often confused with *sarcasm*, which means words used to insult or scorn

irrevocable—impossible to reverse

J

jeopardize—to endanger

judicious—sensible; having good judgment

juxtapose—to place things next to each other in order to compare or contrast

K

keen—quick-witted; sharp

kudos—compliments for achievements

L

languish—to become weak; to become disenchanted

lavish—(*adj*) elaborate and luxurious; (*v*) to freely and boundlessly bestow

lenient—easy-going; tolerant

listless—characterized by a lack of energy

lithe—gracefully slender

loathsome—offensive; disgusting

loquacious—very talkative or rambling

M

magnanimous—courageous or generous

malevolent—purposefully wishing harm on others

manifest—(*adj*) clearly recognizable; (*v*) to make clear; (*n*) a list of transported goods or passengers used for record keeping

melancholy—glumness; deep contemplative thought

melodramatic—overly emotional or sentimental

metamorphosis—a transformation or change

meticulous—devoting a high amount of attention to detail

minuscule—extremely small; unimportant

mollify—to calm down or alleviate

monotony—repetitive; lacking variety

moral—(*adj*) based on standards of good and bad; (*n*) a rule of proper behavior

mundane—occurring everyday; routine

munificence—the act of liberally giving

mutability—the ability to transform

N

naive—lacking experience in life or the world

narcissism—being conceited or having too much admiration for oneself

negligent—having a habit of behaving carelessly

negligible—meaningless and insignificant

nonchalant—behavior that is indifferent or unconcerned

noxious—unwholesome or harmful

nurture—to support or help in development

O

obdurate—firm; stubborn

obtuse—an angle larger than a right angle

onerous—very troublesome

oracle—someone of great wisdom or authority

ostracize—to eliminate from a group

overt—obvious and clearly shown

P

paradox—a statement that seems contradictory but is actually true

paragon—an example of excellence

penchant—a tendency or fondness

perceive—to become aware of something, usually through the senses

percolate—to slowly pass through

peripheral—located in or near a boundary

periphery—the outermost boundary of an area

peruse—to examine or review something

pervasive—capable of spreading or flowing throughout

phenomenon—an event or circumstance that is significant or extraordinary

plagiarize—to copy another's work and pretend that it is original

plausible—reasonable; likely

pragmatic—concerned with facts; practical

preceding—coming before

precipitate—to cause something to happen very suddenly

predominant—having superior strength; paramount

preliminary—precedes or comes prior to

prerequisite—required beforehand

prestigious—having honor or respect from others

prevail—to triumph or come out on top

prevalent—commonly used or occurring

primordial—happening first or very early

procure—to acquire something

promulgate—to publicize

protagonist—the main character of a story or tale

prototype—an original form of something

protract—to lengthen or prolong

prowess—great skill or ability in something

Q

querulous—characterized by constant complaining or whining

quixotic—unpredictable and impractical

R

rapt—being completely occupied by or focused on something

reciprocate—to give and take in equal amounts

relevant—logically connected; pertinent

reluctant—unwilling and resistant

remedial—intending to correct or remedy

renunciation—a rejection

reparation—compensation given to make amends

reproachful—expressing disapproval

repudiate—to reject or refuse as valid

resolute—definite; determined

resonant—strong and deep; lasting

rife—very frequent or common

rudimentary—very basic or not fully developed

S

sacrilege—to misuse something that is considered sacred

salient—extremely noticeable

sanctimonious—hypocritical

scrutinize—closely examine

sedition—creating or inciting an uprising

shrouded—covered; concealed

simultaneously—happening or existing at the same time

skepticism—an attitude of doubt or disbelief

solace—comfort; safety

speculators—people who form theories based on uncertain evidence; those who purchase something with the hope of reselling it later at a profit

stagnant—not moving or changing; stale

stoic—indifferent or unaffected

strident—offensively harsh and loud

subjective—depending on a person's attitudes or opinions

surfeit—an overabundance or excessiveness

suppress—to restrain or reduce

sustenance—things that provide nourishment for survival

synchronized—occurring at the same time and at the same rate

synthesis—combining separate elements to form a whole

T

tacit—an expression that uses no words

tenuous—very thin or consisting of little substance

terrestrial—relating to dry land as opposed to water; relating to the Earth as opposed to other planets

timorous—shy; hesitant

transcend—to go above and beyond; to rise above

transgress—to exceed or violate

translucent—enabling light to pass through but clouded or frosted in such a way that objects on the other side are not clearly visible; often confused with *transparent*, which means clear

trivialize—to make something appear insignificant

tyrannize—to oppress, intimidate, or harshly rule over

U

uniform—(*adj*) continuing to be the same or consistent; (*n*) identical clothing worn by members of a certain group

unilaterally—performed in a one-sided manner

unprecedented—having no previous example

utilitarian—useful or practical

V

variegated—having a variety of colors or marks

versatile—having many uses or a variety of abilities

vindication—the act of clearing someone or something from blame

virtually—in almost all instances; simulated as by a computer

W

wane—to gradually decrease

wary—cautious and untrusting

wily—very sly; deceptive

Z

zealous—very passionate or enthusiastic

Math Reference

It is assumed that most PSAT test takers will have a basic understanding of certain mathematical concepts and skills. The following reference information should serve as a review of the concepts that are commonly tested on the PSAT.

Numbers and Operations

These questions might involve basic arithmetic operations, operations involving exponents, factoring, absolute value, prime numbers, percents, ratios, sequences, number sets, and number lines.

The Properties of Integers

The following are properties of integers that are often tested on the PSAT.

➤ Integers include both positive and negative whole numbers.

➤ Zero is considered an integer.

➤ Consecutive integers follow one another and differ by 1.

➤ The value of a number does not change when multiplied by 1.

Order of Operations (PEMDAS)

Following is a description of the correct order in which to perform mathematical operations. The abbreviation PEMDAS stands for Parentheses, Exponents, Multiplication, Division, Addition, Subtraction. It should help you to remember to do the operations in the correct order, as follows:

1. P: First, do the operations within the *parentheses*, if any.

2. E: Next, do the *exponents*, if any.

3. M: Next, do the *multiplication*, in order from left to right.

4. D: Next, do the *division*, in order from left to right.

5. A: Next, do the *addition*, in order from left to right.

6. S: Finally, do the *subtraction*, in order from left to right.

Fractions and Rational Numbers

The following are properties of fractions and rational numbers that are often tested on the PSAT.

➤ The reciprocal of any number, *n*, is expressed as 1 over *n*, or $1/n$. The product of a number and its reciprocal is always 1.

➤ To change any fraction to a decimal, divide the numerator by the denominator.

➤ Multiplying and dividing both the numerator and the denominator of a fraction by the same non-zero number will result in an equivalent fraction.

➤ When adding and subtracting like fractions, add or subtract the numerators and write the sum or difference over the denominator. So, $\frac{1}{8} + \frac{2}{8} = \frac{3}{8}$, and $\frac{4}{7} - \frac{2}{7} = \frac{2}{7}$.

➤ To simplify a fraction, find a common factor of both the numerator and the denominator. For example, $\frac{12}{15}$ can be simplified into $\frac{4}{5}$ by dividing both the numerator and the denominator by the common factor 3.

➤ To convert a mixed number to an improper fraction, multiply the whole number by the denominator in the fraction, add the result to the numerator, and place that value over the original denominator. For example, $3\frac{2}{5}$ is equivalent to $(3 \times 5) + 2$ over 5, or $\frac{17}{5}$.

➤ When multiplying fractions, multiply the numerators to get the numerator of the product, and multiply the denominators to get the denominator of the product. For example, $\frac{3}{5} \times \frac{7}{8} = \frac{21}{40}$.

➤ To divide fractions, multiply the first fraction by the reciprocal of the second fraction. For example, $\frac{1}{3} \div \frac{1}{4} = \frac{1}{3} \times \frac{4}{1}$, which equals $\frac{4}{3}$.

➤ A rational number is a fraction whose numerator and denominator are both integers and the denominator $\neq 0$.

➤ Place value refers to the value of a digit in a number relative to its position. Starting from the left of the decimal point, the values of the digits are ones, tens, hundreds, and so on. Starting to the right of the decimal point, the values of the digits are tenths, hundredths, thousandths, and so on.

➤ When numbers are very large or very small, they are often expressed using scientific notation. Scientific notation is indicated by setting a positive number, N, equal to a number less than 10, and then multiplying that number by 10 raised to an integer. The integer depends on the number of places to the left or right the decimal was moved. For example, 667,000,000 written in scientific notation would be 6.67×10^8, and 0.0000000298 written in scientific notation would be 2.98×10^{-8}.

Ratio, Proportion, and Percent

The following are properties of ratios, proportions, and percents that are often tested on the PSAT.

➤ A ratio expresses a mathematical comparison between two quantities. A ratio of 1 to 5, for example, is written as either $\frac{1}{5}$ or 1:5.

➤ A proportion indicates that one ratio is equal to another ratio.

➤ A percent is a fraction whose denominator is 100. The fraction $\frac{25}{100}$ is equal to 25%.

➤ When working with ratios, be sure to differentiate between part-part and part-whole ratios. If two components of a recipe are being compared to each other, for example, this is a part-part ratio (2 cups of flour:1 cup of sugar). If one group of students is being compared to the entire class, for example, this is a part-whole ratio (13 girls:27 students).

Squares and Square Roots

The following are properties of squares and square roots that are often tested on the PSAT.

➤ Squaring a negative number yields a positive result. For example, $-3^2 = 9$.

➤ The square root of a number, n, is written as $\sqrt{n}$, or the non-negative value a that fulfills the expression $a^2 = n$. For example, the square root of 7 is expressed as $\sqrt{7}$, and $\sqrt{7}^2 = 7$.

➤ A number is considered a perfect square when the square root of that number is a whole number. For example, both 9 and 144 are perfect squares because the square root of 9 is the whole number 3 and the square root of 144 is the whole number 12.

Arithmetic and Geometric Sequences

The following are properties of arithmetic and geometric sequences that are often tested on the PSAT.

➤ An arithmetic sequence is one in which the difference between one term and the next is the same. To find the nth term, use the formula $a_n = a_1 + (n - 1)d$, where d is the common difference.

➤ A geometric sequence is one in which the ratio between two terms is constant. For example, $\frac{1}{2}$, 1, 2, 4, 8..., is a geometric sequence where 2 is the constant ratio. To find the nth term, use the formula $a_n = a_1(r)^{n-1}$, where r is the constant ratio.

Sets of Numbers

The following are properties of number sets that are often tested on the PSAT.

➤ A set is a collection of numbers. The numbers are elements or members of the set. For example, {2, 4, 6, 8} is the set of positive, even integers less than 10.

➤ The union of two sets includes all of the elements in each set. For example, if Set A = {2, 4, 6, 8} and Set B = {1, 3, 5, 7, 9}, then {1, 2, 3, 4, 5, 6, 7, 8, 9} is the union of Set A and Set B.

➤ The intersection of two sets identifies the common elements of both sets. For example, if Set A = {1, 2, 3, 4} and Set B = {2, 4, 6, 8}, then {2, 4} is the intersection of Set A and Set B.

Factors and Multiples

The following are properties of factors and multiples that are often tested on the PSAT.

➤ A prime number is any number that can only be divided by itself and 1. For example, 2, 3, 5, 7, 11, 13, 17, and 19 are prime numbers.

➤ Factors are all of the numbers that will divide evenly into one number. For example, 1, 2, 4, and 8 are all factors of 8.

➤ Common factors include all of the factors that two or more numbers share. For example, 1, 2, 4, and 8 are all factors of 8, and 1, 2, 3, and 6 are all factors of 6. Therefore, 8 and 6 have common factors of 1 and 2.

➤ The Greatest Common Factor (GCF) is the largest number that will divide evenly into any 2 or more numbers. For example, 1, 2, 4, and 8 are all factors of 8, and 1, 2, 3, and 6 are all factors of 6. Therefore, the Greatest Common Factor of 8 and 6 is 2.

➤ A number is a multiple of another number if it can be expressed as the product of that number and a second number. For example, $2 \times 3 = 6$, so 6 is a multiple of both 2 and 3.

➤ Common multiples include all the multiples that two or more numbers share. For example:

Multiples of 3 include 3, 6, 9, *12*, 15, 18, 21, and *24*.

Multiples of 4 include 4, 8, *12*, 16, 20, *24*, and 28.

Multiples of 6 include 6, *12*, 18, *24*, 30, and 36.

12 and 24 are common multiples of 3, 4, and 6.

➤ The Least Common Multiple (LCM) is the smallest number that any two or more numbers will divide evenly into. For example, the common multiples of 3, 4, and 6 are 12, 24, and 36. The smallest multiple is 12; therefore, 12 is the Least Common Multiple of 3, 4, and 6.

➤ The arithmetic mean is equivalent to the average of a series of numbers. Calculate the average by dividing the sum of all the numbers in the series by the total count of numbers in the series. For example, a student received scores of 80%, 85%, and 90% on 3 math tests. The average score received by the student on those tests is 80 + 85 + 90 divided by 3, or $\frac{255}{3}$, which is 85%.

➤ The median is the middle value of a series of numbers when those numbers are in either ascending or descending order. In the series (2, 4, 6, 8, 10), the median is 6.

➤ To find the median in an even set of data, find the average of the middle two numbers. In the series (3, 4, 5, 6), the median is 4.5.

➤ The mode is the number that appears most frequently in a series of numbers. In the series (2, 3, 3, 4, 5, 6, 7), the mode is 3.

➤ The Commutative Property of Multiplication is expressed as $a \times b = b \times a$, or $ab = ba$. For example, $2 \times 3 = 3 \times 2$.

➤ The Distributive Property of Multiplication is expressed as $a(b + c) = ab + ac$. For example, $x(x + 3) = x^2 + 3x$.

Outcomes

Following is a property of outcomes that is often tested on the PSAT.

➤ Two specific events are considered independent if the outcome of one event has no effect on the outcome of the other event. For example, if you toss a coin, there is a 1 in 2, or $\frac{1}{2}$ chance that it will land on either heads or tails. If you toss the coin again, the outcome will be the same. To find the probability of two or more independent events occurring together, multiply the outcomes of the individual events. For example, the probability that both coin-tosses will result in heads, is $\frac{1}{2} \times \frac{1}{2}$, or $\frac{1}{4}$.

Algebra and Functions

These questions might involve rules of exponents, factoring, solving equations and inequalities, solving linear and quadratic equations, setting up equations to solve word problems, and functions.

Factoring

The following are properties of factoring that are often tested on the PSAT.

➤ The standard form of a simple quadratic expression is $ax^2 + bx + c$, where a, b, and c are whole numbers. $2x^2 + 4x + 4$ is a simple quadratic equation.

➤ To add or subtract polynomials, simply combine like terms. For example, $(2x^2 + 4x + 4) + (3x^2 + 5x + 16) = 5x^2 + 9x + 20$.

➤ To multiply polynomials, use the distributive property, expressed as $a(b + c) = ab + ac$. Also remember the *FOIL* Method; multiply the *F*irst terms, then the *O*utside terms, then the *I*nside terms, then the *L*ast terms. For example,

$$2x(4x + 4) = 8x^2 + 8x; \text{ and } (x + 2)(x - 2) = x^2 - 2x + 2x - 4, \text{ or } x^2 - 4.$$

➤ You may be required to find the factors or solution sets of certain simple quadratic expressions. A factor or solution set takes the form $(x \pm \text{ some number})$. Simple quadratic expressions will usually have two of these factors or solution sets. For example, the solution sets of $x^2 - 4$ are $(x + 2)$ and $(x - 2)$.

➤ To find the common factor, simply look for the element that two expressions have in common. For example, $x^2 + 3x = x(x + 3)$.

➤ You may have to find the difference of two squares. For example, $a^2 - b^2 = (a+b)(a-b)$

Exponents

The following are properties of exponents that are often tested on the PSAT.

➤ $a^m \times a^n = a^{(m+n)}$

➤ $(a^m)^n = a^{mn}$

➤ $(ab)^m = a^m \times b^m$

$$\left[\frac{a}{b} \right]^m = \frac{a^m}{b^m}$$

➤ $a^0 = 1$, when $a \neq 0$

➤ $a^{-m} = 1/a^m$, when $a \neq 0$

➤ $\frac{a}{b}^{-m} = ab^m$, when $b \neq 0$

Inequalities

The following are properties of inequalities that are often tested on the PSAT.

➤ Greater than is expressed with this symbol: $>$

➤ Greater than or equal to is expressed with this symbol: $\geq$

➤ Less than is expressed with this symbol: <

➤ Less than or equal to is expressed with this symbol: ≤

➤ Inequalities can usually be worked with in the same way equations are worked with.

➤ When an inequality is multiplied by a negative number, you must switch the sign. For example, follow these steps to solve for x in the inequality $-2x + 2 < 6$:

  ➤ $-2x + 2 < 6$

  ➤ $-2x < 4$

  ➤ $-x < 2$

  ➤ $x > -2$

Word Problems

The following are properties of word problems that often appear on the PSAT.

➤ When solving word problems, translate the verbal statements into algebraic expressions. For example:

  ➤ "greater than", "more than", "sum of" refer to addition (+)

  ➤ "less than", "fewer than", difference means subtraction (–)

  ➤ "of", "by" means multiplication (×)

  ➤ "per" means division (÷)

Functions

The following are properties of functions that are often tested on the PSAT.

➤ A function is a set of ordered pairs where no two of the ordered pairs has the same x-value. In a function, each input (x-value) has exactly one output (y-value). For example, $f(x) = 2x + 3$. If $x = 3$, then $f(x) = 9$. For every x, there is only one $f(x)$, or y.

➤ The *domain* of a function refers to the x-values, whereas the *range* of a function refers to the y-values.

Geometry

These questions might involve parallel and perpendicular lines, circles, triangles, rectangles and other polygons, as well as area, perimeter, volume, and angle measure in degrees.

Coordinate Geometry

The following are properties of coordinate geometry that are often tested on the PSAT.

➤ The (x,y) coordinate plane is defined by two axes at right angles to each other. The horizontal axis is the x-axis, and the vertical axis is the y-axis.

➤ The origin is the point $(0,0)$, where the two axes intersect.

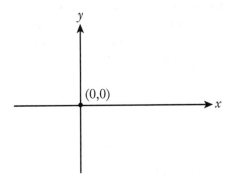

➤ The slope of a line is calculated by taking the change in y-coordinates divided by the change in x-coordinates from two given points on a line. The formula for slope is $m = (y_2 - y_1) / (x_2 - x_1)$, where (x_1, y_1) and (x_2, y_2) are the two given points.

➤ A positive slope will mean that the graph of the line will go up and to the right. A negative slope will mean that the graph of the line will go down and to the right. A horizontal line has slope 0, whereas a vertical line has an undefined slope.

➤ Two lines are parallel if and only if they have the same slope.

➤ Two lines are perpendicular if and only if the slope of one of the lines is the negative reciprocal of the slope of the other line. In other words, if line a has a slope of 2, and line b has a slope of $-1/2$, the two lines are perpendicular.

➤ The slope-intercept form of the equation of a line is y = *mx* + *b*, where *m* is the slope of the line and *b* is the y-intercept (that is, the point at which the graph of the line crosses the y-axis).

➤ To find the distance between two points in the (*x,y*) coordinate plane, use the formula $\sqrt{([x_2 - x_1]^2 + [y_2 - y_1]^2)}$, where (x_1, y_1) and (x_2, y_2) are the two given points.

➤ To find the midpoint of a line given two points on the line, use the formula $(\frac{[x_1 + x_2]}{2}, \frac{[y_1 + y_2]}{2})$.

➤ A translation slides an object in the coordinate plane to the left or right, or up or down. The object retains its shape and size and faces in the same direction.

➤ A reflection flips an object in the coordinate plane over either the x-axis or the y-axis. When a reflection occurs across the x-axis, the x-coordinate remains the same, but the y-coordinate is transformed into its opposite. When a reflection occurs across the y-axis, the y-coordinate remains the same, but the x-coordinate is transformed into its opposite. The object retains its shape and size.

Triangles

➤ In an equilateral triangle, all three sides have the same length.

➤ In an isosceles triangle, two sides have the same length.

The following are properties of triangles that are often tested on the PSAT.

➤ The sum of the interior angles in a triangle is always 180 degrees.

➤ The perimeter of a triangle is the sum of the lengths of the sides.

➤ The area of a triangle is A = $\frac{1}{2}$ (base)(height).

➤ The Pythagorean Theorem states that $c^2 = a^2 + b^2$, where *c* is the hypotenuse of the triangle and *a* and *b* are two sides of the triangle.

➤ The following are angle measures and side lengths for Special Right Triangles:

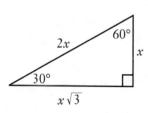
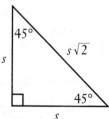

Quadrilaterals, Lines, Angles

The following are properties of quadrilaterals, lines, and angles that are often tested on the PSAT.

➤ In a parallelogram, the opposite sides are of equal length, and the opposite angles are equal.

➤ The area of a parallelogram is A = (base)(height).

➤ A rectangle is a polygon with four sides (two sets of congruent, or equal, sides) and four right angles. All rectangles are parallelograms.

➤ The sum of the angles in a rectangle is always 360 degrees.

➤ The perimeter of both a parallelogram and a rectangle is P = 2*l* + 2*w*, where *l* is the length and *w* is the width.

➤ The area of a rectangle is A = *lw*.

➤ The lengths of the diagonals of a rectangle are congruent, or equal.

➤ A square is a special rectangle where all four sides are of equal length. All squares are rectangles.

➤ When two parallel lines are cut by a transversal, each parallel line has four angles surrounding the intersection, that are matched in measure and position with a counterpart at the other parallel line. The vertical (opposite) angles are congruent, and the adjacent angles are supplementary (they total 180°). Please refer to the following diagram:

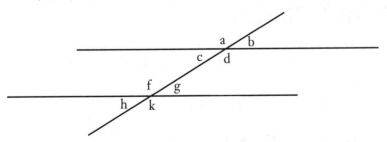

➤ a = d = f = k

➤ b = c = g = h

➤ a + b = 180°

➤ c + d = 180°

➤ f + g = 180°

➤ h + k = 180°

➤ An acute angle is any angle less than 90 degrees.

➤ An obtuse angle is any angle that is greater than 90 degrees and less than 180 degrees.

➤ A right angle is an angle that measures exactly 90 degrees.

Circles

The following are properties of circles that are often tested on the PSAT.

➤ The radius (r) of a circle is the distance from the center of the circle to any point on the circle.

➤ The diameter (d) of a circle is twice the radius.

➤ The area of a circle is A = Πr^2, where r is the radius.

➤ The circumference of a circle is C = $2\Pi r$, or C = Πd, where r is the radius and d is the diameter.

➤ The equation of a circle centered at the point (h,k) is $(x - h)^2 + (y - k)^2 = r^2$, where r is the radius of the circle.

➤ The complete arc of a circle has 360°.

➤ A tangent to a circle is a line that touches the circle at exactly one point.

Special Symbols

Special symbols are sometimes defined on the PSAT. Read the definition carefully and evaluate the mathematical expressions given in the question. For example:

➤ Let $a \clubsuit b = \dfrac{1}{ab}$. What is the value of 2 $\clubsuit$ 3?

To solve, simply substitute the numbers given in the problem for a and b.

➤ 2 $\clubsuit$ 3 = $\dfrac{1}{(2)(3)}$ = $\dfrac{1}{6}$.

Data Interpretation

The following are properties of data interpretation questions that often appear on the PSAT.

➤ Carefully read the labels on the tables, charts, or graphs.

➤ Make sure that you understand the relationships between the data represented in the graphs and tables before you answer the test questions. For example:

Projected Sales for Computer W	
Price of Computer W	Projected # of Computers Sold
$400	250
$600	100

1. Based on the projections, how much more money would be received from sales of Computer W when the price is $400 than when the price is $600?
   - (A) $10,000
   - (B) $40,000
   - (C) $60,000
   - (D) $100,000
   - (E) $250,000

The correct answer is B. $100,000 will be received from the sales of Computer W at $400, and $60,000 will be received from the sales of Computer W at $600. $100,000 - $60,000 = $40,000.

Need to Know More: Additional Resources

. . . .

The purpose of this book is to help you prepare for the PSAT. Although this book provides you with helpful information about the test and realistic practice materials to get you ready for the real thing, the following additional resources might also be useful in your preparation:

➤ The College Board website at http://www.collegeboard.com offers a wealth of up-to-date information about the PSAT. Once you get to the "PSAT/NMSQT" section in the "For Students" area of the website, you can find out when your school is administering the PSAT, try practice questions from past tests, and even access MyRoad, an online program designed to help you explore different majors, colleges, and careers.

➤ The primary purpose of the PSAT is to qualify students for the National Merit Scholarhip. Each year, approximately 10,000 students receive scholarships worth a total of $50 million for college undergraduate study. Find out more about this program by visiting http://www.nationalmerit.org.

➤ The PSAT is often used as preparation for the SAT. Therefore, *The Official SAT Study Guide for the New SAT* (ISBN 0-87447-718-2), published by the College Board is a great source of practice material for both the PSAT and the SAT. This book is usually available at all the major bookstores. Pick one up as a great complement to *PSAT Exam Cram*. Order it online at http://study-smart.com/hsbooks.htm.

➤ Advantage Education offers many programs for college-bound students, including programs that prepare students for the PSAT, SAT, and ACT, as well as Admissions Counseling and College Preparation. To learn about individual tutoring, workshops, courses, and other programs for college-bound students, visit http://study-smart.com.

➤ We've discovered two books that take a unique approach to learning vocabulary words that are often tested on both the PSAT and the SAT. These books are designed to make learning vocabulary words fun and interesting by using them in exciting mystery novels. Check out *Tooth and Nail* (ISBN 0-15-601382-7) and *Test of Time* (ISBN 0-15-601137-9), both usually available at major bookstores. Order them online at http://study-smart.com/hsbooks.htm.

➤ Middle school and high school textbooks are extremely valuable resources. The content areas tested on the PSAT are the same content areas that you've been studying in school. Hence, textbooks cover many of the relevant skills and subjects you will need for success on the PSAT. If you do not have your textbooks, your school library should have copies that you can use.

➤ Don't forget to talk to teachers and older students who have some experience with the PSAT. They might be able to shed some additional light on getting ready for the test. It is in your best interest to be as well-prepared as possible on test day.

Scoring Worksheets and Tables

Following is detailed information regarding scoring your PSAT. A Scoring Worksheet for each of the Practice Exams is also included. Once you've taken the Practice Exams, tear out the Worksheet page that corresponds to the exam and follow the instructions for scoring. Use the Scoring Tables to calculate your scores on each exam.

Even though great care has been taken in creating these Practice Exams, the Scaled Scores are all approximate. Actual PSAT scoring scales vary from one administration to the next based on several factors, including the difficulty level of questions within each section. Scores on the exams in this book should not be used as exact predictors of your actual PSAT score.

SCORING YOUR PSAT PRACTICE TEST

The actual PSAT Score Report includes Scaled Scores for each section in the following ranges:

SECTION	QUESTIONS PER SECTION	SCALED SCORE RANGE
Critical Reading	48	20 - 80
Math	38	20 - 80
Writing	39	20 - 80
Selection Index (The sum of your three Scaled Scores)	----	60 - 240

The Selection Index is the score that is reported to the National Merit Scholarship Committee. To arrive at your Scaled Scores and Selection Index, you must first calculate your Raw Scores. Your Raw Score for each multiple-choice section is the number of questions you answered correctly, less a fraction of the number you answered incorrectly.

STEP 1: To calculate your Raw Scores for Critical Reading, Math, and Writing, first count the number of questions you answered correctly and the number of questions you answered incorrectly for each section. Calculate your totals as indicated below, and then enter those totals into your PSAT SCORING SHEET.

Note: Answers that you leave blank do not affect your score. Do not count blank answers as incorrect or correct; simply ignore them.

Critical Reading—Sections 1 & 5

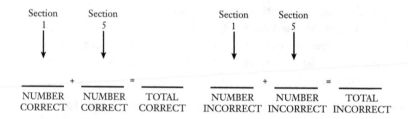

Section 1		Section 5			Section 1		Section 5		
NUMBER CORRECT	+	NUMBER CORRECT	=	TOTAL CORRECT	NUMBER INCORRECT	+	NUMBER INCORRECT	=	TOTAL INCORRECT

Writing—Section 3

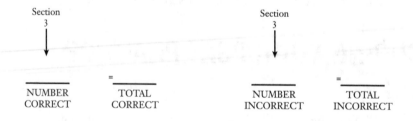

Section 3			Section 3		
NUMBER CORRECT	=	TOTAL CORRECT	NUMBER INCORRECT	=	TOTAL INCORRECT

Multiple Choice Math ONLY—Section 2 & Questions 1–8 of Section 4

Count the number of correct and incorrect answers for all of Section 2 and the first eight multiple-choice questions of Section 4 ONLY.

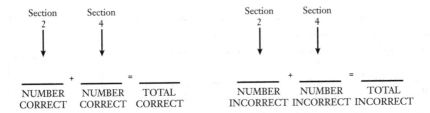

Section 2	Section 4			Section 2	Section 4	
NUMBER CORRECT	+ NUMBER CORRECT	= TOTAL CORRECT		NUMBER INCORRECT	+ NUMBER INCORRECT	= TOTAL INCORRECT

Student-Produced Math ONLY—Questions 9-18 of Section 4

Only count the number of Student-Produced Response questions that you answered correctly. There is no penalty for incorrect responses.

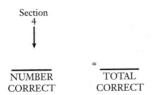

Section 4	
NUMBER CORRECT	= TOTAL CORRECT

STEP 2: After you enter your totals into the PSAT SCORING SHEET on the following page, perform the operations indicated and round your Raw Score to the nearest whole number according to normal rules. For example, a Raw Score of 32.75 should be rounded up to 33 and a Raw Score of 33.25 should be rounded down to 33.

STEP 3: Once you have determined your Rounded Raw Scores, you can determine your Scaled Scores using the three PSAT SCORING TABLES that follow your PSAT SCORING SHEET. Enter your Scaled Scores in the boxes to the right on the PSAT SCORING SHEET.

STEP 4: The Selection Index is the sum of your Critical Reading, Writing, and Math Scaled Scores. Add your three Scaled Scores and determine your Selection Index at the bottom of the PSAT SCORING SHEET.

Practice Exam 1 Scoring Worksheet

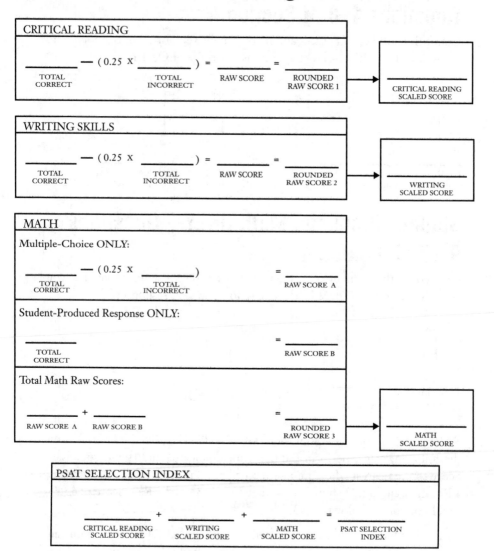

CRITICAL READING

_____ — (0.25 X _____) = _____ = _____

TOTAL CORRECT   TOTAL INCORRECT   RAW SCORE   ROUNDED RAW SCORE 1

CRITICAL READING SCALED SCORE

WRITING SKILLS

_____ — (0.25 X _____) = _____ = _____

TOTAL CORRECT   TOTAL INCORRECT   RAW SCORE   ROUNDED RAW SCORE 2

WRITING SCALED SCORE

MATH

Multiple-Choice ONLY:

_____ — (0.25 X _____) = _____

TOTAL CORRECT   TOTAL INCORRECT   RAW SCORE A

Student-Produced Response ONLY:

_____ = _____

TOTAL CORRECT   RAW SCORE B

Total Math Raw Scores:

_____ + _____ = _____

RAW SCORE A   RAW SCORE B   ROUNDED RAW SCORE 3

MATH SCALED SCORE

PSAT SELECTION INDEX

_____ + _____ + _____ = _____

CRITICAL READING SCALED SCORE   WRITING SCALED SCORE   MATH SCALED SCORE   PSAT SELECTION INDEX

Practice Exam 2 Scoring Worksheet

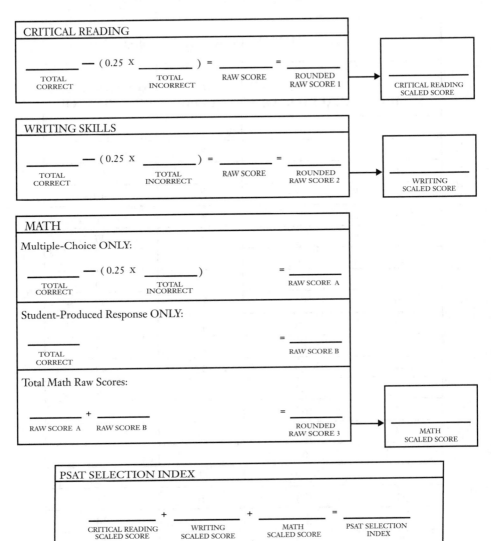

CRITICAL READING

_____ — (0.25 X _____) = _____ = _____
TOTAL CORRECT .... TOTAL INCORRECT .... RAW SCORE .... ROUNDED RAW SCORE 1

→ _____
CRITICAL READING SCALED SCORE

WRITING SKILLS

_____ — (0.25 X _____) = _____ = _____
TOTAL CORRECT .... TOTAL INCORRECT .... RAW SCORE .... ROUNDED RAW SCORE 2

→ _____
WRITING SCALED SCORE

MATH

Multiple-Choice ONLY:

_____ — (0.25 X _____) = _____
TOTAL CORRECT .... TOTAL INCORRECT .... RAW SCORE A

Student-Produced Response ONLY:

_____ = _____
TOTAL CORRECT .... RAW SCORE B

Total Math Raw Scores:

_____ + _____ = _____
RAW SCORE A .... RAW SCORE B .... ROUNDED RAW SCORE 3

→ _____
MATH SCALED SCORE

PSAT SELECTION INDEX

_____ + _____ + _____ = _____
CRITICAL READING SCALED SCORE .... WRITING SCALED SCORE .... MATH SCALED SCORE .... PSAT SELECTION INDEX

PSAT SCORING TABLES

CRITICAL READING SCORING TABLE			
RAW SCORE	**APPROXIMATE SCALED SCORE**	**RAW SCORE**	**APPROXIMATE SCALED SCORE**
48	80	23	51
47	78	22	51
46	76	21	50
45	75	20	49
44	73	19	48
43	71	18	47
42	70	17	47
41	68	16	45
40	67	15	45
39	66	14	44
38	65	13	43
37	64	12	42
36	63	11	41
35	62	10	40
34	61	9	39
33	60	8	38
32	59	7	37
31	58	6	35
30	58	5	34
29	57	4	33
28	56	3	31
27	55	2	30
26	54	1	27
25	53	0	24
24	52	Below 0	20-23

WRITING SKILLS SCORING TABLE

RAW SCORE	APPROXIMATE SCALED SCORE	RAW SCORE	APPROXIMATE SCALED SCORE
39	80	19	53
38	78	18	52
37	77	17	51
36	75	16	50
35	74	15	49
34	72	14	48
33	70	13	46
32	69	12	45
31	68	11	44
30	67	10	42
29	66	9	41
28	64	8	40
27	63	7	39
26	62	6	37
25	60	5	36
24	59	4	35
23	58	3	34
22	57	2	33
21	55	1	30
20	54	0 or Below	20-29

MATH SCORING TABLE			
RAW SCORE	**APPROXIMATE SCALED SCORE**	**RAW SCORE**	**APPROXIMATE SCALED SCORE**
38	80	18	51
37	77	17	49
36	74	16	49
35	73	15	47
34	70	14	46
33	69	13	45
32	67	12	44
31	65	11	43
30	64	10	42
29	63	9	41
28	62	8	39
27	60	7	38
26	59	6	38
25	58	5	36
24	57	4	34
23	56	3	32
22	55	2	31
21	54	1	28
20	53	0	26
19	52	Below 0	20-25

Index

Specific Detail questions, 9
text vs. assumptions, 8
Vocabulary In Context questions, 9
PEMDAS, 67, 285
percents, 71, 287
perimeters, 86, 294
perpendicular lines, 81, 293
pictographs, 89
pie charts, 88
place values, 69, 287
plane figures, 82
points, 294
polygons, 295
polynomials, 75-76, 290-291
positive slopes, 293
practice exams. *See individual section entries*
practice questions. *See individual section entries*
prime numbers, 289
probability, 71
process of elimination, 7-8
pronouns, 33
proportions, 70, 287
Pythagorean theorem, 82, 294

Q - R

quadrilaterals, 295
question stems, 4

radius, 296
range (functions), 78
rational numbers, 286-287
ratios, 70, 287
Raw Scores, 302
reading comprehension section. *See* Passage Based Reading section
reciprocals, 286
rectangles, 83, 295. *See also* squares
reflections (geometry), 294
rhetoric, 34
right angles, 85, 296
right triangles, 82, 294

S

scoring
practice tests, 301
Raw Scores, 302
Selection Index, 302-303

self-assessment questions. *See* individual section entries
Sentence Completion section
description of, 2
difficulty levels, 4
general strategies, 2-3
practice exams, 108-109, 139-141, 186-187, 220-221
practice exams answer keys, 155-159, 180-184, 235-239, 260-265
practice questions, 11-12
practice questions answer keys, 20-22
self-assessment questions, xxii-xxv
word recognition, 2
sequences (mathematics), 72, 288
sets of numbers, 288
simplifying fractions, 286
slopes, 80, 293-294
solution sets, 76, 291
special right triangles, 82
special symbols, 296
Specific Detail questions, 9
square roots, 69, 287, 291
squares (geometric), 295. *See also* rectangles
stimuli (Passage Based Reading), 4
Student-Produced Response section
overview, 90-91
practice exams, 137-138, 217
practice exams answer keys, 176-179, 257-259
practice questions, 97-98
practice questions answer keys, 101-104
self-assessment questions, xl-xliii
subject-verb agreement, improving, 31
symbols (mathematics), 296
synonyms, 2
systems of equations, 74-75

T - U - V

tangents, 296
Test of Time, 300
Tooth and Nail, 300
translations (geometry), 294
transversals, 85
trapezoids, 84
triangles, 82, 294

universities
applying to, 270-271
considering, 268-270
recommended high school classes, 272

How can we make this index more useful? Email us at indexes@quepublishing.com